Exodusters

Exodusters

Black Migration to Kansas after Reconstruction

Nell Irvin Painter

 Alfred A. Knopf / New York / 1977

703738

This Is a Borzoi Book
Published by Alfred A. Knopf, Inc.

Copyright © 1976 by Nell Irvin Painter

LIBRARY OF CONGRESS CATALOGING IN PUBLICATION DATA

Painter, Nell Irvin.
Exodusters: Black migration to Kansas after Reconstruction.

Bibliography: p.
Includes index.
1. Afro-Americans—Kansas—History. 2. Afro-Ameri-
cans—History—1877–1964. I. Title.
E185.93.K16P34 1976   978.1′004′96073   76–26858
ISBN 0–394–40253–7

Manufactured in the United States of America

First Edition

For Frank and Dona Irvin

Contents

Part III: *Emigration*

Illustrations appear following page 100.

Acknowledgments

Afro-Americans migrating to Kansas in the Exodus of 1879 came from four states, Mississippi, Louisiana, Texas, and Tennessee. In searching out the origins of that movement, therefore, I have limited my exploration to those states, and more especially to the particular regions affected by the Exodus. Although conditions prevailing there often resembled those of other Southern states and other times, I make no general claim to their wider applicability. affected by the Exodus. Although conditions prevailing there often resembled those of other Southern states and other times, I make no general claim to their wider applicability.

Thanks to a grant from the Ford Foundation for the writing of dissertations in minority history, I researched most of this work during the academic year 1971–72. In my travels across the country, Della Phillips of Austin, Texas, Harry Howe and Nancy Ransom of Nashville, Tennessee, and Fred and Tanya Banks of Jackson, Mississippi, offered me their kind hospitality. I am still pleased to count them among my friends. To archives and libraries I owe many debts but would like to offer especial thanks to the staffs of the Kansas State Historical Society, to Ed Langsdorf, in particular; of the National Archives, especially to Robert Clark and Debra Newman; of the Barker Collection of Texas History; and of the Harvard College Library, to Ed Peterson and Don Brown. At Mother Bethel African Methodist Episcopal Church in Philadelphia, I would like to thank the members of the church's Historical Commission for their help and fellowship. Thanks, too, to Ashbel Green, for helping a thesis become this book.

My greatest debts, however, are to my thesis adviser and my parents. Frank Freidel has offered moral support and professional guidance, striking a fine balance between much-appreciated concern and much-needed criticism. My parents have long stood by me with friendship, support, and love; to them this book is dedicated.

Nell Irvin Painter
Philadelphia
December, 1975

Part I
Reconstruction's Aftermath

1
After Slavery

In the spring of 1879 the John Solomon Lewis family lived and worked in Tensas Parish, Louisiana, a heavily Black, heavily Republican parish in which Blacks had suffered a vicious campaign of political violence during the previous autumn. That spring, though, debt, not politics, weighed most heavily on John Solomon Lewis's mind as he and his family burst the bonds of serfdom and joined the many thousands of their race leaving home, leaving Mississippi, Louisiana, Texas, and Tennessee, seeking a less elusive freedom. "You see," wrote John Solomon Lewis, "I was in debt, and the man I rented land from said every year I must rent again to pay the other year, and so I rents and rents, and each year I gets deeper and deeper in debt. In a fit of madness I one day said to the man I rented from: 'It's no use, I works hard and raises big crops and you sells it and keeps the money, and brings me more and more in debt, so I will go somewhere else and try to make headway like white working-men.'

"He got very mad and said to me: 'If you try that job, you will get your head shot away.'

"So I told my wife, and she says: 'Let us take to the woods in the night time.' Well, we took [to] the woods, my wife and four children, and we was three weeks living in the woods waiting for a boat. Then a great many more black people came and we was all together at the landing.

"Boats came along, but they would not stop, but before long the *Grand Tower* hove up and we got on board. Says the captain, 'Where's you going?'

"Says I, 'Kansas.'

"Says he, 'You can't go on this boat.'

"Says I, 'I do; you know who I am. I am a man who was a United States soldier and I know my rights, and if I and my family gets put off, I will go in the United States Court and sue for damages.'

"Says the captain to another boat officer, 'Better take that nigger or he will make trouble.' "

Thus John Solomon Lewis and his family joined the Exodus to Kansas of 1879, and found themselves among the thousands of Black Southerners leaving home that spring. The Lewises, on reaching their new land, found that their emotions transcended preoccupations with mere debt and prosperity. "When I landed on the soil," said Lewis, "I looked on the ground and I says this is free ground. Then I looked on the heavens, and I says them is free and beautiful heavens. Then I looked within my heart, and I says to myself I wonder why I never was free before?

"When I knew I had all my family in a free land, I said let us hold a little prayer meeting; so we held a little meeting on the river bank. It was raining but the drops fell from heaven on a free family, and the meeting was just as good as sunshine. We was thankful to God for ourselves and we prayed for those who could not come.

"I asked my wife did she know the ground she stands on. She said, 'No!'

"I said it is free ground; and she cried like a child for joy."[1]

Fourteen years after emancipation, many thousands of rural Black people, like the Lewises, struck out for their freedom, real freedom. They congregated by the hundreds on the banks of the Mississippi River as the Lewises had, awaiting boats to take them to St. Louis and from there to Kansas. Some migrants, called "Exodusters," left home on the strength of their faith in their ultimate deliverance from the terrorists and extortionists of the white South. Others, like the Lewis family, studied the flight of the believers and asked themselves, "Why stay?" All the migrants together registered the first, massive repudiation of the Democratic South. Reconstruction, following the Civil War, inaugurated social—if not economic—reordering of Southern life. Black men

---

[1] John Solomon Lewis, Leavenworth, Kansas, June 10, 1879, Boston *Traveller* in New Orleans *Southwestern Christian Advocate,* July 3, 1879.

In Louisiana, counties are called parishes.

voted and began, as political beings, to conceive of their own interests. To the extent that those interests conflicted with those of the whites of the South, the whites opposed the new order. They called their recapturing the reins of power from the Republicans "Redemption," for they saw themselves "redeeming" their South from Negroes. Although it is convenient to date Redemption from the Compromise of 1877, which put Rutherford B. Hayes in the White House, the Democratic takeover proved to be a long process, advancing by fits and starts from the early 1870s into the 1880s. With a parallel unevenness, Black people lost hope for their prospects in that same South. The 1860s, in contrast, had seemed to promise a new and brighter future.

Slavery and the old order sagged perceptibly before emancipation and Congressional Reconstruction swept them aside, ushering in the new order, for by the second year of the conflict, war-wrought changes had begun to gnaw away at bondage. In Washington the Confiscation Acts, and in the Mississippi Valley the presence of Union Armies in New Orleans and northwestern Mississippi, loosened the cords of uncompensated labor. Northern teachers, Black and white, inaugurated the long work of unfettering minds from the ignorance of slavery. Thus, by 1865, when the vast majority of Southern slaves received their freedom, many had already gained a first hold on literacy, seen service in the Union Army, and earned a little cash—enough to shape ideas about the meaning of freedom. More than anything, freedom meant being for oneself, individually and collectively, no longer the creature of another's will.

The freedpeople insisted on being treated in a new way, no more as chattels, but as people. They resolved, wrote an Army officer, "that in their present condition as freemen their former masters and present employers should address them in a more respectful manner than formerly."[2] Now they refused the whippings that had been their lot as slaves. They "stoutly resisted" beatings, exhibiting an "independence and fearlessness" that

---

[2]Charles H. Gilchrist to W. G. Gordon, Jackson, Mississippi, September 17, 1865, United States Senate, 39th Congress, 1st session, Executive Document no. 2 (reprint eds., Carl Schurz, *Report on the States of South Carolina, Georgia, Alabama, Mississippi, and Louisiana* [Washington, 1865], in *Condition of the South* [New York, 1969], p. 69.)

showed them clearly cognizant of the difference between being slaves and being freedpeople, and willing to care for themselves.[3] They meant no harm toward their former masters, for the most part; rather they wanted simply to do for themselves and act in their own interests.

This reorientation of freedmen's activities confused many white Southerners, some of whom at first believed that emancipation would only temporarily obstruct their accustomed way of life. In Texas it was reported that whites commonly told "their former slaves, now free, that the proclamation of emancipation would be set aside."[4] And even after recalcitrant masters accepted the fact of the Thirteenth Amendment, they found it difficult to adjust to the substance of their ex-slaves' freedom.

Carl Schurz noted immediately after the war that white Southerners could not fathom Blacks working for themselves, doing what they wanted, particularly if it meant subsistence farming. Former masters still thought that "the negro exists for the special object of raising cotton, rice and sugar *for the whites,* and that it is illegitimate for him [the Black man] to indulge, like other people, in the pursuit of his own happiness in his own way."[5] Blacks acting in their own interests would ultimately lead to enormous misunderstandings between them and Southern whites, the first of which revolved around that basic Southern commodity, land. Whatever the importance of the new race relations of the postwar South, the issue of land remained one of the most crucial, to both Blacks and whites.

Farming one's own land on one's own account meant being one's own master. Indeed, even the United States Congress seemed, with the 1865 Freedmen's Bureau Act, to recognize the need to ease the newly freed people into land ownership. Land division and reform was a commonsense proposition in 1865, since the freedpeople made up the only massively loyal contingent of the Southern population, and their former masters—the owners of large plantations—exhibited a marked anti-Unionist spirit. What

---

[3]Stephen Powers, Cincinnati *Commercial* correspondent, United States House of Representatives, 39th Congress, 1st session, Report no. 30, *Report of the Joint Committee on Reconstruction* (Washington, 1866), IV (Florida, Louisiana, Texas): 148. (Hereafter referred to as *House Report 30.*)

[4]Christopher C. Andrews, *House Report 30,* IV: 24.

[5]Schurz, *Condition of the South,* p. 21. (Emphasis in original.)

better means of assuring the independence and strength of these loyal Southerners than by settling them on abandoned and confiscated lands? Whether the logic of land division decided the freedpeople or they were informed of the Freedmen's Bureau legislation by Black Union soldiers, late in 1865 the certitude spread throughout the South that there would be a general division of the land, which would take place over the Christmas holidays. United States Army officers reported the freedpeople's belief that "some great change was going to take place about Christmas," when they expected that "the government intended to make some further provision for their future welfare, especially by ordering distributions of land among them."[6] In anticipation of owning their own land, freedpeople hesitated to sign contracts which would bind them well after the impending land reform. In Louisiana they were said to be "indisposed to labor very steadily" during 1865, certain as they were that "they were going to cultivate land of their own, or to do something for themselves."[7] The key phrase, "to do something for themselves," meant land ownership, first and foremost.

But Southern white determination that Blacks must not own farmland at any cost matched the freedpeople's desire to own it. This is not to say that numbers of former masters did not willingly divide their plantations, for long lease or sale among Black farmers, often their former slaves. In Mississippi in 1865, for instance, a planter made three-year contracts with a number of his former slaves, at the expiration of which he agreed to divide and lease his plantations to them. Shortly after the contracts had been signed, however, the Mississippi State Black Code outlawed the selling or leasing of land to Negroes. The Black employees left the land, deserting the contracting planter and accusing him of having purposely misled them in order to extort their labor.[8] Although these particular freedmen seem to have blamed their former master unjustly, the case underscores the skepticism with which former slaves regarded their old masters and also their readiness to make long-term contracts provided they stood to gain land at the end. The planter's willingness to enter such a contract with them is unusual.

---

[6]Ibid., p. 31.

[7]Charles C. Dolittle, *House Report 30*, IV: 70.

[8]J. W. Shaffer, ibid., p. 52.

The Mississippi Black Code's legislative ban on selling or leasing farmland to freedmen embodied the prevailing Southern white view on the matter. Although the Reconstruction legislatures invalidated the Black Codes, neither they nor Congress took significant steps toward land reform, and the reluctance of whites to relax their hold on the land endured.[9] It stemmed in part from their view of Blacks as the region's labor force, solely a labor force. "All the trickery, chicanery and political power possible are being brought to bear on the poor negro, to make him do the hard labor for the whites, as in the days of old," wrote a Union officer in Vicksburg immediately after the war. The whites "steadily refuse to sell or lease lands to black men. . . . The whites know that if negroes are not allowed to acquire property or become landholders, they must ultimately return to plantation labor, and work for wages. . . ."[10] The idea of large numbers of freedpeople owning land seemed so foreign that a rumor spread among the whites, countering the Blacks' expectation of land distribution at Christmas 1865. Instead of land reform, the white rumor threatened Negro insurrection.

Southern whites viewed the Blacks' anticipation of fundamental change as the very antipode of good times to come. Whereas Blacks expected that land distribution would round out their freedom, whites foresaw a Negro rampage. Perhaps to their minds the ultimate unfolding of Black freedom necessarily implied insurrection. Certainly they awaited insurrection, for whatever motives. Their fear of revolt permeated the South, matching the breadth of the Blacks' belief in land reform. Northern officers handled the anticipated threat in various ways.

In Natchez, Mississippi, the head of the occupying forces called in prominent Black men and asked them whether their people were planning an uprising. When the Black representatives assured him that "there would be no insurrection upon the part of the blacks; [that] if there were any insurrection it would be gotten up by the whites," the difficulties simply died away.[11] In

---

[9]Carol Bleser discusses South Carolina land reform in detail in her excellent study *The Promised Land: The History of the South Carolina Land Commission, 1869–1890* (Columbia, S.C., 1969).

[10]Samuel Thomas to Carl Schurz, Vicksburg, Mississippi, September 28, 1865, Schurz, *Condition of the South*, p. 82.

[11]W. A. P. Dillingham, *House Report 30*, III: 118.

Texas, however, the white authorities of Lamar County requested and received six hundred Enfield rifles, pleading the need to "suppress an intended insurrection of the freedmen of that section." Here the situation led to a tragic and foregone conclusion, for "on this pretext the freedmen were disarmed, plundered, and many of them were killed," according to the local Union officer in command.[12] That general pattern occurred in many other areas, well after Christmas 1865 had passed and Blacks had adjusted to the necessity of wage labor. In the very same way that whites interpreted Black hopes for land as insurrectionary, they misunderstood Black solidarity—a new thing in its scope—as antiwhite militance.

Blacks reacted to their freedom by coming together in many self-help organizations and gestures. In voting, as in economic activities, they were not notably antiwhite. "We colored folks thought that if we were allowed to be voters we could, of course, express our own opinions," said a Black Louisianian. "We did not want to do anything against our masters, but we wished the privilege of voting according to our judgement and knowledge."[13] A kindred desire to help their own led Blacks to form cooperative stores and societies.

Many of the freedpeople's new associations were benevolent organizations, often named Union Aid Societies, serving as burial or social groups. Frequently, however, their very existence antagonized white sensibilities. In Columbus, Mississippi, whites broke up the January 1 emancipation celebration of the local Union Aid Society.[14] Other groups, of more pronounced self-help proclivities, ran even greater risks.

In Oktibbeha County, Mississippi, about one hundred Blacks collectively owned a freedmen's exchange, having purchased shares worth five dollars to twenty dollars each. When the Reconstruction state government took over the Northern missionary

---

[12]T. J. Mackey, ibid., IV: 159.

[13]Solomon White, United States House of Representatives, 41st Congress, 2d session, House Miscellaneous Document no. 154, *Testimony Taken by the Sub-Committee of Elections in Louisiana* (Washington, 1870), II: 165. (Hereafter referred to as *House Misc. Doc. 154.*)

[14]Robert Gleed, United States Senate, 42d Congress, 2d session, Senate Report no. 41, *Testimony Taken by the Joint Select Committee to Inquire into the Condition of Affairs in the Late Insurrectionary States* (Washington, 1872), XII: 723. (Hereafter referred to as *Senate Report 41.*)

schools in 1870, shareholders employed the Northern white minister who had been teaching school to act as their agent in the day-to-day running of the store. Local whites, resenting both the cooperative venture and the white man's participation, beat up the agent, forced him to leave Mississippi, and menaced the store.[15] Although they did not pretend to see the cooperative store as a threat of violence, whites reacted to the seeming danger in Black cooperation.

Black solidarity, especially in interracial confrontations, frightened whites and, by extension, furnished a pretext for their binding together in White Leagues and Ku Klux Klans. White Southerners complained that Blacks drilled and marched in the streets on holidays and blindly supported one another "without any inquiry . . . relative to the merits of the difficulty." These apparently inflammatory activities, together with the Union Aid Societies and co-ops, moved local whites to form organizations "as a check upon these other [Black] organizations."[16] "Directly after the surrender," explained a Mississippi white, "the negroes organized what they called freedmen's aid societies, which were understood to be purely charitable. In a little it began to be public and understood among the people that black people swore in that society to stand up to each other, and support each other—to support their color in all contests; and whenever a difficulty occurred in the country between a white man and a black man, the blacks invariably rallied *en masse.* . . ."[17] But Mississippi whites discounted the violent and racial character of their attacks on Blacks. When Blacks did not stand together, they ran the risk of individual victimization.

Despite all their efforts at self-protection, Blacks fell prey to nightriders, who picked them off one by one if they appeared concerned with the political well-being of their people. Leaders of Republican clubs stood out as especial targets of these terrorists, who also silenced or drove away white Republicans. Immediately after the war, white Republicans, mostly Northern but many Southern, worked with the freedmen politically, but by the late 1860s, nightriding (or "bulldozing," as it was called) had markedly thinned their ranks. Of necessity, Blacks depended on one another

[15]Homer C. Powers, ibid., pp. 993–94.
[16]James H. Rives, ibid., XI: 555–56.
[17]Ibid.

politically, and men who had been in the Army or who could read the newspapers discussed politics with the less informed. The partisan clubs and freedmen's societies were favorite arenas for discussion.

In St. Mary's Parish, Louisiana, Radical or Republican clubs existed on every third or fourth plantation in the late 1860s, and nearly every Black man belonged at least nominally to a club on his own or a nearby plantation. "We organized those clubs with the intention of teaching the people what they were to vote for and what the constitution meant," said a Black Louisianian. "We had those meetings weekly all the time, and we had men of the most influence and intelligence among our people to speak to them, and to tell them what the constitution meant."[18] One man of "influence and intelligence," John Kemp, numbered among the many thousands of active Black men who met violent deaths precisely because of their political activities among their people.

John Kemp, said one of his old comrades, "was president of a republican club at Tangipaho [St. Helena Parish, Louisiana]. He devoted his time, whenever it was suitable, to instructing the colored people what was to their interests, and what steps they should take. He could read and write." A "true-hearted republican," John Kemp walked and breathed, a living provocation to local whites. "The white democrats were opposed to him on account of his politics, and did everything they could to injure him. . . . They hated him worse than any person ever hated a rattlesnake."[19] Kemp died at the hands of nightriders, a victim of the massive violence aimed at the elimination of coherent, self-interested political action among the freedpeople. It is worth noting that John Kemp, like many of his fellow victims, was not a minister.

In stark contrast to the heavy preponderance of ministers among outstanding Black men by the end of the nineteenth century, the generation serving as guides in the interracial world of the late 1860s and very early 1870s had very few preachers. Two explanations account for this difference, one of which concerns the evangelization of the freedpeople.

Before the Civil War, Black churches existed only on the mar-

---

[18]John J. Moore, *House Misc. Doc. 154*, I: 637.
[19]Mumford McCoy, ibid., p. 684.

gins of Southern life, the precarious creatures of cities with large free Black populations. Slaves attended their masters' churches and sometimes enjoyed their own "shouts" at night, but, for all intents and purposes, organized Black congregations began only after the war, growing from two directions. For the most part, freedpeople came together in their own community churches, often Baptist churches, which required no outside organizers. These churches grew up spontaneously among people acting on their own behalf. On the other hand, two Episcopal churches centered in the North sent missionaries South as the war progressed: the African Methodist Episcopal Church (A.M.E.) and the Methodist Episcopal Church (North), one Black, one white. Originating in the cities and towns, these two centralized churches gradually reached into the countryside, in a proselytizing effort extending over several decades. In the late 1860s and early 1870s their firmest footholds were still in urban areas. At that point, many rural freedpeople belonged to no organized Black church, for the process of primary organization lasted well into the 1880s (and in some Southwestern areas into the early twentieth century). Thus the small proportion of preachers among Black political men in the years following the Civil War reflected the relatively low number of preachers among the freedpeople as a whole.

A second reason for the late-nineteenth-century increase in Black ministers concerns the demise, or rather the harassment, of secular cadres. Southern white resentment explains the relative increase of preacher-politicians and the elimination of nonreligious partisans. As nightriders assassinated political organizers or forced them into exile or inactivity, the growing ranks of preachers inherited the Black public arena by default. Black political activity did not cease in the face of bulldozing, for even after the Compromise of 1877, Blacks continued to search for means to express themselves politically. However, independent Black politics carried on by purely political organizers came under fire from white Democrats early on, and the campaign proved a long and ultimately a losing one. The attrition of men whose primary public activity was political organizing, coupled with economic pressure and election chicanery, explains the defeat. While the symbol of protection, the Union Army, restrained Southern white violence, Black political organizers acted in comparative freedom. Once the Army withdrew, activists faced increased danger. More and more, men encumbered with religious responsibilities shouldered what they could of the political burden. But the preachers (who, like the political activists, generally supported themselves by farming) had less time to give to politics; in addition, they were more likely to view continual day-to-day organizing tasks as incidental to the life of a good Christian. In short, politics seldom took first place in ministers' lives. Although preachers viewed politics as an end in itself less than did secular cadres, numbers of them took partisan duties seriously enough to attract the ire of local whites. As preachers assumed political responsibilities they, too, ran the risks of white retribution, suffering exile and assassination. Whoever articulated Black solidarity and independence stood a good chance of offending the great number of white Southerners, even though that solidarity was never complete.

The decade of Reconstruction witnessed cultural and political fissures among Black Southerners. Although few in number, Black Democrats—voluntary Black Democrats, that is—irritated the masses of Blacks who shared ardent Republican sentiments. Republican Blacks distinguished between their brethren who were forced to vote Democratic against their will and those who did so for money or from conviction. The latter sort attracted considerable hostility, for most Blacks viewed the Democratic party as pro-slavery and anti-Black. Oscar J. Dunn, lieutenant governor of Louisiana in the late 1860s, explained that Blacks thought Democrats opposed their voting, and "we regarded the loss of suffrage as being the loss of freedom. My people, as a general thing, believed that if the democratic party were to get into power they would try to do away with all the laws passed by the republican Congress, and that they would be returned to a condition of slavery."[20] Given this viewpoint, Blacks almost by definition inclined to the Republican party.

The basic problem with Black Democrats lay with the party's principles, said a Republican Black Mississippian. "If the democratic party accepted the situation, and were willing to accord to the black man the right to vote and to hold office, or the right in common with other citizens; then we would think they had a right to acquiesce with that party. But we don't believe they have a right to acquiesce with a party who refuse to recognize their right

---

[20]Oscar J. Dunn, ibid., pp. 181–82.

to participate in public affairs; that is why we brand them as traitors. . . . They are generally pretty high, because they feel they are sustained by the white community, and sometimes they say a good many things we [Black Republicans] cannot bear from them."[21] That Black Democrats pursued their own self-interest, assuring their own bodily protection, in no way mitigated their being considered "traitors." To the contrary, it seems to have damned them even more. "I have never heard of an instance of . . . a white democrat nor a black traitor—we don't consider a black democrat, we simply call them traitors—I have not heard of a white democrat or black traitor being punished by these parties in disguise."[22]

Ill-considered by most Blacks, Negro Democrats existed in nearly every community, where they suffered resentment and dislike for their politics but were not likely to be molested by their Republican fellows—in part, perhaps, because the Democrats enjoyed the protection of well-armed whites. To some degree, their apostasy was shrugged off, as when a Mississippi Black man dismissed his brother's voting Democratic, saying, "some few vote with the white people."[23] Politically, Black Democrats posed little threat to Republicans, vastly outnumbered as they were by white Democrats who took matters into their own hands. However, while the partisan split in Black ranks remained a local irritant, the growing cultural cleavage between unschooled rural Blacks and assimilated individuals confused intraracial and interracial relations for the rest of the century.

Black America had never been culturally monolithic, for Western-educated or at least culturally assimilated Negroes played a prominent part in the abolitionist crusade. In the South, however, where most Blacks were slaves, they shared a rural, nonliterate folk culture, which of course endured well past the Civil War. Firmly egalitarian and marked by strong racial cohesion, they commonly spoke of "our race," "the colored people," and "our color," manifesting an enduring communal identity.

Despite common nineteenth-century views, rural Black folk culture was not merely a faulty edition of Euro-American cul-

---

[21]Robert Gleed, *Senate Report 41*, XII: 725–26.
[22]Ibid., p. 722.
[23]Peter Cooper, ibid., XI: 497.

ture.[24] Admittedly syncretic, it combined Euro-American traditions with what had persisted of West African traditions after more than a century's separation from their sources. It was a whole culture, but in one aspect it was subject to deliberate change. Whereas they had been nonliterate, Blacks sought purposefully to learn reading and writing when the opportunities presented themselves after the war. Literacy, after all, stood as the one essential skill of a free person.

The desire to read and write did not in itself signal rejection of the rural folk culture, it merely indicated a desire to protect oneself in a literate world. But the process of formal schooling in the late nineteenth century carried with it implied assimilation to Euro-American culture and values. As Black individuals acquired formal education—beyond the acquisition of fundamental tools of literacy—they often tended to take on the additional baggage of Euro-American life.

Late-nineteenth-century newspapers, Black and white, spoke of assimilated Negroes as "representative colored men," meaning that they represented the best the race had to offer. "Representative colored men" by no means constituted a class; one encountered "representative" individuals, rarely whole families, and the individuals were few except in a handful of cities such as Washington, D.C., and New Orleans.[25]

The distinction between rural Black folk and "representative colored men" would be less useful had it been widely recognized in the nineteenth century as a *cultural* difference. There did indeed exist a limited, tacit recognition of the difference between unschooled Blacks and acculturated "representative colored men" in the titles accorded the latter in print. Whites often granted them the title "Mr." or called them "leading colored men," in the sense that they functioned as actual leaders of the

---

[24]Two recent studies, John Blassingame's *The Slave Community* (New York, 1972) and Eugene D. Genovese's *Roll, Jordan, Roll* (New York, 1974), describe this rural folk culture in detail.

[25]The most exact terminology derives from twentieth-century French colonialism, in which natives and *évolués* occupy the two extremes of non-French colonial life. Natives in their "savage" state were only natives *(indigènes),* but with exposure to French culture, natives "evolved" into civilized beings, thus becoming *évolués.* The term *évolué* roughly translates as "civilized native," and it fits the individual Afro-Americans who took on Euro-American culture in opposition to Afro-American folk life very well indeed.

Negro people. In fact, however, the terms served only to label Blacks who spoke to whites in a language they could readily understand. "Representative colored men" were articulate Blacks; rural Black folk were by and large inarticulate. The danger lies in confusing the views or rhetoric of "representative colored men" with the authentic voices of rural Blacks.

Although assimilated Blacks could in no sense be equated with white Democrats in the scale of mischief against the rural Black folk, they came to criticize the folk for deviating from "civilized" Victorian values and conventions. They denigrated folkways and agreed with many whites that rural Blacks must change culturally before they could expect to enjoy their basic citizens' rights, thus furnishing a handy peg for the demagoguery of white supremacists. Instead of unequivocally demanding enforcement of state and federal laws protecting rural Blacks' rights, persons, and property, "representative colored men" and whites asked unschooled Blacks to change their way of life. In effect, they told rural Blacks to accommodate themselves to the illegal activities of the white bulldozers. Thus, the burden of political violence slipped from the bulldozers and assassins to their victims. Whites and "representative colored men" discussed legal and political questions on the cultural level, faulting the people. Few rural Blacks swallowed whole the "representative colored men's" exhortations to get schooling, money, and temperance first, suffrage later. But as Reconstruction and voting faded, "representative colored men" came increasingly into their own. As much as Henry Grady, they typified the new South and called for commerce and industry to sweep away the old, including the old Negro way of life.

From the vantage point of 1877, Reconstruction appeared to falter in about 1871 in Louisiana, Mississippi, and Texas. Black solidarity and a real, if guarded, optimism (bolstered by relative prosperity) marked the period preceding 1871, but nightriding and a corresponding loss of hope among rural Blacks prevailed in the later years. By the late 1870s the South had begun to take on the feudal usages which shaped race relations economically and politically throughout the rest of the century.

2
Fictions of Black Life
and Southern
Race Relations

Immediately after the Civil War, observers in the South noted "the irrepressible conflict, the antagonism of interest, thought, and sentiment between the races."[1] The great majority of Southern whites continued to resent emancipation, and their resentment first found expression in senseless rapine and later in attacks calculated to undermine the freedpeople's newfound independence. As Republican-dominated Reconstruction tottered and Democratic Redemption solidified, Southern white Democrats elaborated an ideology that supported their brutal takeover. Contending that Blacks could enjoy their civil rights in the Democratic South, they drew upon a series of fictions, each with its adjuncts and corollaries. The whole fabrication ultimately insisted that Blacks ought to accede to the new order of things—an order said to be divinely ordained and entirely natural —white supremacy and a fast-hardening color line. Implicit in these fictions that whites and some "representative colored men" held about Southern race relations were the assumptions of an identity of interest between Southern Blacks ("the labor of the South") and Southern whites ("the wealth and intelligence of the South"), and, by extension, that rural Black people fundamentally differed from other (normal, white) people. Numbers of Southern

---

[1]Major General Q. A. Gillmore to General Carl Schurz, Hilton Head, South Carolina, July 27, 1865, *Condition of the South,* p. 48.

whites convinced themselves that Blacks cared less, or at least ought to care less, for their own opinions, their own lives, and their own rights than did whites. The myth of white paternalism undergirded the cant about post-1877 racial harmony.

The concept of upper-class white paternalism persisted from slavery days, but with Redemption it re-emerged. Feeding into the identity-of-interest line of thought, it bridged the gap between the two seeming contradictions of Southern life: the color line, on one hand, and interracial cooperation, on the other. For despite increasingly pervasive racial segregation stemming from white-supremacy campaigns of the early 1870s, interracial contacts persisted. On the individual level, whites might, indeed, show fatherly solicitude toward certain familiar Blacks. They proffered help, advice, warnings of impending danger, even safe harbor in times of trouble. Nor was this aid limited only to inoffensive Blacks. Individual whites might shelter Blacks of extraordinarily independent views, if they were personal friends. John Milton Brown, for instance, a Black candidate who had been involved in a political riot in Mississippi, unaccountably escaped his pursuers unharmed. Although he was one of the most-hated Republicans in Coahoma County, whites nevertheless forewarned him whenever he was endangered by mobs. Brown explained, "I had some friends there among both the whites and blacks."[2]

John Milton Brown's experience was hardly unique. This interracial cooperation worked most smoothly between Black employees and their white employers, the most common tie linking Southern Blacks and whites, and it solidified the fiction of the paternalistic "better class" of whites. But between poor whites and poor Blacks, residential separation and the absence of the employer-employee relationship reduced noncompetitive contact and, hence, friendships. Here, institutionalized antagonism took the place of the paternalistic rapport linking the "better class" of whites to Blacks. Whether resentment between poor whites and Blacks or paternalism between the "better class" and their servants was borne out in fact, Re-

---

[2]J. Milton Brown, *Report and Testimony of the Select Committee of the United States Senate to Investigate the Causes of the Removal of the Negroes from the Southern States to the Northern States* (Washington, 1880), II: 374. (Hereafter referred to as *Senate Report 693.*)

deemers made great show of the second tie.

In the wider world of public opinion, the ballyhoo accorded individual shows of decency shored up an optimistic view of Southern race relations. This view gained a certain currency among reconciling whites and some Northern and urban Southern Blacks whose lives were relatively secure. Tucked safely away in the fastness of Northern cities, even former freedom fighters sometimes mellowed. Although Black abolitionists were less susceptible than their white counterparts to Southern propaganda of blossoming racial harmony, they nevertheless grew weary of unmitigated racial strife and welcomed hopeful signs. Staunch activists like the Reverend Henry Highland Garnet in New York City elaborated shreds of good news into portents of good times to come:

There is already a large class of whites in the South who are strongly opposed to the outrages upon our race. You know that these outrages are committed by the lowest class of the whites. It is only here and there that there are men of good position and of intellect who prompt them and profit by them, but they do not openly countenance such methods. The upper class down there is increasing, and my hope is . . . that the present state of things will not always exist.[3]

Blacks in the rural South usually took a less sanguine view. While they might allow that the "better class" of whites did not actively engage in bulldozing and terrorism, Blacks seldom regarded this upper class as a reliable shield of protection. Indeed, many Black people saw "good" white people as "accessories before and after the fact because they all sit quietly and see these men come in from other parishes, and do not attempt to drive them out, or to protect the colored people against them."[4] In the same vein, the opening address of a Tennessee State Convention of Colored Men impugned the vaunted good intentions of upper-class whites:

While this convention is firm in the faith that the representative white men of the State are disposed to accord them justice and entertain the kindest feeling for them, yet [the convention] is compelled to ascribe the evils from which its race suffers to the inactivity and lukewarmness, in some measure, of these representative men, and is decided in its convic-

---

[3]New York Daily *Herald*, April 3, 1879.
[4]William Murrell, *Senate Report 693*, II: 530.

tion that the irresponsible and ignorant white men of the State are resolved that the colored men shall not attain to the full measure of their
rights as citizens.[5]

The resolutions of the convention noted the hollow ring of claims
"that the more respectable white people are disposed to accord
justice, yet none will dare say that they have ever made a single
effort to prevent outbreaks against people of color, too frequent
in the State."[6]

This hard-headed skepticism corresponded closely to the actual state of affairs in the South in the late 1870s. While the body
of the bulldozing mobs consisted of ordinary, working-class whites,
they were led, encouraged, and often joined by white citizens of
the most respectable sort, the very "better class" of whites
reputed to be the best protectors of Black people. George T.
Downing of Rhode Island put little faith in them: "The white
might show consideration—he could pat the black man; he could
under certain circumstances, be even merciful; but these were
regarded as voluntary acts and feelings to be indulged in at pleasure. There was no sense of bounded duty—no feeling of a legal
binding force in the matter."[7] A Black Southerner said more suc-
cinctly: "There is not a pledge a Southern white man will keep,
in case it is a question where a negro is concerned."[8]

Blacks like William Murrell of Delta, Louisiana, repudiated
entirely the concept of the paternalistic better class of whites.
He claimed that the bulldozers' very existence depended directly on upper-class white backing. Rich whites instigated the
terrorism that they claimed to witness in utter helplessness,
Murrell charged, and they actually employed nightriders as
mercenaries, who in turn made their living policing the colored people:

The class of men that do the bulldozing are a set of men who enter
the country for this very purpose, and none of them enter the country
except they make money by murdering and bulldozing generally, and
they would not come into these parishes unless their expenses were paid....
There is a class of rich men in the parish that pays the expenses of these
men. I know one case of these bulldozers where they got mad . . . these

[5]Nashville *Union and American*, May 20, 1875.
[6]Nashville *Republican Banner*, May 21, 1875.
[7]New York Daily *Herald*, April 11, 1879.
[8]John G. Lewis, *Senate Report 693*, II: 436.

bulldozers went to a certain rich man of the parish and said, "By God, we have done the work, and now you have got to pay us, and if you don't settle up we will do to you as we done to the niggers!"[9]

Impoverished white mercenaries, propertyless and living "on peanuts and sweet potatoes and one thing and another where they come from," proved difficult to prosecute in election cases, but they accounted for only a portion of the white mobs.[10] In several instances men of the "better classes" took an active part, rarely running the risk of conviction for bulldozing. Black and white Republicans often testified to the hopelessness of prosecuting bulldozers in state and local courts, where judges and lawyers invariably exonerated the offenders, if they even came to trial. In one such case, the wife of one of Natchitoches Parish's leading white Republicans charged that the district judge was a leader of a mob which broke up a Republican meeting and forced her husband's flight.[11]

In Louisiana, lack of counsel seriously impeded the United States attorney's prosecution of election cases. Although the United States grand jury had indicted several prominent whites for election-law violations, the U.S. attorney found most respected lawyers reluctant to argue the government's case. The defendants, members of the "better class," were the lawyers' own friends and colleagues:

. . . there are of course able counsel [in New Orleans], but their sympathies are with the accused and it should be remembered that the cases now pending here are against the leaders of society, against District and Parish Judges, prominent lawyers, large planters, well-known merchants, State officials high in position—*In short the accused as a rule belong to and indeed in their various localities constitute the*

---

[9]William Murrell, ibid., p. 517. Blacks were not alone in observing the collusion of the respectable elements of the Southern white population with the supposedly lower-class nightriders. In 1871 the United States district attorney for the northern district of Mississippi gave testimony to the same effect: "I think the organization [of the Ku Klux Klan] is divided into two classes. There is the working or executing class who ride, who do the raiding and whipping, and shooting. Another class is composed of respectable citizens, who point the finger of scorn at some certain persons or designate a man, and influence these parties to commit these deeds of violence." (G. Wiley Well, *Senate Report 41*, XII: 1158.)

[10]William Murrell, *Senate Report 693*, II: 517.

[11]Mrs. J. Ernest Breda to Jack Wharton, U.S. marshal, Natchitoches, Louisiana, September 30, 1878, Record Group 60, Department of Justice, Source-Chronological Files, Louisiana, box 434, National Archives.

higher class. It is difficult to get prominent lawyers here to prosecute such men.[12]

Ultimately, loyalties between whites, especially of the same class, prevailed over any commitment to the legal rights of Negroes. This loyalty, rather than friendliness with individual Blacks, molded race relations in the post-Reconstruction South. The mass of Blacks could not rely upon protection from "the best people" as a class, for almost without exception, kindness across the color line stemmed from face-to-face relationship alone. It furnished no institutionalized guarantee of constitutional rights whatever. Nevertheless, every Black person who had been succored by a kind white knew the inviolable color line to be fiction.

Another idea basic to Southern racial politics contended that unschooled Blacks were unable to think for themselves. It held that rural Blacks, ignorant of their own best interests, easily misled, and generally unreasoning, failed to assess changes in the political climate. To varying degrees, "representative colored men" shared this view with many Northern and Southern whites. They fulminated against country preachers and unscrupulous politicians who, they charged, duped the poor colored people at every turn.

In actual fact, when uneducated Blacks needed to take public community action, they invariably reached commonsense conclusions hammered out in mass meetings. Ideally, everyone had license to speak, and once participants had expressed and discussed all their options, the meeting would reach a consensus and decide upon a course of action, designating an able speaker or organizer to execute policy on its behalf. "Representative colored men" and whites sometimes called the spokesman, organizer, or executor "the leader of the colored people," but the role of executor did not at all imply dictation of policies to the people without their prior consent. Executorship was tenuous, and it was strictly conditional upon the people's agreeing beforehand on the actions in question. Because the executor's mandate was exceedingly limited, he necessarily had to remain in close contact with his constituency.

This executor-constituency system sometimes seemed to

---

[12]A. H. Leonard, U.S. attorney, to Charles Devens, U.S. attorney general, New Orleans, February 14, 1879, Record Group 60, Department of Justice, Source-Chronological Files, Louisiana, box 435, National Archives. (Emphasis added.)

thrust forth identifiable leaders, especially when Blacks shared a common interest among themselves—in the late 1870s, for instance, in politics. Here cleavages were most likely to occur along the color line. In interracial issues, a Black person more experienced in manipulating white culture—a former soldier, or a teacher, perhaps—might well be accorded sustained respect precisely because of this expertise. But his influence nevertheless remained narrowly circumscribed, and the apparent distinction between leaders and followers broke down in questions involving only Blacks. In intraracial concerns, Blacks with valuable skills in dealing with whites enjoyed no special hearing by virtue of those skills alone. Each member of the community had equal footing.

A secret meeting held in Madison Parish, Louisiana, and its aftermath provide a good example of the egalitarian manner in which the members of a Black community reached political decisions and delegated authority. Having learned of an imminent attack of bulldozing sparked by the gubernatorial election, some eight hundred Black men met deep in the woods in Hackett Swamp late in 1879. The assembly debated the wisdom of resisting the impending assault.

Several longtime residents of Madison Parish favored resistance. In light of the military preparedness of Louisiana whites, however, they realized the folly of standing alone. The whites were not only well armed, they were also well drilled. One man at the secret meeting later said:

The white people in Louisiana are better armed and equipped now than during the war, and they have a better standing army now in the State of Louisiana than was ever known in the State, and I defy any white man in Louisiana, Democrat or Republican, to deny that assertion. We have brigadiers all over the State, and we have not got a ragged corporal and not a colored militia company in all the State, not one. And we have an excellent army [in Louisiana]. You see them parade the streets of New Orleans with their gray uniforms on, and with their improved Winchester rifles and their Gatling guns, and they have now got everything except the rebel flag—even to the gray uniform.[13]

---

[13]William Murrell, *Senate Report 693*, II: 521. The White League in Louisiana, well organized from the mid-1870s, managed to seize a huge cache of arms from the arsenal in New Orleans. The material, worth about $67,000, was never recovered. No Blacks could ever aspire to such armed might as that which the Louisiana White Leaguers stole from the United States Government:

The meeting decided not to oppose the bulldozers unaided and moved on to consider appealing to the "better class" of whites. Some Blacks with long-standing ties to whites in the parish hoped planters would honor their earlier pledges to repel an armed attack. But men who had moved to Madison from previously bulldozed parishes cautioned against that solution; they had tried that course and found that

it was of no use asking the white people to help us, for that would only give publicity to the fact that we had held a meeting, and were talking about resisting; that the whites would misconstrue our purpose, even if we appealed to the better class of white people, while it would give the other class the very excuse the bulldozers wanted for coming in on us.[14]

Once the alarm was raised among the whites of any class, Blacks would entirely lose control of the situation, even if they had only considered resistance in the most abstract terms:

The telegraph operators would get hold of it and would send it abroad all over the country that the negroes were rising and preparing to murder all the white people; but the facts of the case, if they got them, they would never send them. It was of no use talking about resistance; we had had a very sad experience of that thing all through the State of Louisiana; the more resistance the more colored men were killed—that was all there was of that.[15]

Although approaching the whites about self-defense could easily precipitate disaster, political compromise might stay the violence. The meeting discussed the wisdom of splitting the ticket and letting the Democrats field a local slate unopposed, in return for their allowing the Republicans to nominate a Congressional candidate. The meeting agreed upon this course and delegated a

---

		value	
2 12 lb. Brass Howitzers		$	350.00
624 Springfield B. L. Rifles with bayonets			15,600.00
301 Winchester Rifles with bayonets			15,555.00
664 Enfield Rifles with bayonets			10,000.00
93 Spencer Carbines			2,325.00

Also cartridges, sabres, Gun slings, waist belts, etc.

(J. R. G. Pitkin to Justice Department, New Orleans, December 11, 1876, Department of Justice Source-Chronological Files, Louisiana, box 432, National Archives.) Black men, by contrast, were seldom owners of anything more lethal than hunting guns and buckshot.

[14]*Senate Report 693*, II: 522.
[15]Ibid.

committee to parley with leading Democrats. From the outside, the members of the committee to implement the strategy might well have appeared to be the leading colored men, but the meeting had already reached a consensus communally. (The emissaries ultimately failed to strike a bargain, for the Democrats were unyielding in their determination to nominate and elect the entire ticket. The election spawned widespread violence; bulldozers murdered one of the most visible political figures among the Blacks and whipped several others, "made good negroes out of them," in bulldozing parlance.)

One of the delegates selected to parley with the whites was William Murrell, who fancied himself a leading man. At a subsequent secret meeting, however, Murrell learned the exact extent of his leadership. Assembling on the heels of the bulldozing incident, Madison Parish Blacks considered the import of letters from former neighbors who had quit Louisiana for Kansas. They read the letters aloud, discussed them, and closed in favor of migration. Murrell, however, remained in opposition and tried to persuade the people not to leave Louisiana:

I went out and made speeches against their going, and tried to reason with them. And then I found out one thing that was very peculiar—one thing that I would not have believed if I had not seen it—those who had been leading these colored people in political matters could not lead them any more when it came to this matter; the colored people would not pay any attention to them whatever.[16]

Earlier, Murrell's views had generally been in accordance with the people's opinions; now he sought to contradict them. Had he attempted to do so before, even on political questions, he would have found himself equally isolated. Since his position was no longer theirs, he argued with them in vain. "Lord of Heavens," he said, "I might as well have been singing psalms to a dead mule!"[17]

Bulldozers later paid Murrell a personal visit: "When they came to my door, to the door of my own house, and committed such outrages, then I gave up all hope," he said.[18] Having shared that experience, Murrell reversed his anti-migrationist stand. He rejoined Black popular opinion and could again play a prominent role. Thus Murrell learned that his "leadership" hinged upon his

---

[16]Ibid., p. 528.
[17]Ibid.
[18]Ibid., p. 529.

continued agreement with the people. He was not a leader who could decide for the people, but a mouthpiece and a sounding board for the less articulate. Plain people were very seldom led by the nose or duped into something they did not agree with. A Black newspaper editor in New Orleans said of plantation workers, "I have seen some exhibitions of very marked intelligence among them, sir,—not much knowledge of books, perhaps—but exhibitions of very marked natural intelligence."[19]

Negro leadership suffered similar misunderstanding on the national level. Black men whom white public opinion usually singled out as the great national leaders of the colored people were first and foremost those who symbolized what whites thought Black people should think and must be. Needless to say, estimates of exactly who constituted the leaders of the colored people varied. Many white journals in the North—and even in the South in the late 1870s—often quoted Frederick Douglass as the greatest leader of the colored people. But his opinions by that time were unswervingly conservative and often anti-Black. Many Blacks disowned Douglass's latter-day views, notably his shrill denunciations of the Exodus. Senator Blanche K. Bruce of Mississippi, another of the favorite leading colored men in the eyes of the Northern white press, was also a conservative.

In the late 1870s, the nation's concept of a leading colored man was of one who had achieved success in the white majority's terms, very likely one who had attained high political office, such as P. B. S. Pinchback, who had been lieutenant governor of Louisiana, or John H. Rainey, who had been a congressman from Alabama. But by this time the Raineys and Pinchbacks were no longer in touch with their constituencies of poor, rural Blacks. As Democrats took over their state governments, these men lost their elective offices and turned to national Republican patronage, surviving in appointive offices. (Pinchback, for instance, was an inspector for the Internal Revenue Service in New Orleans in 1878–79.) Whether they resided and worked in Washington or in the capitals of their states, they fell ever further out of tune with the everyday living conditions of ordinary Blacks. Once they no longer lived among the people or attended their local meetings, speaking to them and listening to them, they ceased to represent them. These "leading

---

[19]George T. Ruby, ibid., p. 65.

colored men" could hardly be termed the spokesmen of the colored people, much less their leaders.

Whether a leader is taken to mean one exercising delegated power or one swaying public opinion to his point of view, Black people had no *national* leaders. Since leadership depended upon close and constant contact between leaders and people, the idea of a national leader was a contradiction in terms. Public concerns differed from one locality to another, even within the South. Rural conditions generated particular problems of everyday life that varied enormously from parallel concerns in Southern cities. Yet, self-styled race leaders spent most of their time in Southern cities, if not in New York or Washington. They were simply too far removed even to discuss solutions to rural problems. In addition, the personal, empirical nature of individual decision making widened the rural/urban gap. As in the case of William Murrell, who opposed emigration until he had himself experienced bulldozing, the positions that prominent colored men adopted were directly linked to their own narrow experiences.

New York was as different from New Orleans as both of them were from Caddo Parish, Louisiana, or Davidson County, Tennessee. Yet, unless they closely conformed to concrete, local conditions, political strategies proved irrelevant in practice. Although a unified, national Black political stance conceivably might have made sense before 1876, the Compromise of 1877 set Southern Black voters apart from their Northern brethren. With the possibility of military intervention as a curb to political violence effectively ruled out, rural Southern Black voters faced dangers virtually unheard of in Northern or Southern cities, for bulldozing was a characteristically rural phenomenon. Not surprisingly, therefore, questions of sheer bodily safety obsessed rural Black people; in contrast, urban dwellers could afford to theorize about political practice in comparative safety. Black men in town might tire of the bloody shirt and press for fiscal reform in government, but in the country the bloody shirt remained the most compelling issue of the day.

After 1877 the federal government concerned itself less than ever with the welfare of Southern freedpeople. Among Blacks themselves, however, only a few liberal Republicans followed national political trends calling for economy in government and internal improvements. These policies were of little immediate import to working-class Blacks in the country (who were Radical

Republicans and strong Grant men). Their single, persistent demand of the federal government was for protection, and the government's other activities affected them only marginally. Certainly they cared very much whether a Democrat or a Republican occupied the White House and whether a Democratic or Republican majority controlled Congress. Partisan power arrangements in Washington had clearly discernible local repercussions on the issue of whether bulldozers felt emboldened or cautious. But in the elections of presidents or Congressional majorities, nationally known "leading men" carried very little weight. To the extent that Black people could affect Congressional representation or presidential nominations, their influence worked on the *local* level. Ordinary Black people realized this, and they prized the vote for that very reason.

Because political problems were amenable to local or regional activities alone, many Blacks perceived little sustained need for national race policies, hence little need for national spokesmen. Among their number, a Nashville Black man completely rejected the concept of national race leaders:

Now I have this to say, that the colored people have no national leaders. The leaders of the colored people are those who are directly located and associated with the colored people.

. . . It used to be, and is yet, represented in the newspapers of this country, that Frederick Douglass and John M. Langston are the leading colored men of the United States. This assertion is not true. Neither Douglass nor Langston are leaders; they are nobody but Douglass and Langston. Whenever they go among the colored people they charge them well for it. All those fellows that lay around Washington City and represent that they are the power of the colored nation are frauds and false. . . . So far as there being any national leaders among the colored people, there are none. . . .[20]

The correspondent took issue with the basic assumption of the May 1879 National Convention of Colored Men, charging that it was the creature of self-seekers, "those men who keep their names always in the newspapers and in the Associated telegraph news. . . ." The convention

is only for all the defeated colored Congressmen and all other office seekers who are disappointed, to give vent and expression, as if they were

---

[20]"A Colored Man," Nashville Weekly *American,* April 3, 1879.

the leaders of the colored people and could control their votes. I will repeat, the only leaders among the colored people are those whom they personally know and live and associate among them.[21]

Ideally, then, leadership did not pose serious problems on the local level, where Black communities reached unanimous decisions after unlimited, egalitarian exchange. While the town-meeting technique worked more or less well where participants shared the same preoccupations, it served poorly on a larger scale. Despite this difficulty, however, Black political ideals remained rooted in wide-ranging discussion and ultimate unanimity, even in the face of incongruent realities—hence, the constant and futile calls for race unity. Unanimity on any question not so general as to be meaningless proved, of course, unattainable. Yet unity persisted as the ideal mode of race action; it engendered considerable acrimony, as partisans for each position castigated dissenters as frauds.

In practice, the ideal of limitless debate often suffered, even on a small scale. When the great majority of the group in question shared the same general viewpoint, it simply disregarded divergent positions. Blacks conducted their meetings on an egalitarian footing, but they tacitly circumscribed the breadth of opinion accorded a hearing. In the meetings of the Colonization Council of Caddo Parish, Louisiana, participants aired many points of view, but the variety of opinion was not limitless. The Council regularly reached important policy decisions beforehand, in its secret meetings. The president, Henry Adams, said of the closed meetings, "We didn't allow nobody in there but our friends. If he was not a member he couldn't get in until we came out in public." Even the public meetings were subject to qualified participation:

When we called a public meeting we came out to the park or anywhere, and didn't care who heard. *Then anybody could participate who believed in our movement.* There was no meetings held of our members that allowed anybody but our members *unless it was somebody that wanted to give us some of their views.* . . . When we held our meetings we would not allow the politicians to speak. We would not allow any one to speak but in our favor.[22]

In short, the group controlled the flow of opinion, narrowing

---

[21]Ibid.

[22]Henry Adams, *Senate Report 693*, II: 105. (Emphasis added.)

it to exclude completely opposing views. While this limitation compromised the ideal of truly open discussion, it did not obscure the fact that rural Blacks deliberately discussed public policies and action.

Two other persistent fictions of Southern race relations concerned voting. One view held that Blacks were not "intelligent" voters because they slavishly followed the Republican ticket. They voted, it was said, to feel important or out of mindless habit, not reflection. This reasoning held that since Blacks did not prize suffrage for any sound motives, they might as well vote Democratic as Republican, or not vote at all. This devaluation of Black voting meshed nicely with the second conviction—that "good Negroes," who let politics alone, would generally prosper.

"Representative colored men" and whites sometimes assumed that rural Blacks voted for frivolous reasons, to feel important, to make a show, and that they were ill informed of the relationships between their ballots, the local and state governments, and the federal government. The Senate report on the election outrages of 1878 voiced this common view:

The right to vote is a privilege more highly prized by the colored voter than by voters of any other class; and he will make sacrifices to exercise this privilege that few white men will. It is by the exercise of the right of suffrage that he assures himself that he is a free man, and not a slave. It gives him an increased idea of his importance in social and political affairs. *It gratifies his pride . . .*[23]

Yet this same report included testimony showing that rural Blacks in Louisiana had elaborated a strategy two years in advance to assure that their ballots would be counted in the national elections of 1880. "Our idea [in 1878] was that we wanted to elect a good, honest police jury against 1880," said one of the organizers, "so that when the Presidential election comes on we can have the ballot-box where we can get to it and put tickets into it."[24]

Working-class Blacks were far from ignorant of their self-interest in political issues. In fact, it was their correct understanding of

---

[23] *Report of the United States Senate Committee to Inquire into Alleged Frauds and Violence in the Elections of 1878* (Washington, 1879), I: xxviii. (Hereafter referred to as *Senate Report 855.*) (Emphasis added.)

[24] Lafayette Thorpe, ibid., p. 36.

the use of suffrage which drove the Southern whites to extralegal means of distorting the Black vote. During the 1876 canvass in Louisiana, Black Republican organizers were working in Claiborne Parish, near Homer. They reactivated Republican clubs—the local party unit—and rallied Republican voters. Whites who objected to Blacks organizing politically disrupted a meeting, sending many of the audience home. But several men reconvened at a nearby church and continued their exchange of views. "I also went in the church," said one organizer, "and some who knew me by name, asked me to ask an educational speech; so I consented, and began to say something respecting us freedmen. . . . I further said we ought to elect men to office that would always give us free schools."[25] At that point, "Three white men came in and leaned upon the benches in the church, and some of the colored men who had been run by white men that night, jumped over the benches and ran out of the church." The whites reacted not only to the organizer's stand on the school issue, but also to his rejection of permanent white supremacy. In the church he had mentioned "how long we had been free; how fast we had improved in citizenship, and that we would soon overtake some of the white people if we continued as we had started."[26] They were, indeed, growing into considerable political sophistication.

While Blacks appreciated the value of political organization and voting, they also took advantage of means other than the ballot to impress their point of view on officials at all levels. The Caddo Parish Colonization Council, for instance, wrote to senators and congressmen, sent petitions to Presidents Grant and Hayes, and presented its views to conventions of colored men in race assemblies.

Indeed, Southern Blacks utilized a whole array of political techniques to organize, disseminate their views, and vote. They understood very well that Southern whites "[did] not believe the negro votes 'intelligently' because he [wouldn't] support them," and that according to whites, "when [Negroes] vote the Democratic ticket it is all right, but when they vote the Republican ticket it is all wrong."[27]

---

[25]Henry Adams, *Senate Report 693*, II: 188.
[26]Ibid.
[27]John G. Lewis, ibid., p. 440; George T. Ruby, ibid., p. 73.

Most Republicans agreed with the dictum "Show me a negro who votes the Democratic ticket and I will show you either a hypocrite or a fool."[28] The vast majority of Black voters preferred Republican candidates, but some Blacks were coerced into voting Democratic, and a handful cast Democratic ballots voluntarily.

One Black Democrat, R. L. Faulkner, had voted with the Republicans in Natchitoches Parish, Louisiana, immediately after the war. At that time, he said, "The respectable class of colored people all participated." Later, however, hoi polloi took over, and he withdrew. By the late 1860s "there came so many strangers among [the Republicans] and then the ignorant class of people—simply the ignorant class of people—they were partial to get in the lead, so that the respectable class has withdrew and took no part. . . ."[29] Faulkner contrasted the old speech days, when the better class of colored people stood out, with the later years when the clamjamfry took over: ". . . days when there would be speaking, when I would know we would have the best men in the place marshals during a procession you know, sir, but in the last days it was just bird of a feather."[30] It is worth nothing, perhaps, that Faulkner was free before the war.

While Faulkner voted with the Democrats primarily out of snobbery—he did not like being associated with what he termed "the ignorant class of people"—prosperous Gilbert Myers of Caddo Parish voted with the Democrats for material reasons. He did not necessarily prefer Democratic candidates, but he intended to stay in the good graces of the most powerful and prestigious men in the parish. He called them "the majority," but he meant the electoral majority *as returned,* for Blacks were in the numerical majority in the parish. For Myers, voting Democratic seemed a kind of insurance for his continued economic well-being: "I sympathized with my own self, knowing that I expected to stay with them to make property if I could, and the South had always

---

[28]James M. M'Gill, *Senate Report 855,* I: 216.

[29]R. L. Faulkner, *Senate Report 693,* III: 244. An active Republican in the late 1860s, R. L. Faulkner headed a Grant-Colfax club in Natchitoches Parish before he was Ku-Kluxed in 1868. In 1869 he still considered himself a Republican and stated his concept of the principles of the Democratic party like this: "(to put it in a common way,) that if they licked [if the Democrats won the election], there would be no more voting for Mr. Nigger; . . . it was a white man's country." (*House Misc. Doc. 154,* I: 523.)

[30]R. L. Faulkner, *Senate Report 693,* III: 244.

been kind to me. . . . I thought my interest was to stay with the majority of the country whom I expected to prosper with."[31] Myers showed himself a most uncommon Black man, however, for when asked which he valued more, his freedom or his property, he answered, "Well, if I had to get shet of either of them, I would rather have my property."[32]

Remaining inoffensive in the eyes of local whites opened the most usual route to peaceful survival for Southern Blacks. It meant renouncing political organization and perhaps even voting. Politics increasingly became white folks' business, and nightriders "disastered dem what meddled wid de white folks."[33]

Shunning Republican politics offered no sure guarantee of safety, however, and the best of Negroes might occasionally and unaccountably fall foul of bulldozers. In Shreveport, James Butler was worth nearly seven hundred dollars in real estate and livestock. He kept to himself, made money, and whites considered him a good enough Negro to make him a commissioner at the polls for city elections and a representative of the colored people on the local jury committee. Nonetheless, one of his employees was capriciously murdered in cold blood in a racial incident.[34] Radicalism and political independence, however, accounted for a disproportionate part of the slaughter.

The single document most vividly recording the enormity of Black bloodshed between 1866 and 1876 was kept by Henry Adams and the committee that he headed in northern Louisiana. The list of beatings and murders enumerates 683 briefly described incidents, and eleven affidavits of about one paragraph each. It includes numerous examples of politically motivated violence in Louisiana parishes:

164th. Nathan Williams (colored), badly whipped and his cotton taken away without any cause by Bill Mark, a white man, on his place, in 1874, because he voted the Radical ticket.

228th. Old man Jack Horse and son was badly beat and shot at by white men—they were as bloody as hogs—at or near Jack Horse's place, going to the election November 7, 1870.

333d. Abe. Young, shot by white men on Angels plantation, spouting about voting Republican ticket, in 1874.

---

[31]Gilbert Myers, ibid., II: 584.
[32]Ibid., p. 587.
[33]Isaac Stier, W.P.A., *Ex-Slave Narratives*, vol. IX (Mississippi), p. 148.
[34]James Butler, *Senate Report 693*, III: 167–68.

442n. Jones (colored), shot about voting a Radical ticket at or near Haynesville, by white men, 1874.[35]

Not all the violence sprang from political motives:

454th. Ben. Gardner (colored), badly beaten by white men, on Mr. Gamble's plantation, because he refused to stay on the place another year. This was in 1874.

518th. Henry Moore, colored, killed by white men and burned; accused of living with a white girl near Homer, in 1873.

559th. Jack, colored, was hung dead, by white men, on De Loche's plantation, about three miles from the town of Saint Martinville, because he sauced a white man. The white man wanted him to leave his crop and he refused, thereupon the white man got a crowd of white men and hung him, and taken his crop from his family; 1875, July.

[AFFIDAVIT] NO. 9.
DE SOTO PARISH,
STATE OF LOUISIANA:

My name is Hiram Smith; I lived on Joe Williams' place, about two miles southeast of Keachie. I asked Mr. Williams to pay what he owed me on my cotton; also seventy-five dollars he had taken away from me, what another man had paid me. He jumped on me and beat me so badly I fear I cannot live. He made me crawl on my knees and call them my God, my master, the God of all power. They then drew revolvers on me; all because I had asked for a settlement. This was done on the 16th of March, 1876.

Hiram Smith[36]

Extralegal violence served primarily to keep Blacks in line politically, but its usefulness spread to a variety of interracial contacts, before and after Redemption. In print and in speeches, white Democrats insisted that once they ran the South, bulldozing would die away. Quite to the contrary, the practice persisted throughout the rest of the nineteenth century, as long as Black voters—or maverick white ones—sought to exercise their suffrage in their own interests, as they saw them. The attempt to close Blacks and uncooperative whites out of public life did not stop at bulldozing, however, for a hardening white solidarity drove Black and white voters into separate, narrow channels of political expression.

---

[35]Henry Adams, ibid., II: 196, 198, 201, 202.
[36]Ibid., pp. 204, 206, 208, 213.

3
Politics
and the Color Line

Blacks did not automatically vote Republican out of gratitude for emancipation. They clung to the party of Lincoln more than a decade after the end of the Civil War because on the state and local levels it represented the interests of working people, supporting free public schools and exemption laws (which placed personal property beyond the reach of creditors). The Democracy's policies were anti-working-class as well as anti-Black. On the other side of the color bar, Democrats constantly whipped poor whites into line in the name of white solidarity, although they often contradicted their interests as poor people. Exceptions to this rule occurred from time to time, of course, but for the most part, white Democrats rode the color line with vigor and considerable success. In 1878 the Brenham Weekly *Banner*, a Washington County, Texas, Democratic newspaper, beat the drums for lily-whiteness:

—The question to be decided by this county election is, Shall we have a white man's or a colored county government?
—Capt. J. M. Williams is the Democratic nominee for representative from this county; his opponent is a colored man. Let every *white* man vote for Williams.

And later in the same issue:

The name of W. H. Billingslea appears as the nominee of the Republican party of this county, in the manifesto recently issued by the colored people, therefore he cannot expect any Democrat to vote for him.[1]

Despite the *Banner's* urgings, the results of the election humiliated the lily-whites. Black candidates won the offices of both county representative and "floater" (representative at large), although white voters enjoyed a majority of nearly five hundred in the county.[2] Republicans had united and fared so well that in the election's aftermath, the piqued *Banner* whined: "Hereafter, county conventions should be abandoned in this county and men run on their merits for county offices. So long as the colored elements are united and the whites divided, the colored elements and their manipulators will have everything their own way."[3] For the *Banner,* the splintered Democratic vote explained its losses in the 1878 county elections, and the paper ignored the class interests of the party's platform and candidates.

The Texas Democratic party, like its counterpart in Louisiana, spoke all too often to the especial interests of the old planter class. As a result, nonplanter, Democratic whites lent their strength to the Greenback party, which also drew on the remnants of the Republican organization. In addition, they supported Republican and independent candidates who addressed the interests of poor men. During the winter of 1878–79, coalition or "fusion" politics prospered, but, as was to be the case in other interracial political efforts—especially those that were the fruit of hard times—cooperation was short-lived. By the year of the presidential election, the Greenback party was on the decline in Texas. But during its brief heyday, its success frightened Democrats into contemplating disfranchisement, and not only for Blacks.

Failing to realize their expectations in the 1878 local elections, a number of Democratic papers in Texas began agitating for a poll tax as a voting prerequisite. The *Banner* agreed entirely:

A poll tax law would work like a charm in the counties where there is a

---

[1]Brenham (Texas) Weekly *Banner,* October 11, 1878. (Emphasis in original.)

[2]Washington County was the richest county in the state at the time, and the most thickly settled. Its white voters included both Republicans and Democrats, for the Republican party in Washington County embraced the large German population of the area. In addition to at least one Black faction within the Republican party of the county, there were two white ones, one German, and one native American.

[3]Brenham Weekly *Banner,* November 29, 1878.

large negro population. About all the enjoyment some negroes have in the world is voting; it is a part of their existence, and they never allow an opportunity to vote to pass. A very large majority of them pay no taxes and also avoid road working. If they were compelled to exhibit their poll tax receipts before voting, the probability is there would be fewer of them vote [*sic*]; the people generally would be better off.

To critics who feared the poll tax's spill-over effects on whites, the *Banner* retorted: "In regard to the whites, the votes of those who are unwilling or unable to pay a poll tax could be dispensed with, without any serious detriment to the public good."[4] No wonder many Democrats favored Greenback and Republican candidates at the ballot box. To agree with the *Banner* that the Greenback and Republican parties were the same thing might be going too far, but it is noteworthy that the elected representatives of both parties sponsored legislation favorable to the poor working classes.

Washington County Democrats lamented the 1878 election of a state representative named Sledge, merely because he was Black. But during his first winter in the legislature, Sledge introduced an exemption bill aimed at mitigating the worst aspects of the crop-lien law.[5] Had it passed, the bill would have exempted two hundred bushels of corn and five hundred pounds of bacon per family at forced sales. As mild as it was, Texas Democrats considered the exemption excessive. In 1872 a Black legislator in Louisiana, J. Henri Burch, successfully introduced a "homestead law," which operated as an exemption law, "prevent[ing] a person from taking [from] any labor[er]—white or colored, it made no difference—any of his implements—that is, his horse, his wagon, his stock, his wife's furniture, and such as that—to the value of six hundred dollars." With Redemption, the Democratic legislature repealed the act, "one of the first laws they repealed," said Burch. As a result, "there is nothing safe for the laborer now, if [the landlord] chooses to move upon him and take away his goods and implements of agriculture."[6]

---

[4]Ibid., December 20, 1878.

[5]Crop-lien laws protected the merchants and landowners, not the tenants or sharecroppers. See chapter 5 for more discussion of renting contracts.

[6]J. Henri Burch, *Senate Report 693*, II: 219–20. Burch, a Black carpetbagger from New England, married the widow of Oscar Dunn. He had been forced to accept modification of the exemption law in 1874, releasing the city of New Orleans from its provisions.

In several such instances, then, the Republican party of these Southern states functioned as the party of the "workingmen," as they were often termed. This was principally due to its roots in a largely Black—and therefore working-class—constituency. The elected representatives of this constituency of laboring people, however, were often much better off materially and educationally. In order to function effectively among white elected officials they needed to have mastered white language and mannerisms, which sometimes distanced them from the Black masses. While Black Republican representatives did not unfailingly take progressive positions, they often inspired coalition attempts between poor Blacks and poor whites. A noteworthy example was the broad appeal of the Reverend A. R. Blount of Natchitoches Parish, Louisiana.

Blount was a propertied Baptist minister, worth some seventy-four hundred dollars. A mulatto, he had represented the Natchitoches district in the Louisiana legislature in 1872 and in the state senate between 1872 and 1876. As president of the Natchitoches Parish Republican Central Committee, he worked to bring poor whites into the parish's Republican majority. Although the Black registered voters in the parish's Republican party outnumbered whites by three to one, Blount attracted some five hundred white voters to a prospective fusion ticket in 1878. His success brought bulldozers to his door, and he was forced to flee the parish well before the elections. The Natchitoches White League complained that he was "not only controlling the negroes, but duping the white men." According to a Black New Orleans newspaper: "This was an allusion to the attitude of the poorer whites towards the Democracy, in that the passage of a hog law, impounding and confiscating swine, and a stock law, obliging the poor people to keep their animals away from pasturage, had made naturally this class opposed to the Democratic rule."[7] And poor whites sought him out for additional reasons: "As Mr. Blunt [*sic*] had been the State Senator, and was besides generally known and respected, it was quite natural for these people to talk with and endeavor to receive such advice about their common grievances as he could give."[8] Before bulldozing wrecked their cooperation, representa-

---

[7]New Orleans *Observer*, n.d. [about October 17, 1878], quoted in Department of Justice Source-Chronological Files, Louisiana, box 434, National Archives.
[8]Ibid.

tives of Democratic clubs of whites "from the pine woods" were forging a coalition with Black Republicans that would have outpolled the regular Democrats by fifteen hundred to two thousand votes. Had terrorism not nipped the fusion in the first bud, "all their bulldozing could not defeat us."[9] Alive to their own interest, the Democrats struck before the graft could take.

Biracial bipartisanship, such as this aborted effort in Natchitoches Parish, was comparatively rare in the post-Reconstruction South. While it occurred in various third-party movements, such as the Greenbackers in the late 1870s, the Farmers' Alliances in the late 1880s, and the People's Parties of the mid-1890s, interracial politics remained the exception, the color line, the rule. The rule progressively hardened, burying the economic interests of poor whites beneath an avalanche of white solidarity and placing Blacks more and more on the defensive. According to a United States marshal in Louisiana, the color line worked "to compact the blacks, to constran [*sic*] them to find refuge in thier [*sic*] own numbers, to fortify themselves by local legislation and to station in the offices, as in so many sentry-boxes, stewards who should not be indifferent to thier [*sic*] interests. They have been and are politically in a state of siege."[10]

Extreme conservatism resulted, and by the late 1870s many articulate Blacks advised Black voters to play safe and avoid third parties. Richard Nelson, editor of the Galveston *Spectator,* and W. W. Jackson of Jackson, Mississippi, warned against the vague promises Greenbackers held out to Blacks:

There is a party now split from the Democrats who style themselves "Greenbackers;" but I think the proper name to give them would be "forlorn Democrats." They are now seeking to get the colored Republicans to join hands with them and help them to win. Now I may be wrong, but I think it would be best for all colored men to let these two sore head parties fight their own battles. These two parties at the last election joined freely in the slaughter of the poor colored man; and if it is necessary they will join again. There is no use for them to say that "we will stand by you" for this has been the say all along, and it was only to get the poor ne-

---

[9]A. R. Blount, *Senate Report 855,* I: 140, 142.

[10]J. R. G. Pitkin to Alphonso Taft, New Orleans, November [21?], 1876, Department of Justice Source-Chronological Files, Louisiana, box 432, National Archives.

gro's vote and then the shot gun policy and bulldozing went on all the same.[11]

Like Jackson, the vast majority of Blacks remained loyal Republicans; only occasionally, when there was no Republican slate in the field, they might grudgingly support third parties or independent tickets. A token Black candidate on the ticket would encourage this kind of voter. Black Republicans in Texas, for instance, worked to elect Greenbackers in the absence of a Republican ticket. One called it the best he could do "under the circumstances": "Well, I am something like some Democrats, in one respect; I have heard some of them say if you were to put up the Devil on the Democratic ticket they would vote for him. The Republican party had no nomination in the field in that contest, and I was ready to do anything to beat the Democrats; so I worked for the Greenback ticket."[12] But as Southern Republicans found themselves cut off from election successes, some sought permanent allies outside the Republican party.

Abandoned by Republicans of the North and the South, Southern Blacks cast about for remedies to their political isolation and eventual neutralization. "Southernizing" was the solution favored by conservative Blacks. They advocated permanent fusion with the less objectionable elements of the Democratic party, instead of retrograde struggling for political autonomy and unswerving Republicanism. The prime apologist of Southernizing was P. B. S. Pinchback, a "representative colored man" and Louisiana's leading Black Republican in the late 1870s. Pinchback was the editor of the New Orleans Weekly *Louisianian,* through whose columns the only outright advocates of Southernizing spoke.

At best, Southernizing meant facing up to the realities of post-Reconstruction politics. It recognized that if Blacks acted alone, they had their backs to the wall, and that unless they combined with Southern whites of some stripe, they faced a crush between the two wheels of Northern indifference and Southern violence. Pinchback counseled Blacks to cultivate friendly relations with

---

[11]Brenham Weekly *Banner,* May 17, 1878; New Orleans *Southwestern Christian Advocate,* August 28, 1879.

[12]H. Ruby, *Senate Report 693,* III: 422–23. H. Ruby was not the same person as G. T. Ruby, although both were born in New York and had resided in Texas. H. Ruby, at the time he testified before the Senate select committee, lived in Oswego, Kansas.

conservative Democrats and elect men who would not only represent the "wealth and intelligence" of the South, but look after the welfare of Blacks as well.

In 1878 Pinchback claimed that early in the second Grant administration he had seen the handwriting on the wall, even while a Republican majority controlled Congress. At that time, Southern whites had been anxious for biracial alliances, he said, but Black politicians and voters had let their chance slip away by not voluntarily relinquishing their political clout while they still wielded considerable power. Now, in 1878, wrote Pinchback, "with their power and prestige gone, disheartened and demoralized, their manhood crushed and their votes practically suppressed, it will require more sagacity and skill than the race has heretofore exhibited to accomplish that much to be desired end."[13]

In 1876, however, Pinchback's criticism of Black voters was far more accusatory than he remembered. He denied that the federal government had turned its back on Blacks in the South; rather, "it has said to the negro—'Halt.' It has said to the negro, that your corruption in office must cease. As long as you put to the front men incompetent to discharge the great duties that devolve upon them, we give you no protection. This is what it means—nothing more, nothing less." He charged that Blacks, not whites, had drawn the color line, inaugurating a "long train of evils and outrages." The fault lay squarely with Blacks themselves, for in every instance in Louisiana that "the colored man has shown a disposition to be guided by his own convictions, an incessant war has been carried out against him, both inside and outside the Republican party. We are not only impoverished, not only bankrupt, but worse—immeasurably worse. The black people have lost all their manhood."[14] Only a few other conservatives reached Pinchback's level of vituperation.

Other Black supporters of Southernizing left anti-Black invective aside and advocated the tactic for reasons of expediency. A contributor who signed himself "NOUNA" in the *Louisianian* took his cue from President Hayes's Southern Policy.[15] He equated

---

[13]New Orleans Weekly *Louisianian,* December 14, 1878. The proposal that anyone voluntarily hand over political power remains unrealistic to this day.

[14]Nashville Weekly *American,* April 13, 1876.

[15]Hayes urged that Southerners, Black and white, should cooperate politically for the good of the section as a whole. He took for granted that whites would

working-class Grantism with Northern domination and served notice on radical Black Republicanism: "Surrounded by prejudice at home he [the Southern colored Republican voter] must needs incur the hatred of those who employ him if he continues to go with and take instructions from, northern idols and gods. What must he do then? There is only one thing left for him to do and that is to *southernize his ideas.*" Black voters must arouse themselves and seek new political friends among the bulldozers:

I mean by that, that the negro must understand his new relations now that he is out of power. These new relations are close political association and sympathy with southern men, and southern ideas of commercial progression. But will it do to act with men who murder and kill? . . . I say boldly and frankly as a negro that all things considered it is better to trust those with whom you live, even if they are stained with your blood, than to link your political fortunes to a set of cold, heartless and hypocritical leaders in the north, as represented by the present executive and the class of men he has around him.[16]

"PELICAN," another proponent of Southernizing, further shifted the burden of readjustment onto Black shoulders. Exceeding NOUNA's approval of alliances with former enemies, PELICAN insisted that Blacks must also foreswear complaints of ill-treatment. Challenging the very basis of democratic government, he argued that Blacks were not sufficiently experienced to deserve full political rights, for "comparatively speaking, the negro is but an infant in politics, and like an infant knows nothing of the duties and responsibilities of government." Since Blacks were economically dependent on whites in the South, he contended, Blacks must conform to present circumstances. "We must stop this cry of intimidation, in order to remove the sores which infest the body politic in the South." PELICAN assigned additional tasks to Black voters:

---

provide most of the leadership and hold almost all the offices—since they enjoyed a near monopoly of the "wealth and intelligence" of the South. It was also urged that Blacks renounce support of their own candidates and accept indirect representation in local, state, and national assemblies. They would support the whites in power who, in turn, would protect Blacks from violence and look after their interests in some unspecified manner.

[16]New Orleans Weekly *Louisianian,* December 14, 1878. (Emphasis in original.)

We must vote for the conservative and independent thinkers of the South, in order to break down the wall of prejudice which surrounds the Democratic party, and which makes its ranks impregnable [in the South]. By so doing, we will force both parties to make economy in the administration of government, internal improvements and commercial development their aim, instead of inflaming the passions and prejudices of sections, classes and races one against the other.[17]

But none of these Southernizers lived in the countryside, among the bulldozers. PELICAN was lamentably out of touch with the preoccupations of the great majority of Black voters. While he advocated favorite planting and mercantile reforms, he entirely ignored the two major concerns of ordinary Blacks: enforcement of laws protecting life and liberty, and free public schools. Internal improvements and commercial development were the pet projects of what would soon be termed the "New South."

Understandably, rural Blacks rejected Southernizing as either irrelevant or repugnant on anything more than a temporary and purely local basis. This position found clear statement in the words of John R. Lynch of Mississippi:

The name "Democracy," affording to it modern perverted application, is synonymous with every species of political crime, outrage, and inhumanity which has ever disgraced our government or brought reproach upon our civilization. It not only sustained and upheld the inforced degradation and subjugation of a large portion of the inhabitants of the country, but which, to say nothing of what may now be regarded as dead issues, has been the bane and curse of the South for the last quarter of a century.[18]

Southernizing was stillborn in the late 1870s, for the combined pressure of common Black political aims and the color line increasingly isolated Black voters. White supremacy divorced poor Blacks from poor whites, militating against their waging joint campaigns that would reflect their economic self-interest. Blacks struggled on alone, although their three central preoccupations—earning a living, voting in peace, and seeing their children educated—depended on effective political action.

---

[17]Ibid., December 21, 1878. PELICAN is possibly J. Henri Burch of New Orleans.

[18]John R. Lynch to Colonel Mason, Natchez, Mississippi, November 20, 1878, New Orleans Weekly *Louisianian,* April 5, 1879. Lynch was a Black Republican from Mississippi, twice United States representative from the Natchez ("Shoestring") district of that state.

4

Schools and Politics

Wide-scale public-school educa-
tion, an innovation of the Reconstructed state legislatures in the
South, stood high among the aspects of freedom that Blacks prized
most. To educate themselves and their children, freedpeople resorted to a variety of expedients, but the public schools provoked
sustained political concern. Blacks considered education their key
to the future, and, as such, a critical responsibility of government.
Although the school issue assumed somewhat different urban and
rural aspects and varied in states where Reconstruction ended
before or after 1874–75, it unfailingly evoked sharp racial and
partisan responses.

Partly because antebellum laws walled slaves off from schooling, freedpeople regarded education with unbounded enthusiasm. One Black man vowed: "I am going to school my children if
I have to eat bread and water."[1] For others it was a matter of
clearheaded self-defense:

I wants my children to be educated because then I can believe what they
tells me. If I go to another person with a letter in my hand, and he reads
it, he can tell me what he pleases in that letter, and I don't know any
better. I must take it all for granted; but if I have got children who read
and write, I will hand them the letter, and they will tell me the contents
of that letter, and I will know it's all right, as he says it.[2]

Immediately after the Civil War, Black people of all ages
flocked to the schools that opened across the South. In those first

---

[1]Gilbert Myers, *Senate Report 693*, II: 585.
[2]Quoted in John G. Lewis, ibid., p. 437.

postwar years, the Methodist Episcopal Church and other Northern white-church missionaries, freedmen's aid societies (mostly white, but some Black), the Freedmen's Bureau, and the Union Army operated schools. At the same time, literate Blacks, often migrants from the North, opened schools wherever they could secure a room; pupils paid teachers by subscription. Years later, a former slave remembered attending just such a school in Tennessee: "The colored people who had been in the North were better educated than the people in the South. They would come down to the South and help the rest of us. . . . I went to a subscription school. We would all pay a man to come to teach us. . . . There were no Government schools then that were free.[3]

This system persisted outside towns and cities well after Redemption. But the expense—paying the teacher consumed a substantial portion of a family's paltry cash earnings—combined with the need for children in the fields, severely restricted the number of children in private schools. In Bossier Parish, north Louisiana, for instance, on a plantation with some three or four hundred children, only forty attended the local private school. The young teacher and his even younger assistant collected one dollar per month per pupil. Meanwhile, the parish's handful of public schools opened only two or three months a year in 1879; many stayed closed throughout 1880. The remaining two or three hundred children either did without education entirely or relied on the Sabbath school.[4]

Black churches commonly operated schools alone or in cooperation with city councils, particularly in Texas towns. In Denison, the Reverend Mr. Marmet was pastor of the African Methodist Episcopal church and the town's only Black teacher (he was retained as a teacher by the Denison City Council). Although his school was considered the best colored school in north Texas, it met in the church, and the Reverend Mr. Marmet taught over one hundred children.[5]

Sabbath schools also helped fill the enormous gaps in formal education. Colored teachers in the local schools often held Sunday

---

[3]Clayton Holbert, W.P.A., *Ex-Slave Narratives*, vol. VI (Kansas). Booker T. Washington's first schooling in West Virginia occurred in this sort of school, run by a Black teacher.

[4]Henson Alexander, *Senate Report 693*, II: 563, 572.

[5]Denison (Texas) Daily *News*, October 15, 1879, and January 6, 1880.

schools, which both children and adults attended. Generally Sunday schools taught reading and sometimes writing, taking the Bible as a text. A former Tougaloo University student wrote:

I have a day school of forty-nine scholars, a majority of them can write and cipher. My S[unday] S[chool] is much larger and more interesting than my day school. I have eighty-three Sunday Scholars and only a few of them are ever absent.

I have charge of the Bible class which includes my two assistant teachers, Miss Hannah Williams, and Mr. Calvin R. Nicholson who is also the Superintendent. The youngest member of my Bible class, a boy, is 13 years of age, and the eldest, a man, is 51, tho' he doesn't look to be so old. There were nearly a hundred passages of scripture repeated in school last Sabbath. Only four scholars were absent; one was sick, two accompanied their grandmother "over the creek," the fourth is a girl who lives a long way from school. . . .[6]

Yet subscription schools, Sabbath schools, and all the teachers' and scholars' dedication in the world could not substitute for fast-disappearing public education.

The Reconstruction legislatures of Tennessee, Mississippi, Louisiana, and Texas had written provisions for public schooling into the new state constitutions in the late 1860s, thereby taking over the primary schools opened and financed by Northern missionary societies and the Freedmen's Bureau.[7] But by the early

---

[6]Robert C. Martin to M. E. Strieby, Sallie Station, Attala, Mississippi, May 25, 1877, American Missionary Association Papers, Mississippi.

[7]Although public schools had existed to a very limited extent in the antebellum South (in Louisiana, for instance, only within New Orleans), for all intents and purposes the Reconstruction constitutions of the late 1860s brought public education to large numbers of youngsters for the first time. The states' serious commitment to public instruction, however, did not outlive the Republican administrations. Once Democrats regained control of state legislatures, they substantially reduced support for schools, either de jure, as in Mississippi, or de facto, as in Louisiana, where school appropriations dropped precipitously. The cuts resulted from Democratic opposition to publicly financed schools, especially for Black children, from protests against high taxes from Democratic constituencies, and from the economic hard times of the 1870s. In theory, the parish and local governments supplemented state appropriations, as, indeed, they were to have done during Reconstruction. While local rural governments were no more conscientious in supporting public schools after 1877 than before, the slashing of state assistance rendered their failure all the more grievous. Since private philanthropy like the Peabody Fund made little impact on public education in Louisiana in the 1870s and since school funds were favorite targets of embezzling local officials both before

1870s the public schools were already in jeopardy, especially in Tennessee; there, what little Reconstruction the state underwent ended with Democratic takeover in 1870.

In Tennessee the question of public education come to a head in 1874, embroiled in the Federal Civil Rights Bill controversy.[8] The bill sparked acrimonious debate among the factions of the state Republican party, with the white leadership in adamant opposition, the Black rank-and-file in ardent support.

The state constitution of 1870 had already enfeebled the Republican party in Tennessee with its inclusion of a poll-tax provision. (Although it was dropped in 1873, the poll tax dealt a permanent blow to Tennessee Republicanism.) Yet the Republican party held on, despite overwhelming Democratic victories after 1870 and the eventual desertion of most of its white supporters to the ascendant Democracy. The leader of the Republican party, United States Senator William G. "Parson" Brownlow, had been Tennessee's Reconstruction governor.

After Brownlow had attacked the Civil Rights Bill in Senate debate, the State Convention of Colored Men took up the issue at its Nashville meeting in 1874. The convention rejected a suggestion that it leave the Republican party entirely in order to form a Black man's party, but it severely reprimanded Brownlow Republicans for their anti–civil-rights stand. Samuel Lowery, a Nashville delegate, opposed walking out over the Civil Rights Bill at that time, but he conceded that "unless the Republican party of Tennessee adopted the civil rights measure, the colored people could not go hand in hand with them any longer." Although the whole bill carried great weight for Blacks, as well as for whites, the public schools lay at the heart of the matter. Lowery thought that "if the policy of Brownlow was adopted, their children would be

___

and after Redemption, the state's children had to wait until this century to see anything approaching adequate schools.

[8]The Civil Rights Bill of 1875—introduced and championed by Charles Sumner—aimed at insuring equal access to public schools and transportation. Blacks, quite naturally, supported it strongly. They had already begun to encounter color lines and instances of racial exclusion in scattered areas of public life. They saw the Civil Rights Bill as a sort of last hope for the preservation of civil rights and equality of access to public institutions. Congress passed the bill in 1875; Texas immediately declared it unconstitutional. In 1883 the United States Supreme Court invalidated it in a move that, more than any other single act, condoned the color bar and racial exclusion.

deprived of the privileges of the public schools."[9]

The incompatability of adequate schools for children in rural areas, on the one hand, with racially segregated education, on the other, presented Tennesseeans of two races with a terrible dilemma, given limited school funds. The state superintendent of education admitted as much in a reply to the colored men's convention: "I cannot regard the action of the colored convention as other than hostile to the public school system of Tennessee," he said, "and really at war with the best interest of such of the colored people as desire to give their children the benefit of a common school education." But his concept of "equal schooling" was lopsided:

If it be complained that colored children are not permitted to enter the white schools, it might with equal propriety and force be complained that white children are not allowed to enter the colored schools, as they are not. . . . It is impossible to so locate the schools at present, as to place them within convenient reach of all the children in every neighborhood in the State, owing to the sparseness of the population in many sections. The consequence is, in some localities one race suffers; in others, the other— the colored the more frequently, being the more sparse.[10]

He never considered the expedient of racially mixed schools in lightly settled areas.

As the school controversy heated up, opponents of the Civil Rights Bill introduced their arguments of last resort. Senator Brownlow lashed back at a critic, who,

though a white man, seems to regard the black race as entitled to *superior privileges* to his own. I do not believe that the personal freedom of all the white people of the South, and all their rights of local self-government, should be sacrificed to accommodate a few thousand insolent negroes, or to gratify the caprices of negro-worshiping white men and selfish politicians.[11]

The Nashville *Union and American* took Brownlow's side in several editorials, asserting, "The fact is, Brownlow represents the sentiments of nine-tenths of the white Republicans of the State . . ." and "the fanatics [among the colored people], in attempting to force the establishment of mixed schools through

---

[9]Nashville *Union and American,* April 29, 1874.

[10]Ibid., May 1, 1874.

[11]Ibid., June 4, 1874. (Emphasis added.)

Congressional legislation, are simply inaugurating a social war of races in which, as all history demonstrated, the superior must win."[12]

The state's school-segregation bill short-circuited the Civil Rights Bill in Tennessee and laid the issue of school desegregation to rest for several decades. In fact, by the late 1870s segregated schools were the rule throughout the South and in the border states. Even in most Northern states (including Kansas), racially segregated schools were normal, if not the rule. For Blacks the issue was no longer enrolling all Black children in accessible schools; that was a lost cause. Two other campaigns continued, however, safeguarding existing but segregated schools and securing Black teachers.

As early as 1877, Blacks in St. Louis petitioned the Board of Public Schools to place only Black teachers in Black schools. Protesting the poor quality of whites teaching Black children, they charged that qualified Black teachers were passed over in the hiring process, with preference given to whites merely because they were white. On the other hand, well-qualified white teachers avoided Black schools because of the "social stigma attached to such a position."[13] Throughout the late 1870s and into the 1880s, Blacks waged the campaign for Black teachers, usually on the grounds of the successful St. Louis case. At the National Convention of Colored Men in Nashville in 1879, the cause received renewed impetus when Ferdinand L. Barnett of Chicago summarized the issue for a national Black audience:

White teachers in colored schools are nearly always mentally, morally, or financially bankrupts, and no colored community should tolerate the imposition. High schools and colleges are sending learned colored teachers in the field constantly, and it is manifestly unjust to make them stand idle and see their people taught by those whose only interest lies in securing their monthly compensation in dollars and cents. Again, colored schools thrive better under colored teachers. The St. Louis schools furnish an excellent example.[14]

---

[12]Ibid., May 3, 29, 1874.

[13]New Orleans *Southwestern Christian Advocate*, April 12, 1877.

[14]Ferdinand L. Barnett, "Race Unity—Its Importance and Necessity—Causes Which Retard Its Development—How It May Be Secured—Our Plain Duty," *Proceedings of the National Conference of Colored Men of the United States* (Washington, 1879), p. 85. Barnett was a Chicago attorney who later married the journalist and anti-lynching activist Ida B. Wells.

Barnett's report encouraged Blacks in cities with segregated schools where they had not yet begun to agitate for Black teachers. One such city was Topeka, Kansas, where Blacks had nursed hopes for school desegregation. Now they bowed to reality; they met and passed resolutions to the effect that since they had no alternative to segregated schools, they would insist on Black teachers for the good of the students and the community. Black teachers, they said, "would introduce an additional number of educated men and women whose presence would greatly benefit our society as well as excite a laudable emulation in our children."[15] Similar resolutions and memorials circulated in San Antonio, Texas, New Orleans, Louisiana, Lexington, Kentucky, and Nashville, Tennessee. For the most part, city school boards voiced little opposition, and the movement for Black teachers for Black pupils met with considerable success.

But in the foreseeable future, regenerating state financial support for rural public schools was a losing battle. For several reasons, Black leverage influenced state legislatures far less than city school boards. In the cities, schools were often supported by municipal taxes levied on comparatively wealthy populations. City and town schools were likely to be run by local school boards, and throughout the South, where Blacks managed to retain any vestiges of political power, it was on the local rather than on the state level. Rural schools depended directly upon the state administrations, where local political pressure was diluted. In the country, the Black population was poorer, more isolated, more vulnerable, and almost universally engaged in farming the land of local planters. Ties of dependence most nearly resembled the old master-slave relationships, and there was relatively little occupational diversity. By the late 1870s, the representatives of well-to-do whites effectively controlled state legislatures and executives. They set about undermining public schools, arguing that taxing whites to educate Black children was unfair, for Blacks supposedly paid little or no taxes. Repeatedly Blacks argued that they did, indeed, pay taxes, directly and indirectly, for tenant farmers paid property taxes in their land rents.

Progressive strangulation of the public schools also aggrieved Southern Blacks because literacy carried juridical value. Once the Reconstruction amendments made freedmen United States citi-

---

[15]Topeka *Tribune*, October 7, 1880.

zens, many Southern states, such as Texas, required literacy of prospective jurymen. The importance of both bench and jury was not lost on any segment of the Black population, for the courts played a role in Southern life that exceeded mere law enforcement. Thus, literacy and the state of the public schools were inextricably tied to Southern politics and to the perpetuation of the old social system based on Black dependency. It is hardly surprising, then, that schools were a topic of discussion at nearly every meeting at which Blacks considered their public stance.

A Texas conference of colored men held in Houston in the summer of 1879 underscored the centrality of the public-school question:

Within a few of the cities and towns of the south schools have been maintained for colored children, but in the rural districts, where the great masses of our people follow agriculture, there has been no opportunities for general education. We therefore justly infer, from the universal opposition of our former masters to the general education of our race, that they desire to perpetuate our ignorance and poverty in order to control our labor and retain our people in a state of vassalage and dependency.[16]

In response to Democratic unwillingness to tax whites to educate Blacks, the Report of the Committee on Address offered the following arguments:

First—That by the fruits of our labor the great majority of the finest educated white gentlemen of the past and present generations of the south mainly owe their education and prosperity.
Second—That not only in the past, but at the present time, the white people of the south control our labor, and that it would be but a small return to aid our people to educate their children.[17]

In this report, and in common parlance, the term "the whites of the south" indicated the old master class that had profited from slave labor. While it is true that the leading Democrats in the states under review here very often belonged to that class, or at least shared its interests, the white Democratic rank-and-file had not gained from slavery. Now these people faced educational deprivation along with poor Blacks when public schools closed down. In Dallas, a Black Kansas migrant named Joseph Giddings expected a white exodus to Kansas to result:

---

[16]Galveston Daily *News,* July 5, 1879.
[17]Ibid.

Governor Roberts [of Texas], has knocked the free-school system in the head, and he has crippled the State to a fearful extent. . . . Now mark what I say to you, Mr. Reporter, it won't be long before you see poor white people, honest, hard-working men, leaving Texas. They have children that should be educated, and they will go where they will give it to them.[18]

In Mississippi, as in Texas, withholding state appropriations weakened the state public-school system. In Texas, the bill vetoed by the governor would have appropriated for the schools one fourth of the general revenue of the state. In Mississippi, similarly, the state legislature refused to appropriate special revenue to support the schools. According to John R. Lynch, Democrats could seriously weaken the financial support of the public schools without tampering with the state's constitution. The constitution provided that certain revenues be reserved for the support of the schools, for instance, proceeds from the sale of public lands, fines, and licenses, but this fund alone hardly sufficed. During Reconstruction, the Republican-controlled legislature instituted a school tax of two mills; this tax, supplemented by special appropriations, provided school revenue. When the Democrats came to power in 1875, however, they not only refused to appropriate special revenues, but they also effectively abolished the school tax. Consequently, the schools limited the length of their term, which by 1879 was as little as two to four months per year in some rural areas. Town schools, in contrast, sometimes remained open, thanks to special municipal taxes.[19]

The work of dismantling the public-school systems was not entirely that of Democrats. White Republicans acquiesced, swayed by economy-in-government convictions or white-solidarity campaigns. Redeemed state governments progressively withdrew financial support from Black country schools, condemn-

---

[18]Dallas *Herald*, quoted in Denison Daily *News*, December 11, 1879. The free schools of Texas were no longer free; in fact, a fee had been charged per pupil even before 1879. In Washington County, pupils had had to pay about $1.50 each for the school year. In the 1879–80 year, the estimated fee was $3.00 per pupil. This apportionment was levied by the county court, which ran the schools and certified the teachers. The increase in school apportionment in Washington County was due to the veto of the state school apportionment by Governor Roberts. The opposition failed to rally the two-thirds majority necessary to override the veto. (Brenham Weekly *Banner*, May 2 and August 8, 1879.)

[19]New York Daily *Herald*, April 10, 1879.

ing vast numbers of school-age children to ignorance. Poor people saw schools as a route to autonomy, and ignorance as the most crippling brand of slavery. "Representative colored men" looked to education as a civilizing tool and thus valued it all the more. But if illiteracy had been the badge of slavery, it still invited economic victimization. The land-tenure and crop-lien systems typical of Southern agriculture were the most salient causes of Black poverty, but illiteracy implied a further vulnerability. Both aggravated the abuses pertaining to an economy run entirely on credit.

5

The Economics of Oppression

In 1865 most Southern Blacks faced their freedom with nothing but their labor as capital. Years passed, but they grew little richer. The burdensome land-tenure and credit systems of the Southern agricultural economy kept them poor. Despite the immense difficulties of realizing a profit and accumulating property, some rural Blacks were able to purchase lots and build homes; a narrower minority bought farmland, and they were more likely to live in Texas than in Louisiana, Mississippi, or Tennessee. For the vast majority of freedpeople, merely getting out of debt represented an accomplishment. "We are hard working people here in [the] South," wrote a Black Texan, "and give hige rent and big interest for everry thing we get and we work and work and everry year we jest cand come out eaven."[1] In the long run, many came out worse than even. During the 1860s and 1870s, Black farmers preferred to rent land from planters, the tenure under which the vast majority worked. In succeeding decades, however, their economic condition deteriorated, so that the proportion of sharecroppers to renters steadily gained.

---

[1]Jasper Arnold to Governor John P. St. John, Sabine County, Texas, n.d. [about September 30, 1879], Correspondence Received, Subject File (hereafter referred to as CRSF), box 10, Kansas State Historical Society, Topeka, Kansas (hereafter referred to as KSHS). Here, as in many other quotations to follow, spelling and grammar deviate from standard usage. *Sic* will not be used in such quotations, partly because of the value judgment implied by its use and partly because it would occur so often as to obliterate the meaning.

Exorbitant rents for land and the crop-lien system were the two most common grievances of Southern Blacks in the immediate post-Reconstruction South. Indeed, crop mortgaging and endless debt financing were familiar evils of Southern agriculture. Although it originated in the colonial period and persisted well past the turn of the twentieth century, the credit system especially oppressed the people at the bottom in economic hard times, such as the years between 1873 and 1879. The particulars of renting varied infinitely across the Gulf States in the late 1870s, but they can be summarized.

Around the first of the year, the laborer would sign a contract with the landowner to rent a given number of acres for a specified sum. Ordinarily the farms, really portions of plantations, were quite small; Southern cotton cultivation by Blacks was particularly labor-intensive.[2] The usual acreage of a rented farm in the late 1870s in Louisiana, Mississippi, and the heavily settled areas of Texas was only fifteen to twenty acres, seldom as much as forty, and almost never more than fifty acres. Tenants sometimes rented as few as eight acres. The size of the tenant's family (his work force) limited the number of acres he could cultivate, unless he was relatively well off and could hire additional labor. For this small farm of fifteen to twenty acres, the tenant contracted to pay from five to ten dollars rent per acre, usually figured in pounds of lint cotton per acre.[3] Since actual money seldom changed hands, the cotton equivalent served as the functional value. By and large, ratios of dollars to cotton were traditionally pegged and responded to market conditions only sluggishly.

The rent charged the tenant bore a closer relation to local conditions, within certain limits, than to fluctuating cotton prices. Thus, in a very general manner, rent reflected soil productivity. In Hinds County, Mississippi, considered an infertile area, tenants paid rents of from $5.50 to $6.50 per acre, whereas in the parishes bordering the Mississippi River in Louisiana, rents varied between $8.00 and $10.00 per acre in East Carroll Parish, and were $10.00 per acre in Madison and Concordia parishes.[4] For the most part,

[2]Bureau of the Census, U.S. Department of Commerce, *Negro Population, 1790–1915* (Washington, 1918), pp. 557–58.
[3]R. L. Faulkner, *Senate Report 693*, III: 246; John G. Lewis, ibid., II: 455–56; James L. Brown, ibid., III: 49; Clarence Winn, ibid., III: 46; "Eli Perkins," Chicago Daily *Tribune*, April 29, 1879.
[4]R.W.P. (a *Tribune* correspondent), Chicago Daily *Tribune*, May 14, 1879; J. A.

rents amounted to approximately one fourth to one half the value of the cotton crop. Although tenants might grow corn and some garden vegetables in addition, cotton was the only crop that figured in the valuation of land.

Only three other factors counted in the determination of the rent: the generosity of the individual planter, the availability of tenants to rent farms, and the animals and implements the tenant supplied. Rents held within one or two dollars of a local average, whether the customary figure was nearer ten dollars per acre or six, for neighboring planters' rents affected those all around them. In Concordia Parish, Louisiana, one planter's willingness to reduce his rents from the going rate to $6 per acre in cotton produced chaos. Surrounding planters were renting much higher and feared losing their tenants or facing demands for similarly lowered rents.[5]

As might be expected in a situation in which planters were in general accord on rents, tenants perceived the agreement as a conspiracy to keep rents high.[6] But the variety of contracts argues against the possibility of landowners combining to keep rents up to a given figure. There is no doubt, however, that planters reacted to what they saw as a shortage of laborers by reducing rents. (The Exodus to Kansas soon caused a sporadic lowering of rents.)[7]

Willson to Governor St. John, Lake Providence, Louisiana, July 7, 1879, CRSF, St. John, box 10, KSHS; Jet Gibbs, *Senate Report 693*, III: 45, 46; Census Office, Department of the Interior, *Report on Cotton Production in the United States* (Washington, 1884), I: 84, 154.

[5]John G. Lewis, *Senate Report 693*, II: 455; R.W.P., Chicago Daily *Tribune*, May 14, 1879. On the national level, the price of cotton per pound fell between 1869 and 1880: 1869, 16.5¢; 1870, 12.1¢; 1871, 17.9¢; 1872, 16.5¢; 1873, 14.1¢; 1874, 13.0¢; 1875, 11.1¢; 1876, 9.71¢; 1877, 8.53¢; 1878, 8.16¢; 1879, 10.28¢; 1880, 9.83¢. (U.S. Department of Commerce, *Historical Statistics of the United States* [Washington, 1960], p. 302.) These are the average prices on December 1 for the entire American cotton crop per year and do not reflect significant variations on the local level, which affected tenants and planters. Black tenants complained of low cotton prices only rarely, although they often insisted that they were not realizing any profit from their labor —for which they blamed unscrupulous planters and merchants. Considering that planters ordinarily marketed all cotton and that rents did not reflect any decline in prices, this is not at all surprising. Too many hands intervened between the tenant and the market price of cotton for tenants to perceive the fall in prices directly.

[6]J. A. Willson to Governor St. John, Lake Providence, Louisiana, July 7, 1879, CRSF, St. John, box 10, KSHS.

[7]S. A. Hackworth to Governor St. John, Brenham, Texas, August 11, 1879,

The division of the crop and thus the rent (in cotton) depended on traditional terms of sharing, not on the actual productivity of the particular piece of land or the value of particular implements. Terms varied locally, but the basic proportion was one half of the crop for the furnisher of the capital—land, implements, mules— and one half for the labor. In some areas planters set the division on a rough one-third basis, allotting the value of a third of the crop to themselves, a third to the laborer (and his family, of course, since their labor was figured in with his), and a third for whoever furnished the farming implements and the mules. The contract of Orange Pucket, who had been a farmer in Tensas Parish, Louisiana, in 1878, provides a typical example: Pucket and his family rented twenty-five acres of land; on twenty-two acres he grew cotton, on the other three, corn. The contract specified that his wife and children must also work in the field with him, and that the rent would be ten bales of cotton, half for the land, half for the tools and mules:

> 5 bales of cotton . . . . for rent of 25 acres of land
> 2 bales of cotton . . . . for use of 2 mules
> 2 bales of cotton . . . . for feed of 2 mules
> 1 bale of cotton . . . . for use of tools[8]

At about the same time, in Natchitoches Parish, the tenant kept about two thirds of the value of the crop when he supplied everything but the land and the stock; when the landowner furnished land, tools, and animals, the tenant kept only one third of the crop's value.[9]

In short, the permutations were endless, depending on whether the tenant paid a rent or worked on shares, on where and when the contract was made, on the amounts of the various other fees rounding out the agreement. For instance, the tenant usually had to supply seed cotton and was also responsible for keeping up ditches and bridges, and for other improvements. But the landlord ordinarily provided housing, as often as not the hated "quarters," a holdover from slavery. All these variables were subject to local and individual usages. A Chicago *Tribune* correspondent discovered that rents varied "according to the quality of the land, the

CRSF, St. John, box 10, KSHS; R.W.P., Chicago Daily *Tribune,* May 17, 1879.
[8]"Eli Perkins," Chicago Daily *Tribune,* April 26, 1879.
[9]John G. Lewis, *Senate Report 693,* II: 455–56.

rapacity of the owner, and the ignorance of the negro."[10]

Several other economic variables that presumably would have influenced land rents produced effects only after a considerable lag or not at all. High land taxes, for instance, were one of the planters' commonest complaints about Reconstruction. With Redemption, Democratic legislatures generally scaled down property taxes. In Louisiana in early 1879, taxes fell from twenty-one mills on the dollar to five and one half.[11] Yet the rents that landlords charged did not reflect their savings in taxes. David Young, a Black minister, storekeeper, and politician, concluded that "the land-owners get all the benefit and the laborers none from the reduction in taxes."[12]

Tenant farmers' rents also failed to correspond to the fluctuation of cotton prices from year to year. Rents remained stable, fixed according to custom, while the average cotton price per bale varied more than $25.00 between 1874–75 and 1879–80. (In 1874–75 the average price per bale in New Orleans was $65.40— down from $84.37 the previous year; in 1875–76, $52.65; 1876–77, $52.00; 1877–78, $40.05; 1878–79, $43.00; 1879–80, $55.00.)[13] Had tenents shared the profits of good prices as they bore the hardships of bad ones, they would have known good years as well as bad. But the manipulated credit system intervened between the Black tenant farmers and their profits, and they seldom enjoyed really good years.

From top to bottom, Southern agriculture revolved around credit financing. In return for advances of supplies and consumer goods, planters mortgaged the crops they intended to grow to factors (merchants), until their crops were sold. After the Civil War, the system drew in Black tenant farmers. A series of laws, known variously as Vendor's Lien laws or Landlord and Tenant acts, enabled the tenant to mortgage the crop he was about to make to the owner of the land, for rent, and to the storekeeper, for supplies. Ordinarily, the landowner held the first mortgage and the merchant held the second. Theoretically, the tenant collected his share after his rent and supplies had been paid. In practice,

---

[10]John B. Runnion, Chicago Daily *Tribune*, May 28, 1879.

[11]*Appleton's Annual Cyclopaedia . . . 1879* (New York, 1880), p. 562.

[12]Chicago Daily *Tribune*, May 19, 1879.

[13]*Appleton's Annual Cyclopaedia . . . 1880* (New York, 1881), p. 483.

however, landlords and shopkeepers purloined the tenant's share, no matter how large the crop or high the prices.

Occasionally the tenants cleared a little money after meeting both liens on the crop, but the overwhelming body of evidence points to tenants commonly coming out in debt. In 1876 Henry Adams compared notes with farmers from across Louisiana and found the same result—chronic indebtedness—despite relatively good cotton prices in the preceding years. Further, he noted a suspiciously common agreement in the burden of debt per family, even though the sizes of the families and the productivity of the lands differed. The colored people in several Louisiana parishes

worked on sugar and cotton plantations, and made large crops, often varying from fifteen to forty bales of cotton per family. Yet they had not had as much as twenty-five to fifty dollars cash money at the end of any one year. That they always, at the owner's mode of settling, was in his debt. Yet they did not even have half enough to eat or scarcely anything to wear, and their indebtedness never exceeded one hundred and fifty dollars per year on an average per family.[14]

The farmers concluded that the credit system was being manipulated precisely so that they would not realize any return. A closer look at the two-stage mortgage system shows how this occurred.

In the late 1870s, approximately 400 to 450 pounds of ginned lint cotton made a bale of cotton. To raise this amount of cotton required two to eight acres of land, depending on its productivity, weather, fertilizing, and the labor invested. Rents equaled from 80 to 100 pounds of cotton per acre, picked, ginned, and wrapped. The tenant received twenty-five to forty-five dollars per bale, usually closer to thirty-five, although he never actually realized this much in cash.[15] But before he began to figure his return, his picked cotton had to be ginned and baled, which entailed a multitude of abuses.

Ginning was expensive, especially since landlords monopolized it in a thoroughly controlled market. Tenants were forced to gin their cotton at the landlord's gin, at the landlord's rates. These landlord's rights also extended to marketing. "The white people do not allow us to sell our own crops," Black farmers complained, "when we do, we do it at the risk of our lives, getting whipped,

[14]Henry Adams, *Senate Report* 693, II: 185–86.

[15]R.W.P., Chicago Daily *Tribune*, April 30, 1879; "Eli Perkins," ibid., April 29, 1879; Clarence Winn, *Senate Report* 693, III: 46.

shot at, and often some get killed."[16] Several Exodusters cited these practices in interviews in St. Louis:

We had to carry the cotton to the gin of the man who owned the land we rented, and he would take it all from us.[17]

The landowners have their own stores and gin houses on their own plantations, in order to catch all the cotton on each place, and the tillers of the soil can't get their cotton ginned at any other place or buy their supplies at any other place. . . .[18]

These controlled ginning fees ranged from $2.50 to $7.00 per bale and consumed from one seventh to one sixth of the value of each bale a tenant produced.[19]

After the cotton was grown, picked, ginned, baled, and sold, the landlord received his rent, valued in dollars but figured in cotton. This first mortgage, or lien, was legally binding, stipulated by contract between tenant and landlord before the ground was broken. The contract quoted below, from Madison Parish, Louisiana, dates from January 1879 and is typical. The clause in which the tenant waived any legal rights of exemption of his personal property in favor of the landlord is especially noteworthy. In the event of a short crop or very low cotton prices, the landlord could seize or take a mortgage on *all* the tenant's personal property, including his mules and farming implements, which were worth a share of future cotton crops:

This agreement, made and entered into this 18th day of January, 1879, between Solid South, of the first part, and John Dawson, of the second part. *Witnesseth:* that said party of the first part for and in consideration of eighty-eight pounds of lint cotton to be paid to the said Solid South, as hereinafter expressed, hereby leases to said Dawson, for the year A.D. 1879, a certain tract of land, the boundaries of which are well understood by the parties hereto, and the area of which are well understood by the parties hereto, and the area of which the said parties hereby agree to be fifteen acres, being a portion of the Waterford Plantation, in Madison Parish, Louisiana.

The said Dawson is to cultivate said land in a proper manner, under

---

[16]Henry Adams, *Senate Report 693,* II: 185–86. These planters exercised monopoly rights that very much resembled the *banalités* of feudal lords in the European Middle Ages.

[17]Lewis Woods, ibid., III: 52.

[18]J. D. Daniel, ibid., p. 50. Daniel was from Warren County, Mississippi.

[19]R.W.P., Chicago Daily *Tribune,* April 30, 1879.

the general superintendence of the said Solid South, or his agent or manager, and is to surrender to said lessor peaceable possession of said leased premises at the expiration of this lease without notice to quit. All ditches, turn-rows, bridges, fences, etc. on said land shall be kept in proper condition by said Dawson, or at his expense. All cotton-seed raised on said land shall be held for the exclusive use of said plantation, and no goods of any kind shall be kept for sale on said land unless by consent of said lessor. If said Solid South shall furnish to said lessee money, or necessary supplies, or stock, or material, or either or all of them during this lease, to enable him to make a crop, the amount of said advances, not to exceed $475 (of which $315 has been furnished in two mules, plows, etc.), the said Dawson agrees to pay for the supplies and advances so furnished, out of the first cotton picked and saved on said land from the crop of said year, and to deliver said cotton of the first picking to the said Solid South, in the gin on said plantation, to be by him bought or shipped at his option, the proceeds to be applied to payment of said supply bill, which is to be fully paid on or before the 1st day of January, 1880. After payment of said supply bill, the said lessee is to pay to said lessor, in the gin of said plantation, the rent cotton herein before stipulated, said rent to be fully paid on or before the 1st day of January, 1880. All cotton raised on said land is to be ginned on the gin of said lessor, on said plantation, and said lessee is to pay $4 per bale for ginning same. To secure payment of said rent and supply bill, the said Dawson grants unto said Solid South a special privilege and right of pledge on all the products raised on said land, and on all his stock, farming implements, and personal property, and hereby waives in favor of said Solid South the benefit of any and all homestead laws and exemption laws now in force, or which may be in force, in Louisiana, and agrees that all his property shall be seized and sold to pay said rent and supply bill in default of payment thereof as herein agreed. Any violation of this contract shall render the lease void.

> *Solid South,*
> his
> *John X Dawson,*
> mark.[20]

In addition to the extortionate provisions in such a contract, the tenant ordinarily bore responsibility for paying about $2.50 to a lawyer or notary for filling out the contract. (Comparable services outside the South cost between twenty-five cents and a dollar.)[21]

In this contract between "Solid South" and "John Dawson,"

---

[20]Ibid., May 13, 1879. The names in this contract were changed by the correspondent who copied it.

[21]*Senate Report 693*, III: 63.

the landlord was also the supplier of "furnish"—food, clothing, and other consumer goods. But a storekeeper often supplied "furnish," and he then claimed the second lien on the crop. The storekeeper advanced the tenant goods on credit; when the crop was in, the storekeeper received payment according to the accounts he had kept of the tenant's purchases during the previous year. Debts mounted quickly, for the prices in the country stores more than doubled the market value of the goods. Theoretically, there was a "cash" price and a "credit" price for goods, but since practically no one paid cash, the "credit" price was operative.

"Credit" prices for commonly bought goods ranged from $1.50 to $2.00 per gallon for molasses, where 25¢ to 75¢ would represent a fair price; pork sold for $25.00 to $40.00 per barrel, when about $15.00 would have been fair; and corn meal was about $2.00 a bushel where 50¢ to $1.00 would have been fair. These are reasonably representative prices, although they varied widely. Interest charges ranged from 15 to 25 percent.[22] The tenant thus paid twice for buying on credit at the local store, first in the vastly inflated prices, then in the exorbitant interest charged on the outstanding balance. In the depression of the 1870s, merchants and planters who ran plantation stores recouped their agricultural losses by increasing prices and interest charges. They justified the increases in terms of their risks in credit dealings. But in fact, the high prices were an attempt to make what the traffic would bear—for the judiciary and social usages reinforced the claims of whites over Blacks—and to pass on the costs and interests which they paid their own factors or suppliers, with whom they, too, dealt on a credit basis.

Many Blacks suspected merchants and planters of adjusting the availability of credit to fit the projected value of the cotton crop. Further, if tenants did not take advantage of their increased margin of credit, they might well find their accounts doctored to take up the surplus profit nonetheless. In situations like these, the nonlegal sanctions of white supremacy worked in the merchants' and planters' favor, insuring that their claims would "take up all that has been raised on the place. If the tenant has raised ten, fifteen, or twenty bales of cotton the merchant's claim will be

[22]J. D. Daniel, ibid., p. 50; James Brown, ibid., p. 49; C. H. Tandy, ibid., p. 63; R.W.P., Chicago Daily *Tribune,* April 30, 1879; David Young, quoted in ibid., May 19, 1879.

found to be enough to cover it and something to spare," said a Black Mississippian.

Just before picking time comes, the merchant sends men around from place to place to see how the crop is getting along; how many bales will probably be made. By this the merchant knows how large to make his bill. ... If the colored man refuses to pay the bill, which, as I have said, is always made large enough to cover the value of the entire crop, after paying the rent, the merchant comes into court and sues him. The white man brings his itemized account into court; the colored man has no account, and of course he is beaten in the suit, and the cost is thrown onto him. They stand against him, if he cannot pay it. And colored men soon learn that it is better to pay any account, however unjust, then to refuse, for he stands no possible chance of getting justice before the law.[23]

Most out-of-court settlements simply meant that the tenant would begin the succeeding year in debt to the planter or storekeeper. But not every tenant acquiesced in trumped-up debt:

I saw a man they [creditors] were after in the next house to where I lived in Madison Parish, Louisiana; they had been in a fuss with him the day before they came, that night; I saw them when they came to his house; it was about five months before Christmas, 1878; they was about seventy-five men; they surrounded the house; they were armed, I suppose, with muskets, from what I could see—it was dark. I heard the noise before they got there, and with some other men went into the man's house (his name was George Page), and took him away down to the swamp and hid him in a brush pile; after we got him away we went to the house and went to the door, and they asked us if he was there, and we told them no, and they told us to tell him they would give him 12 hours to leave the parish, and 24 hours to leave the State. He had been farming there and they wanted to attach his yoke of oxen for debts, they said, and he wasn't willing to give them up, and they told him if he wasn't willing to give them up they would kill him; he said he didn't owe them anything. I haven't seen him since.[24]

For most rural Blacks, the result of the abused credit system, with its mortgaged crops, inflated prices, and extortionate interest charges, was utter, unending poverty. There were exceptions, of course, men who acquired property and land. Most of them were prudent enough to keep out of politics, paying the price of enjoying their prosperity in relative security. Men of property who still

---

[23]J. Milton Brown, *Senate Report 693*, III: 361–62.
[24]Levi Childs, ibid., p. 48.

functioned politically in the late 1870s were exceptions among the exceptions, men like G. R. M. Newman of St. Mary's Parish, Louisiana. Newman, elected clerk of the third judicial district of Louisiana in 1876, furnished his own $5,000 bond and occupied his office.[25] More often, Black elected officials either had their bonds furnished by prosperous white Republicans or were unable to fill their positions. J. Milton Brown was sheriff, assessor, tax collector, and "old levy tax" collector in Coahoma County, Mississippi, in the early 1870s. For all these offices, he posted total bonds of $91,000, furnished by four white men, one of whom was the son of Governor James L. Alcorn of Mississippi.[26] As Reconstruction receded, sapping the vitality of the Southern Republican party, Black officeholders faced increasing difficulty in finding white men to post bonds for them. Though lack of bond was not limited to Blacks, it affected them disproportionately. For instance, of twenty-three deputy sheriffs in Washington County, Texas, in 1878, three had not yet occupied their offices. Two of the three Black deputies lacked bond, but of the twenty white deputies, only one lacked bond.[27] In a racial situation shot through with overt interferences with suffrage and officeholding, the bond system escaped attack. Nonetheless, it imposed a severe handicap on poor men aspiring to office, a handicap that only increased as the "wealth and intelligence" of the South moved into Democratic ranks.

Although poor, rural Blacks bemoaned their grim economic predicament, they encountered little compassion, North or South. State tax policies aimed at economic reform and financial paternalism stumbled in the 1860s and fell entirely in the 1870s. Blacks had failed to pull themselves out of poverty by their bootstraps in the fifteen or so years since their emancipation, and in many quarters this incapacity only strengthened the economic case against them. Summing up everyday Southern white attitudes toward poor Blacks, an editorial in the New Orleans *Times* saw thriftlessness as an integral part of Negro character:

As a class it is doubtful if they have any just reason to complain of their treatment. They themselves are more to blame for their condition than

---

[25]G. R. M. Newman to Governor St. John, Berwick City, Louisiana, September 7, 1879, CRSF, St. John, box 10, KSHS.

[26]J. Milton Brown, *Senate Report 693*, II: 369–70.

[27]Brenham Weekly *Banner*, August 9, 1878.

anybody else. They are dissatisfied because, at the end of each year they have accumulated nothing and are in debt. They do not seek to find out the cause of this, but jump at the conclusion that they have been denied their rights, robbed and misused generally. The truth is, they are improvident. They are given credit by the country merchants to the extent of their year's earnings, and, while their credit is good, they buy extravagantly and without any regard to their actual wants. Of course, buying on credit, they pay a double price for everything they get. The consequence is, they are always behind hand and have very few of the comforts of life. This improvidence, which seems to be a part of their nature, will keep them poor wherever they may go or in whatever locality they may settle. Before they can hope to better their condition they must become thrifty and economical.[28]

Far from unique to white Southerners, these views enjoyed wide currency among comfortable Blacks and Northern whites, who often tossed them about thoughtlessly.

Respectable men in the later nineteenth century undeniably blamed all the poor for their own poverty; thus deprecation of poor Blacks' prodigality merged into a wider, hardening, Spencerian view of the lower classes and lesser breeds in general. Yet the New Orleans *Times*'s vituperation conjures up visions of freedmen indulging in luxury on an antebellum plantation scale—sumptuous repasts, free-flowing liquor, fancy-dress balls, high-spirited horses. A closer look, however, reveals the pitiable level of the freedpeople's extravagance. "The colored people as a class are dreadfully improvident," charged a Northern white critic. "They do not look ahead, or realize when they contract a debt, how hard it may be to pay it. They will buy anything they can get." But his proof of at least one freedman's self-indulgence provided a paltry feast at best: "I have heard of a negro who, at the end of the year, had to pay for 135 boxes of sardines."[29]

This is not to deny that rural Blacks spent their share on frippery and bad whiskey; they did. Nonetheless, one suspects that the standard of consumption against which freedmen were measured harked back to before the Civil War, to the unadorned, unrelieved subsistence of slavery. The parallel gauge of industriousness also pertained to slavery—work from dawn to dusk—a rule to which few free men, Black or white, would voluntarily adhere. This unspoken standard, the paragon of slavery, hovered behind accu-

---

[28]New Orleans Daily *Times*, March 15, 1879.
[29]R.W.P., Chicago Daily *Tribune*, April 30, 1879.

sations of improvidence or sloth hurled at freedmen by respectable Blacks and whites. Usually, spoiled, pampered Black people numbered very few. At settlement time, said north Louisiana mother-wit:

> ought is a ought,
> figure a figure,
> figure belongs to me
> and the ought to the poor nigger.[30]

On one side, poor Blacks blamed whites for rigging a rotten system and preventing them from earning enough to buy land. Whites, on the other, accused Blacks of shortsighted extravagance and laziness. The conflict stemmed from utterly irreconcilable assumptions about the place of Black people in the South. White owners of the land saw Blacks as nothing other than a labor force. Yet Blacks assumed that they were more than mere units of labor, and they cherished hopes of economic betterment. In their eyes, their ambitions of saving a little money for their old age, of educating their children, and of owning land were entirely appropriate. In the view of most articulate Southern whites, however, the agricultural economy of the region formed an integrated whole, a scheme in which well-to-do whites, "the wealth and intelligence of the South," were to oversee the development of the entire region. Poorer whites were to act as their helpmates, not decision makers, filling the roles of employee and policeman. Nor were Blacks to function as political or economic autonomies, but rather as faceless, docile laborers. According to this arrangement, elabo-

---

[30]New Orleans *Southwestern Christian Advocate*, February 19, 1880. A longer response countered charges of improvidence in more detail:

. . . about the colored people being honesty industrious and economy [honestly industrious and economical], in my opinion if it be Wright I think the word economy signify to make the prudentest use of money that we can   in the 1st place we poor colored people of These low states have been in bondage and destituted of Education and Since we have been Emancipated we have been forced by a combination to rent land at from $8 to $10 per acre and from $3 to $4 for each and every 400 lbs. Bale of cotton as Gined & Baled and forced to deal with our employer under the impression of exorbitant Rates for every Thing we use and that is no more than salt pork & corn meal and the terms of affairs is all ways in such condition that we never gits the money to live economy.

(J. A. Willson to Governor St. John, Lake Providence, Louisiana, July 7, 1879, CRSF, St. John, box 10, KSHS.)

rated from the top, each group worked in a smoothly running agricultural machine. This vision of Southern life nourished the endlessly repeated New South concept of the "identity of interests" of all the units of the Southern economy. It was the keynote of the planter-dominated Vicksburg Labor Convention of 1879.[31]

So long as planters held to this view, landlords and tenants would never work out a mutually satisfactory relationship. There could be no fundamental identity of interests between landlords and tenants as long as landlords were interested only in making lucrative cotton crops and tenants aimed at owning their own farms. Landlords envisioned a permanent and, most important, a *landless* labor force. Although some Southern whites saw the contradiction and grasped the root of Black economic discontent—landlessness—most of them remained blind to it. Planters dreamed of a prosperous South, rationalized to produce abundant, high-priced cotton. Black farmers envisaged a land of small farms, which might incidentally send cotton to the New Orleans market, but which were first and foremost to be subsistence farms assuring their owners economic independence.

Blacks who realized that Southern whites viewed them basically as units of labor, with ultimate claims only to food and cabins, insisted that Negroes would have to leave the South in order to claim rights exceeding those of labor. Even though, a Black Texan wrote,

I am doing tolerably well, my people can never do well and generally become landowners in the South. Our old masters will ever regard us as legal property stolen and forcibly taken away from them, and if they cant get our labor for nothing in one way, they will invent some other plan by which they can, for they make all the laws and own all the best lands. . . . The longer we stay here the worse it will be because our old masters are raising their children to believe and act as they do. We have been free 14 years and still we are poor and ignorant, yet we make as much cotton and sugar as we did when we were slaves, and it does us as little good now as it did then.[32]

The Black dream of a region "all dotted over with prosperous communities of both races, who shall be the owners of the soil on which they live, and all alike interested in the institutions they

[31]St. Joseph (La.) *North Louisiana Journal,* May 10, 1879.

[32]Quoted in S. A. Hackworth to Governor St. John, Brenham, Texas, May 19, 1879, CRSF, St. John, box 10, KSHS.

labor to support" stood as the utter antithesis of the planters' ideal South.[33]

After fifteen years of freedom, Black landownership in Louisiana and Mississippi was negligible; in fact, owning even the houses in which they lived occurred but rarely in those states. In Mississippi, in seventeen counties, not one in one hundred Black laborers owned either house or land; in twelve other counties, not one in twenty; and elsewhere, often not one in fifty. In Claiborne County, tenants were reported "to have no desire to own lands." In Louisiana, the results were dismally similar; in DeSoto, Union, and Franklin parishes, one in twenty families owned homes or land; in Bossier and Claiborne, one in twenty-five or fifty. In other parishes, which included those most affected by the Exodus, "very few" Black laborers owned real property.[34] These proportions stand in stark contrast to the letters to Kansas that Southern Blacks wrote inquiring about migrating there. Almost without fail, the first question concerned terms under which land could be acquired. And of course, the great drawing card of the Kansas Fever Exodus was free land. Unequivocally, Black farmers in the South desired above all else to own their own land and to be independent farmers.

For many rural Southern Blacks, landlessness posed as acute a problem as political oppression. In Tennessee, Benjamin Singleton discovered the futility of trying to purchase farmland, and in Louisiana, political terrorism threatened to paralyze Henry Adams. Theirs were the most common problems and the best-known names of the immediate post-Reconstruction period.

---

[33]H. E. Smothers's "Address to State Convention of Colored Men," Dallas, 1880, quoted in Galveston Daily *News*, February 17, 1880.

[34]*Report on Cotton Production*, I: 84, 154.

Part II
Henry Adams
Benjamin "Pap"
Singleton,
and Postwar Realities

6

Henry Adams and Grass Roots Political Action

Well, any kind of risings and swellings coming on people, I rub them with my hands and blow my breath on them and take 'em away. And you find these wens on people. I take that away; and these old sores on the legs of people that are hard to cure, I make a kind of salve myself and cure it. I have studied it myself; it came to me naturally; it always was with me. And then other diseases, a great many kinds of diseases I could name, backache, toothache, jawache, earache, rheumatism, white swellings, and such things as that I cure. . . . I goes over medical doctors for I takes cases they can't cure. I rather take them kind than any other kind.[1]

Henry Adams of Caddo Parish, Louisiana, enjoyed considerable renown as a faith doctor, but he made his mark historically as an extraordinarily intelligent and intrepid political organizer. Experiencing and observing the hardships common to the Blacks of the lower Mississippi Valley, he belonged to the prosperous and articulate minority of freedpeople. He acted in the public arena during and after Reconstruction, seeking to ameliorate the abysmal conditions entrapping his fellows.

Born a slave in Newton County, Georgia, on March 16, 1843, Adams was known as Henry Houston until he was seven. In 1850 he and his family were taken to Louisiana, where they lived until

---

[1] Henry Adams, *Senate Report 693*, II: 152, 138.

1861, moving back and forth across the Texas border; they were the property of a teenage girl, Nancy Emily Adams, after their master died in 1858 and they were hired out to a planter named Ferguson. By the end of the Civil War, the family was living in DeSoto Parish, Louisiana.

At the time of their emancipation in April 1865, Henry Adams and his father worked on Ferguson's plantation near Logansport, but his mother belonged to his young mistress's brother and lived on one of his plantations. The parents remained apart until 1866, when they were allowed to live together.[2] During his enslavement, Henry Adams married a woman named Malinda, and they had four children, Lucy, Rena, Josephine, and Henry. But Malinda belonged to Columbus Henson, who took them to Texas. By the late 1870s, Adams headed a second family.[3]

Even before his emancipation in April 1865, Henry Adams had managed to collect some property, "three horses and a fine buggey, and a good deal of money, both gold and silver," and he was known as "a rich negro." Already a credible businessman, he was unwilling, as a free man, to continue working on the plantation without compensation. While other freedpeople had signed contracts, as their former masters had urged, Adams attempted to bargain for shares of the crops:

On the same day or the next after all had signed the papers or contracts, we went to cutting oats. I asked the boss could we get any of the oats? He said no; the oats were made before you were free. I said it is some of the crop we made, but we did not get any of it. We made about eight hundred bushels. After that he told us to get timber to build a sugar-mill to make molasses; we did so. On the 13th day of July, 1865, we started to pull fodder. I asked the boss would he make a bargain with me to give us half of all the fodder we would pull and save. He said we may pull two or three stacks and then we could have all the other. I told him we wanted to make a bargain for half, so if we only pulled two or three stacks we would get half of that. He said, "All right." We got that and part of the corn we made. We made five bales of cotton, but we did not get a pound of that. We made two or three hundred gallons of molasses and we only got what we could eat. We made about fifty or seventy-five bushels of pindar; we got none of them. We made about seven or eight hundred bushels of potatoes; we got a few to eat. We split rails three or four weeks, and got not a cent for

---

[2]Ibid., pp. 138, 189–91.
[3]New Orleans *Southwestern Christian Advocate*, June 20, 1878.

that; so in September of [the] same year I asked the boss to let me go to Shreveport. . . .[4]

In Shreveport, Adams joined the fifty or sixty Blacks who came into the city daily, refugees from the slaveholders. He and his companion spent only a few days in that dismal, disorganized city, before wandering along the highways, suffering a robbery, then returning briefly to the Ferguson plantation. Although bands of whites roved the roads, repeatedly stopping, intimidating, and searching freedpeople, and parish law now required Blacks to carry passes, Adams made a success of his peddling business in the last months of 1865. He lost $250 to thieves and sympathized all the more with the peripatetic freedpeople, who wandered the roads rather than live as slaves in the homes they had left:

I ran away, as also did most of the rest, and the white people did not sympathize with us; they would take all the money that we made on their places when we went to leave; they killed many hundreds of my race when they were running away to get freedom. After they told us we were free—even then they would not let us live as man and wife together. And when we would run away to be free from slavery, the white people would not let us come on their places to see our mothers, wives, sisters, or fathers. We was made to leave the place, or made to go back and live as slaves. To my own knowledge there was over two thousand colored people killed trying to get away, after the white people told us we were free, which was in 1865. Many of the colored people were killed, but the white people pretended to know little about it. I seen some shot dead because they left with a white woman. This was after they told us we were free, in the year 1865; this was between Shreveport and Logansport.[5]

Adams continued his peddling during the early part of 1866, but on September 10, 1866, he enlisted in the United States Army and was attached to the Eightieth Volunteers. Utterly powerless before the ill-treatment of Blacks all about him, he "went off and left it."[6] Anarchic whites were turning freedom into a warmed-over version of slavery.

Shortly after his enlistment, Adams was posted to New Orleans to the Thirty-ninth Infantry, which in April combined with the Fortieth to make the Twenty-fifth Infantry. Adams served with the Twenty-fifth at Shreveport, Greenville (near New Orleans),

---

[4]Henry Adams, *Senate Report 693*, II: 190–91.
[5]Ibid., p. 192.
[6]Ibid., p. 101.

and Fort Jackson, and he often traveled the back roads of rural Louisiana. West of Shreveport he found the same callous disregard for Black lives that he had noted elsewhere. On the Jefferson Road, he said, "I saw on an old stump the head of a colored man; I inquired of some colored people why and who put it there? They said that some white men brought from Shreveport a colored man who they killed and put his head on the stump."[7]

In March 1867 Adams was promoted to quartermaster sergeant, the rank he occupied until the end of his tour of duty, in mid-September 1869.[8] He experienced his first formal schooling in the Army, learning to read at Fort Jackson:

> I could not read a bit. I knowed the letters and figures when I seed them, but I could not put them together under no circumstances. We had a teacher when we were stationed at Fort Jackson, in Louisiana. She was a white lady, Mrs. Bentine, and we had a school for the soldiers, and we had three hours a day to go to the school. I never went all that time, but only part of the time; and I learned to read and write a little in one month's time; and after I quit her I never went only two weeks more. . . . I acquired all the rest myself.[9]

Although not all former slaves in the Army shared Henry Adams's facility, most learned to read and write. With literacy and wider experience, they acquired a self-confidence that irritated Southern whites. After his discharge, Henry Adams returned to a slightly less chaotic Shreveport, but he faced a new and acute discrimination precisely because he had served in the United States Army. Most local whites regarded ex-soldiers as corrosive agents in the already precarious social order:

> I landed in Shreveport, Caddo Parish, La., September 25th, 1869, and went about trying to rent a house, but it was rumored all over town that a boat load of discharged Union soldiers had come, and the whites would not rent us their houses. Finally we came up with a Baptist preacher, and he let us have his house. After we had been there a few months the white people began saying they were going to kill us; to kill all the discharged negro soldiers; that these discharged men were going to spoil all the other negroes, so that the whites could do nothing with them. . . .[10]

---

[7]Ibid., p. 178.

[8]Ibid., pp. 128, 153–54. Adams said he would have been promoted earlier but for a long illness that kept him bedridden for two months.

[9]Ibid., p. 154.

[10]Ibid., p. 177.

The economic dependence of Black tenants on planters who exploited their ignorance disturbed Adams almost as much as did the butchery. He and other former soldiers rode across the countryside, reading contracts and bills for illiterates, explaining their legal rights to them, and backing up their demands for fairness from the planters. While the ex-soldiers uncovered abundant evidence of extortion, assuring justice to the plaintiffs in court proved another matter entirely. For that fruitless effort they earned the further hatred of the whites of Caddo Parish:

The colored people would get these discharged soldiers to look over their contracts and agreements they had made with the white people they were working for. I would tell them to go and have a settlement of accounts, and get what was due them, and pay what they owed. I figured up accounts for them, and often seen where the whites had cheated the colored people who had made contracts with them out of more than two-thirds of their just rights, according to their contracts. I told a great many of them to take their contracts to lawyers and get them to force the parties to a settlement; but they told me they were afraid they would be killed. Some few reported to the court, but told me afterwards that it did not do. Some even were whipped when they went home.[11]

As though having their writ questioned (however unsuccessfully) were not enough, local whites also had to contend with Adams's financial prosperity. In December 1869 he and his cousin Moses Bartlett purchased a house and two lots in Shreveport for $1,420. Resentful whites harassed Adams and his fellow ex-soldiers at every turn. At one point a white gang accosted Adams on the road with a girl they thought unsuited to the likes of this former slave:

One day I was riding with a young colored lady along the public road between Shreveport and Greenwood, and a crowd of white men rode between me and her and ordered me to leave, and for her to stand still, and told her she was too pretty a girl for such [a] damn black negro as me to be alongside of her. I told them if they wanted to kill me they could do so, for I was not going to leave her.[12]

A "big, stout, broad-shouldered man," Adams refused to leave the girl without a stiff fight, and the whites backed down this time. Later, however, they confronted another Black man and a girl,

---

[11] Ibid.
[12] Ibid.

forcing the man to "run off and leave the girl he was with, and they then done to the girl what they wanted, and then put her upon her horse and told her to go."[13] This act flowed into the high tide of white savagery, exacting retribution for what seemed to them an intolerable new order in which Black men read and talked back. For Blacks, freedom represented a small, precarious improvement; for whites, that small step was already too far.

After five years of freedom and seemingly endless victimization, a group of ex-soldiers assembled to form what they called simply "the Council" or "the Committee." They decided to collect information on the general condition of Black people, to "look into affairs and see the true condition of our race, to see whether it was possible we could stay under a people who had held us under bondage or not."[14] The Committee functioned as a secret intelligence-gathering body between 1870 and 1874, when as many as five hundred men took part. Although the Committee played a significant, grass roots organizing role, its members did not think of it as "political." They organized Republican clubs and advised voters, but they did not run for important offices. (The Committee had no dealings with the Union League, which the Democratic press reported as active in Louisiana at the time. Adams denied ever coming across the Union League, but he admitted that "the politicians" might have had something to do with it.) Nonetheless, the Committee did function politically, distributing ballots and urging Blacks to vote in their own interests—as the Committee perceived them.

Henry Adams voted for the first time in 1870. While he did not consider himself a public speaker, he was sufficiently respected by Black people in Caddo Parish for them to solicit his views. He insisted that he knew nothing of politics in 1870, but in fact that year marked his entry into the political arena:

I was at an election in 1870, in November, in the city of Shreveport, and I heard white men tell colored men that if they voted the Republican tickets that they would not let them have any more credit, nor would they bond them out of jail; that they would have to go to the d—n Yankees or carpet-baggers to take them out, and the colored men told them that they

---

[13]Andrew Currie, mayor of Shreveport, ibid., III: 81; Henry Adams, ibid., II: 178.

[14]Ibid., p. 101.

were afraid to vote the Democratic ticket because they might make them slaves again. Many of them asked me what did I think was best?

Adams's answer was Lincolnesque in its humility: "I told them I was nothing but a rail-splitter and wood-chopper, and did not know anything about politics; had never seen a poll for an election before." Nonetheless, he gave his best advice, speaking to the people on the issues generally:

. . . but [I] thought if we voted the Democratic ticket we would have to carry passes from one parish to another and from one State to the other. I told them as to our freedom, our rights, and our votes that no Southern man was our friend; only the Northern men, Army officers, and United States troops were our friends; that the Southern people would always be arrayed against us as long as we lived because we were free.

After this speech, given on the Monday before the election, Adams learned that he had been "spotted," that whites had marked him out for assassination for "spoiling the other negroes so [the whites] could not do anything with them." He shrugged off the warning: "I told them if they did kill me only give me my rights while I am living."[15]

During the early 1870s Adams worked as a rail splitter and plantation manager for W. C. Hambleton and Company, with whom he earned as much as a hundred dollars per month splitting rails.[16] His success as a rail splitter and businessman brought him additional responsibilities in 1872, and he ran the wood yard and work force on a plantation about twelve miles outside Shreveport. After a year as "boss" of the plantation, he became the manager, attending to all the business and making monthly reports to the owners. He also purchased the cotton seed and corn and ran the cotton-oil mill. During this period he kept up his activities in the Committee and in grass roots Republican politics. Adams flourished, practicing faith healing in addition to managing the plantation and mill, although his healing was irregular but lucrative. In 1873 he served on the Shreveport grand jury with nine other Black men and six whites. President of the Shreveport Republican club,

---

[15]Ibid., p. 178.

[16]Adams said that he chopped between three and seven cords of wood a day and stacked them. Later, when an incredulous senator questioned the possibility of chopping and cording so much wood per day, day after day, Adams replied, "I didn't say I could cut and split them; I say I have did it." (Ibid., p. 132.)

the "mother club" of the parish in 1874, he witnessed a recrudescent terrorism, reminiscent of 1865–66, but now inflicted by the newly organized White League. The accompanying white-solidarity campaign aimed to exile or assassinate prominent Black men.

In their attempt to exert economic pressure on troublesome Blacks, the White Leagues forbade other whites to employ certain Black men, and Henry Adams lost his job. According to Adams, Hambleton only objected to his politics: "Adams, I think a heap of you as a man; I know you are a true man, and that you will do what you promise to do, but under this order I cannot employ you. . . . You are a good old Republican, and I cannot employ you because you are a Republican. I cannot employ you no more."[17]

Somewhat disingenuously, Adams protested that he was not a political man: "I never had anything to do with politics more than going to vote. . . ." Admitting that he had exercised considerable influence among the people in his neighborhood, Adams insisted that he had not pursued influence—as "politicians" would have done—but "when my men who belonged to the society that I belonged to would come to me and ask what I thought best as to the way they should vote, I would tell them, of course, and I would issue them tickets—all my members; I would issue tickets to them and tell them how I thought they ought to vote." Issuing tickets (ballots) was incontrovertibly political. Candidates authorized their organizers to issue the tickets, which voters would then put in the ballot box. Without the ticket of the candidate he supported, there was no way a man could vote for him. Distributing ballots was one of the most important functions a local organizer performed.[18]

Nonetheless, Adams's denial that he was a politician and his admission that he exercised considerable influence were no mere sham humility. They reveal the basis of his success with his constituency—he identified with them and did not set himself apart from them or above them, as "representative colored men" tended to do. Adams did not gratuitously lecture rural Blacks; rather, he waited until his opinion was sought, then gave it in the plain talk of the people themselves. Adams realized that he was

---

[17]Ibid., p. 114.
[18]Ibid.

not a rhetorician (in the tradition of a Pinchback or Bruce), but credited his success to his honesty and identity with the people: "I can speak to them in my language. . . . They hear me and believe what I tell them; and I aim to tell the truth under all circumstances." He was a leader, he said, because he wanted the same things as the laboring class of people wanted, and he spoke as much for them as for himself, "for I am amongst them there. . . ."[19]

During the summer of 1874, when the White League seriously reduced the state government's authority, Republican Governor William Pitt Kellogg requested federal troops for several locales where the White League exercised control. The Council, too, decided to take positive action. It sent a petition to President Grant and to Congress in September, at the height of the disorder. That appeal, added to Kellogg's call, brought the Seventh Cavalry to Shreveport.

The parish maintained somewhat better order after the arrival of the United States troops, but nevertheless, illegalities still occurred around the election. Adams was a United States supervisor of elections at Tom Bayou, about fifteen miles southeast of Shreveport, and he complained of election irregularities. Once again, he was "spotted" in the Shreveport *Times,* along with several other Black men who had protested the tampering with ballot boxes.

Henry Adams worked as an undercover scout with the Seventh Cavalry while it remained in Shreveport during 1875. He collected information on conditions in the parish, earning a good salary of fifty dollars per month. Yet he found it hard and perilous work, and he continued for only three months, between March and June. It was, he said, "a very dangerous business. I had ten times rather have been employed splitting rails. We daren't let nobody know what we was up to."[20]

As much as the local whites resented the military occupation, the soldiers curbed the carnage: "Troops came down there and [the regulators] stopped killing our people as much as they had been; the White Leagues stopped raging about with their guns so much as we had seen them rage about."[21] While the occupation

[19]Ibid., pp. 138, 141.
[20]Ibid., p. 128.
[21]Ibid., p. 127.

limited some of the grossest excesses of violence against Blacks, other forms of oppression continued. During his service on the Shreveport grand jury, in his work as a government scout, and in his discussions with Blacks from other parts of the state and the South, Adams saw that extortion, intimidation, and injustice still plagued Blacks across the lower Mississippi Valley.

On the Shreveport grand jury in 1873, Adams came face to face with the workings of the criminal justice system. Although the grand jury was composed of ten Black and six white men, the judge, lawyers, district attorney, foreman, and clerk were all white and discriminated in favor of rich, white defendants. Black men, women, and children were jailed before they were indicted; if they were indicted they were usually convicted. The chain gang was the usual punishment for convicted Blacks, women as well as men. Adams noted that all Blacks brought before the grand jury for indictment were brought by whites, and that many Black women came before the jury but never any white women. In all the cases considered by the 1873 session of the grand jury, only one white man was indicted and tried for killing a Black man in cold blood. Yet, after the trial stretched out for a year, the defendant was acquitted.[22]

The trivial nature of the crimes for which Blacks were jailed before arraignment impressed Adams most. Prisoners complained to him of having been beaten by the (white) jailer, and the prison population included several young children. "I saw little colored boys in there," Adams wrote of the Shreveport jail, "for stealing one can of oysters. I seen little girls in there for stealing such things as thimbles, scissors, &c., and [there] was several colored men in prison, and only two white men were put in jail for crimes they had committed. . . ."[23]

During the same year, he witnessed Blacks of both sexes and all ages incarcerated for mere suspicion of guilt in petty crimes. Meanwhile, Black people cheated out of their earnings dared not approach the courts for their just redress. "I saw many colored people swindled out of their crops," said Adams; "I led them into the light how it was done, but they were afraid to make affidavits

---

[22]Ibid., p. 180.
[23]Ibid.

[in court] against them."[24] Even during the occupation, the courts offered poor Blacks no protection of their contractual rights. The presence of United States troops reduced political violence in north Louisiana, but Blacks knew no economic respite.

---

[24]"Tenants complained that instead of settling with them once the crop was made, as was specified in their contracts, planters usually withheld the tenants' share until the following year's cotton was planted. In this way, the tenant was tied to the same planter's land in order to receive his earnings from the previous season. Tenants were not allowed to sell their own cotton; instead, the planter or merchant would ship the cotton to New Orleans and then report to the tenant that the cotton had sold at a false, lower figure. Rather than divide the crop immediately, "they ship it in every bale, and will not divide it at the gins, but ship it to the city; then when the cotton is sold they figure and figure until there is but little left to the colored man; then they do not settle, but wait until the next crop is pitched, say in February, and sometimes even in June, before they will say the cotton is sold." (Ibid.)

7

The Committee
Becomes the Colonization
Council

The Committee gathered information on the condition of Black people between 1870 and 1874 before it began to act. Although it sent petitions to Washington in 1874, 1876 proved a watershed in the Committee's evolution. In that year, its members faced the depressing prospect of more election violence but resolved to seek federal support:

We first organized and adopted a plan to appeal to the President of the United States and to Congress to help us out of our distress, or protect us in our rights and privileges.

And if that failed our idea was then to ask them to set apart a territory in the United States for us, somewhere we could go and live with our families.

When that failed then our idea was to appeal to other governments outside of the United States to help us to get away from the United States and go there and live under their flag.[1]

In late December 1875, Henry Adams accompanied a delegation of Black ministers to New Orleans for a conference that included men and women from several states. Adams's attendance at the New Orleans conference heavily influenced the Committee's new direction, for there Adams learned not only that Blacks were cheated across wide areas of the South, but that a clear pattern of controlled exploitation emerged. Debt, for instance, universally

---

[1] Henry Adams, *Senate Report 693*, II: 104.

served to tie Black families to the same planters year after year, but the burden of debt seldom exceeded a family's hope of getting clear by making a good crop the succeeding year. Further, he saw that everywhere it was possible for individual Blacks to prosper economically, but at a considerable price: "The few that makes anything at all has to aid the white people in cheating the others of his own race and color out of his money and crops. That is when the colored man gets what he makes; they have to do that or not make anything." And the punishment in several states for attempting to sell one's crops on the open market was whipping or assassination.[2] Conditions which had hitherto seemed unique to the environs of Shreveport now emerged as typical of the entire lower South.

Several of the delegates to the New Orleans meeting from Louisiana, Mississippi, Alabama, Texas, Arkansas, and Georgia suggested migration out of the South. The others received the idea warmly. One man asked, "Do you think we will do better if we were to ourselves and out of the South?" And a Georgian replied:

Yes; for we will get what we make, our crops or their value; if we get in jail, we will have a chance to get bond and a chance to prove our innocence, and not be taken out by a mob and hung or shot before they know whether we are guilty or not; and may not have to work on the railroad or levees in chain-gangs when we are not guilty of any crime, and not to be whipped as if we were dumb brutes; not hated because we are black.[3]

The meeting considered migration to territories of the United States and to Liberia. Adams and several others, including a man intending to go to Liberia within the year, favored the African alternative. Adams thought Liberia a good place for American Blacks, for thousands had already gone there "where our forefathers came from," and he liked the idea of "living with our own race and people, and under a government with our race as presiding officers." But whether they left the South for other American soil or for the land of their ancestors, Adams insisted that leaving

---

[2]Ibid., pp. 185–86.

[3]Ibid. In the late nineteenth century, leaving the South for another section of the United States was termed "emigration." Since it was envisioned that large numbers of Blacks would go together and settle together, that process was termed "colonization." A large number of families, Black or white, moving to a new area was called a "colony," without pejorative connotations. Thus, "colonization" was synonymous with collective pioneering.

the South was imperative, for "God of high heaven will put a curse should we continue to live with our former masters and ex-slaveholders, who are not enjoying the same rights as he has ordained that we shall enjoy in our own native soil; for God says in His Holy Work that he has a place and land for all his people, and our race had better go to it. . . ."[4]

Adams described the Committee's activities and its petition to President Grant to the New Orleans delegates, encouraging them to go home and try to carry the 1876 election for the Republicans. Then, he said, "if we find the country no better for us, we must then go to work and try and get our race to leave the Southern States where we have been slaves, working the land for our masters." His proposition came to a vote and carried in a "unanimous voice . . . and yes was echoed by all; and we agreed to it, both women and men that were assembled at that conference."[5] In January 1876 Adams returned home, where in midsummer he and his coworkers began laying the groundwork for the 1876 election.

With a handful of men, Adams rode across several north Louisiana parishes: Caddo, Claiborne, the Baton Rouges, and Bossier. They reactivated local Republican clubs, which would choose delegates to the parochial conventions, which in turn would nominate local tickets and delegates to the state convention. During this grass roots organizational work they encountered tremendous white opposition, not only to Republican organizing but to any organizational activities whatever among Blacks. Time and again, Adams and his companions met threats of "what are you damn niggers doing here? If we catch you damn niggers trying to organize here we will kill half of you; as that is our business."[6] Nonetheless, Adams and his ten or twelve men traveled about, even into Mississippi, Texas, and Arkansas counties bordering on Louisiana, rallying voters for the coming election, garnering support for the position taken at the New Orleans meeting. They kept lists of people willing to leave the South in case their right to vote was interfered with in this coming contest.

As Adams and his companions traveled through north Louisiana they gathered information from Committee members who had been sent out among the people. The members were useful

---

[4] Ibid.
[5] Ibid.
[6] Ibid., p. 187.

sources of concrete information, for they had been advised that "you can't find out anything till you get amongst them. You can talk as much as you please, but you have got to go right into the field and work with them and sleep with them to know all about them."[7] Committee members were able to relay the concerns of the people, for they had come to know them intimately. Many working people, they reported, had already lost hope.

In Claiborne Parish, Adams inquired whether they should try to organize Republican clubs, make Republican slates, and vote. With a single exception, the men answered, "No, and we think it useless to try any longer; for the white men of Claiborne Parish has killed every good black man in our parish that tried to lead us right." Yet, in discussion, they remembered that in the past when one good Black man was assassinated, another had stepped forward to take his place. They recalled when they were marching to the polls to vote in 1874, kept in formation by Peter Williams. When he was shot, Joe Calvin took charge, and they went on to vote anyway. Their experience showed that their strength was in the people, not just in the most visible leaders, and they resolved to try once more.[8]

Again and again, Adams encountered a people demoralized by the omnifarious persecution they faced, political, economic, and judicial. Insults to Black women, petty annoyances, and general insecurity of life and property deepened their depression. Often in 1876, the rural people were more eager to leave the South than were Adams and his men. In East Feliciana Parish, for instance, Adams intended to stay with a friend named Joe Johnson. Arriving at Johnson's house, he found it burned to the ground and Johnson's distraught widow at a neighbor's house. She told Adams what had happened:

She said to me that she had lost her husband; that he was burned to death in his own house; that him and I [his wife] had worked together, but he was gone now to return no more forever; but, thank God, he is gone to rest. He [Johnson] asked me not to grieve for him. They made me and my children wrap our heads up in bed-quilts and come out of the house, and they then set it on fire, burning it up, and my husband in it, and all we had. They then took all my husband's papers from me. There were about fifty or sixty of them terrorists. They killed him because he refused to

[7]Ibid., p. 102.
[8]Ibid., p. 187.

resign his office as constable, to which he was elected on the Republican ticket. They sent him several notices, warning him to leave his place and resign his office, but he said he would not until his time was out. So they warned him the last time, but he did not leave, so they burnt him near to death; at least they thought he was dead, but he was not quite dead; he got out and fell into a hole of water and lay there; but all the skin was burnt off of him. So the white men saw him and shot him, and he lived four days and died, and leaves me, a poor widow with a housefull of children, and no one to help me.

Johnson's widow asked Adams if he thought the white men who had murdered her husband so horribly would be brought to justice:

I told her I did not know, perhaps some day, but not soon, as I knew that white men had been killing our race so long, and they had not been stopped yet; as all whites who had owned slaves believed they could kill as many as they wanted in the States that existed before the war. . . .

At this, she wept aloud, "O, Lord God of Hosts, help us to get out of this country and get somewhere where we can live."[9]

Johnson's widow's plight was wretched, but unfortunately it was not unique. Crossing the parishes of north Louisiana, Adams had considerable difficulty in rallying Black people to try to vote even one more time. Adams would ask people "how they were getting along," and they would answer, "If we cannot do any better than we have been doing here since freedom, we had better leave the country and migrate to Africa."[10]

Many Blacks had already had their one last time, but for Henry Adams, a first turning point came in the year following the election of 1876. (For still other Blacks living in more secure circumstances, that first realization of the hopeless lot of Blacks in the South came with the 1878 elections or the 1879 elections. In some cases, the shock of awakening came only in the 1890s.) For the

[9]Ibid., pp. 184–85.
[10]Ibid., p. 190. According to Hollis Lynch, the Republic of Liberia was anxious to bolster its Afro-American population in the late 1870s—although it lacked the financial means to do so—because it felt threatened by native African polities. Edward W. Blyden, an adopted African of West Indian origin, was well known and well liked by Negro Americans. He favored black but opposed mulatto immigrants. For this reason, he placed more faith in the American Colonization Society than in the South Carolina Joint-Stock Steamship Company, which, he feared, would bring mulatto immigrants to Liberia. More detailed treatment of this issue is in Lynch's *Edward Wilmot Blyden, Pan-Negro Patriot* (London, 1967).

Colonization Council members, the outrages of the 1876 election and the resulting Democratic takeover of the state government were the last straw. In 1877 the Council held several large meetings, the first public meetings it had ever called, in response to a ground swell of despair:

We found ourselves in such condition that we looked around and we seed that there was no way on earth, it seemed, that we could better our condition [in Louisiana], and we discussed that thoroughly in our organization along in May 1877. We said that the whole South—every State in the South—had got into the hands of the very men that held us slaves—from one thing to another—and we thought that the men that held us slaves was holding the reins of government over our heads in every respect almost, even the constable up to the governor. We felt we had almost as well be slaves under these men. In regard to the whole matter that was discussed, it came up in every council. Then we said there was no hope for us and we had better go.[11]

In 1877 Adams made his first serious public speeches advocating emigration from the South. The Colonization Council drew up a petition and circulated it at emigration meetings; according to Adams, ninety-eight thousand men, women, and children enrolled on the emigration lists. All of them wanted to go to Liberia or to a territory of the United States, if the federal government would appropriate land and means of transportation. These ninety-eight thousand lived mostly in Louisiana, but the rolls included people in Texas, Arkansas, and a few in Mississippi. In September 1877, Adams sent the petition to President Hayes.

"At a meeting of the National Colored Colonization Society, held in Shreveport, Caddo Parish, State of Louisiana, held on September 15, 1877, there being as said meeting representatives representing 29,000 colored people of the South, the following preambles and resolutions were unanimously adopted," began the petition bearing 3,000 names. The preambles noted that "we look to the future where in case of war we would feel compelled to fight for that government that looks coolly on our sufferings and see our rights one by one taken away from us, and we cry out with a full heart, the cup is full and running over, and with a loud voice cry to God, O, how long?" Three resolutions expressing the Council's views ended the petition:

[11]Henry Adams, *Senate Report 693*, II: 108.

[1.] That we, the colored race of the South, do call upon the President and Congress of the United States to look back upon the blood shed on the battle-field by our race in defense of the government; to look back on the cotton and sugar raised by our labor; and we, in view of those facts that the rights guaranteed to us by the Constitution be restored to us, and ample protection be given to us in the maintenance of those rights. *If that protection cannot be given and our lost rights restored, we would respectfully ask that some Territory be assigned to us in which we can colonize our race; and if that cannot be done, to appropriate means so that we can colonize in Liberia or some other country,* for we feel and know that unless full and ample protection is guaranteed to us we cannot live in the South, and will and must colonize under some other government, and we put our full trust in God that our prayers and petition will be speedily answered.

[2.] That we respectfully and earnestly call upon Congress to restore back to us the savings of years that our race was robbed of by the failure of the Freedman's Bank, feeling that it is only an act of justice due us.

[3.] *That we as a race will abstain from voting on all national questions and at the elections for national officers unless we have full protection and our own officers to guard our interests and rights.*[12]

Although the petition cited several alternatives, interest among rural Blacks in leaving the country altogether grew apace.

During the summer of 1877, while the Colonization Council enrolled the names of thousands of Blacks seeking to emigrate from the South, Henry Adams initiated correspondence with the American Colonization Society, a white association that had been formed in 1817 to remove free Blacks from the United States. Intimately connected with the Republic of Liberia, the Society functioned throughout the nineteenth century, ordinarily sending about a hundred Afro-Americans to Liberia per year. Now, however, Democratic Redemption of the South stirred Black interest in Liberia on a gigantic scale, overwhelming the American Colonization Society. At the same time that Adams opened negotiations with the Society, similar groups of Liberia enthusiasts gained numbers in Arkansas and in North and South Carolina. In August 1877 Henry Adams wrote to the aged president of the American Colonization Society, John H. B. Latrobe, introducing his Colonization

---

[12]Ibid., p. 156. (Emphasis added.) The military argument was used with varying measures of success after every American war, for Blacks were always called upon to serve in the armed forces.

Council and appending fifty-eight names of members of the Council. Although four of the names bore the title "Reverend," Adams pointed out to Latrobe that they represented working men, and that the Colonization Council had signed up "69,000 men and women who wish to be colonized in Liberia or some other country . . . two thirds of us wants to go to Liberia." New people were signing up every day, and they were all "a class of hard laboring people."[13]

The Colonization Council found the organizing of mass participation and money collecting more difficult than simply accumulating information or rallying voters once a year. A solid financial base and sustained participation were crucial to the success of the ambitious effort. Since the petition to President Hayes had produced no official reaction, nor had Congress taken action on appropriating money to aid the Colonization Council, all funds had to come from the members of the Council and the emigrants themselves. In addition, the furor over the violence accompanying the 1876 elections brought publicity and renewed Justice Department attempts to prosecute election cases. As a result, the measure of peace kindled a guarded optimism among many rural Blacks. The urgent desire to leave the South subsided among those who were only peripherally involved in colonization. By early 1878 Adams encountered difficulty in bringing together the scattered members of the Council. Collecting dues to cover the expenses of delegates to Liberia was yet more taxing.

Before 1877, neither the Committee nor the Colonization Council, which succeeded it, had ever held public meetings. Now, the emigration campaign necessitated massive and sustained support, and it proceeded in the usual manner of rural, Black public action. Large numbers of people met to talk out a policy, then delegated executive responsibility to one or two members. In this case, a few men were to go to Liberia to inspect the country, make reports, and generally act as the eyes and ears of the membership

---

[13]Henry Adams to John H. B. Latrobe, president of the American Colonization Society, Shreveport, Louisiana, August 31, 1877, *American Colonization Society Papers*, Ser. IA, 228: 170. Library of Congress. (Hereafter referred to as *Am. Col. Soc. Papers.*) Of the 58 names, 28 were from Caddo Parish, 8 from De Soto Parish, 7 from Bossier Parish, 6 from Claiborne Parish, 5 from Webster Parish, 3 from Bienville Parish, and 1 from East Baton Rouge Parish. All these parishes lie in north Louisiana, and Henry Adams had personally been active in each of them.

at home in Louisiana. But to send three or four delegates would cost $150 to $200. Raising that much money required contributions from hundreds of working people, and the effort to generate continued financial support exposed the Colonization Council's shortcomings. Some weakness was inherent in any organization of poor, economically dependent, and vulnerable people. The basic problem, of course, was poverty. The people simply had little cash for use on other than necessities, whether for school fees or boat passage.

Other weaknesses were structural in nature. The intelligence work of the Committee had not demanded regular meetings or periodic accounting. The Committee had required few financial outlays, so there was no pressing need for full-time officers, secretaries, or treasurers. When it was merely a matter of ascertaining the condition of the colored people, peace was naturally a good thing.

The emigration campaign was a different matter, for it meant movement and required persistent organization. In this case, when conditions settled down after elections, interest in leaving home dwindled. In addition to flagging enthusiasm, the tyranny of the agricultural calendar tied people to their fields, at least in the absence of any concrete alternative. The lack of a compelling imperative lengthened the miles of poor and insecure roads to be traveled to Colonization Council meetings. If the absent member was the treasurer of his parish council, the business of the whole meeting faltered. In the end, the Colonization Council was not able to complete the transition from an underground cadre of men watching over the condition of its people and organizing them politically on the grass roots level to an emigration bureau, collecting dues regularly, sending representatives across the ocean, and organizing the transfer of thousands of farming people from one continent to another.

Excerpts from Henry Adams's letters covering the seven months following the first attempt to solve racial difficulties by expatriation to Liberia illustrate the nature of the organizational difficulties the Colonization Council faced. Henry Adams wrote all of the following letters from Shreveport to the American Colonization Society:

August 31, 1877
We have now enrolled sixty-nine Thousand (69,000) men and women who

wish to be colonized in Liberia or some other country. Part of them are in the Southern part of Arkansas and the Eastern part of Texas and the remainder in Louisiana. . . .[14]

September 24, 1877
We are getting [a]long very well with our colonization Society, but our people is not paying dues weekly nor monthly because this is a terrible part of the country and our Race can not get money for our labor. . . .[15]

November 26, 1877
Our Treasure is very slender. There have been several meetings held for the purpose of taking up Collections for the cause, and the finance Committee's are several miles apart. I have not heard the reports yet.[16]

February 12, 1878
I hope you will send out some circulars to us to arose the minds of our People again for our people are getting very dull.[17]

April 1, 1878
[A fall from a railroad bridge] laid me up for three weeks and I have not been able to attend to my business since our Council men are so busy with their crops now and we did not have but a very small meeting on the 23d of Mch, and our finance members was not present they all live so far apart and it is a great deal of trouble to get word to them in time and they are all hard laboring men and farmers.[18]

In the early period of public meetings and widespread support, the Colonization Council envisioned sending delegates on the American Colonization Society's voyage to Liberia in January 1878. They were to have been five, including Henry Adams. But as financial difficulties piled up, the number fell to three; then it became obvious that even three delegates could not go in 1878. By mid-December 1877 the number of proposed delegates had been reduced to two because of lack of money, and finally no one was able to go. Instead, another copy of essentially the same petition as that of September 1877 was sent to President Hayes on January 5, 1878. Appended to the bottom was the note that the enrolled

---

[14]Ibid.

[15]Henry Adams to William Coppinger, secretary of the American Colonization Society, Shreveport, Louisiana, September 24, 1877, ibid., p. 251.

[16]Henry Adams to William Coppinger, Shreveport, Louisiana, November 26, 1877, ibid., 229:232.

[17]Henry Adams to William Coppinger, Shreveport, Louisiana, February 12, 1878, ibid., 230: 144.

[18]Henry Adams to William Coppinger, Shreveport, Louisiana, April 1, 1878, ibid., 231: 1.

names now totaled seventy-one thousand who wished "to be colonized in Liberia or some other Territory than in the Southern States."[19] Meanwhile, the Colonization Council resolved that it was "not a proper step to hold so many public meetings," and decided to go back to secret meetings for the time being.[20] The most salient motive for increased secrecy around emigration meetings was the criticism attracted by the South Carolina Liberia movement.

Formed at about the same time the Shreveport-based Colonization Council opened correspondence with the American Colonization Society, the Liberian Exodus Joint-Stock Steamship Company also anticipated large-scale Afro-American emigration from the South, which the white Southern press violently opposed. In light of the adverse publicity and outright hostility that the South Carolinian group provoked among whites, the Louisianians decided that closed meetings would do well. Even though the Liberia movement in Louisiana went underground during 1878, it remained a sensitive issue in race relations until the end of the century.

In its secret meetings, the Council cast about for alternate means of escape, for the federal government had not appropriated funds to aid their emigration to Liberia.[21] Outside financial backing grew even more necessary after Louisiana whites learned of

---

[19]Henry Adams to William Coppinger, Shreveport, Louisiana, January 6, 1878, ibid., 230: 26–27.

[20]Henry Adams to William Coppinger, Shreveport, Louisiana, February 28, 1878, ibid., p. 231.

[21]Throughout the second half of the nineteenth century emigrationists petitioned Congress for appropriations to support their emigration. Many Blacks were convinced that the federal government's failure to protect their rights at home entitled them at the very least to the government's aid in finding a home where they could protect themselves.

President Lincoln and other Republicans had supported Black emigration during the Civil War. And in fact, an 1862 law was still on the statute books which provided that one fourth of the proceeds of the sale of abandoned Confederate lands was to be set aside by the government to support Afro-American emigration. In 1862, $600,000 was actually appropriated for emigration of emancipated Blacks in the District of Columbia.

U.S. legislators periodically introduced bills and resolutions to the same end. The Windom Resolution of 1879 and the Butler bill of 1890 provide two examples. See also James M. McPherson, *The Negro's Civil War* (New York, 1965; Vintage ed., 1967), pp. 89–90, and Edwin S. Redkey, *Black Exodus: Black Nationalist and Back-to-Africa Movements, 1890–1910* (New Haven, 1969), p. 151.

the pervasive interest in Liberia among Blacks: "Since these
Southern white people found out that we are trying to get away
from here," Adams wrote, they have "shut down on the Cotton
and taken all the Cotton and Corn and every thing else from the
Colored people and the majority of our race is now living from
hand to mouth." Adams and his group now thought of turning to
foreign governments for aid; he wrote, "We have a notion of
asking England to help us emigrate to Liberia or any other Government that will do it."[22] The Colonization Council held an important meeting on April 27, 1878, that considered several questions, including voting, sending delegates to Liberia, and ordering
priorities during the coming election canvass.

In the face of faltering interest on the part of the people, and
indeed, on the part of some of the Council members themselves,
the central Colonization Council came to a number of important
conclusions in the spring of 1878. The first was that the Liberia
movement should not be dropped during the balance of the election year. Members should continue working in "every way for
our race to get away from the South." Another decision concerned
the proposed delegation to inspect conditions in Liberia. Since
money was scarce and other Black groups (for instance, in neighboring Arkansas) had sent delegations for the same purpose, it was
decided to await their return before the Council sent delegates of
its own. The third question was a sensitive one for the Shreveport
body and for many other Blacks as well. They chose between
dealing with the new Black-owned and -run Liberian Exodus
Joint-Stock Steamship Company and the older, better-known
American Colonization Society, run by whites.

Poor, financially vulnerable Blacks had wanted to support
Black businesses before, but they were understandably wary of
loss. The Freedmen's Bank failure had worked hardship on many
Negroes, as one of the petitions mentioned. Although it was neither Black owned nor managed, the bank had had a Black president, Frederick Douglass, during its expiring days, and it traded
on its resemblance in name to the Freedmen's Bureau. It accepted

---

[22]Henry Adams to William Coppinger, Shreveport, Louisiana, February 28,
1878, *Am. Col. Soc. Papers*, Ser. IA, 230: 231. The allusion to England was undoubtedly inspired by acquaintance with the British colony of Sierra Leone, which was
adjacent to Liberia, and with Blyden. In addition, the British were generally
thought of as being kindly disposed toward people of color. This concept of the
British played a part in Benjamin Singleton's interest in Cyprus in the 1880s.

the savings of thousands of Blacks across the South but failed in 1874. The closing of its branches in Shreveport and New Orleans cost Black customers three hundred thousand dollars in deposits.[23] Despite the bank's having been mismanaged by whites, its failure nevertheless symbolized the insecurity surrounding Black enterprise.

The Liberian Exodus Joint-Stock Steamship Company touched the same sensitive chords in the Colonization Council. Just as the Council faltered in deciding between an established white company with which they could feel confident of getting their money's worth, and a new, untried race venture, Abraham Cashaw of Vicksburg, Mississippi, faced the same conundrum. He wrote the secretary of the Colonization Society almost sheepishly, "Between I & you please tell me what you think of the steamship company & please tell me if you think it will be safe to get a hundred Dollar share [in] the Charleston Exodus Steamship co. at Charleston S.C."[24] After hesitating and deliberating, the Colonization Council chose the better-known group, with which Henry Adams had been corresponding since 1877.

Aside from some procedural questions, the other business of the April 1878 meeting considered the priorities of the Colonization Council in the coming months—Liberia or the election campaign. The petitions to President Hayes (which had not been acknowledged and were evidently ignored) committed Black voters to boycotting all national elections until protected in their suffrage rights. But Democrats would undoubtedly nominate "ultras"— extreme anti-Black candidates—and seriously threaten to extinguish Negro suffrage. "What shall we do this year about voting," the Council asked, wondering whether to hand the Democrats the election on a silver platter: ". . . shall we vote or not and if yes, shall we vote for white men or shall we vote for colored men or vote for both. The Council voted yes to vote as long as we stay here in the Country."[25] The minutes did not record the meeting's intentions on voting for white or colored candidates, but in the actual election, Council members supported white candidates on a fu-

---

[23]Joe Gray Taylor, *Louisiana Reconstructed* (Baton Rouge, 1974), p. 360.

[24]Abraham Cashaw to William Coppinger, Vicksburg, Mississippi, May 14, 1878, *Am. Col. Soc. Papers,* Ser. IA, 231: 120.

[25]Henry Adams to William Coppinger, Shreveport, Louisiana, April 27, 1878, ibid., p. 83.

sion ticket, in opposition to "ultra" Democrats. On the question of whether to continue talking about Liberia during the election campaign, a large majority wanted to "speak Liberia at all times all over the State during the Campaign."[26]

The Council accomplished very little during the summer of 1878, however. Yellow fever struck with unusual severity, and quarantines isolated one Louisiana town from another, rendering communication and travel nearly impossible. In addition, Henry Adams had another accident and lay immobilized for two months. "So I my self am very badly afflicted at this time," he wrote. "I have not been out of my house for 26 days—I fell of the 10 of July off a new Baptist Church which is Building here and injured both legs and both sides one arm and my head—but I think I will be over it in about fifteen or twenty days."[27] By the time he recovered, the election campaign was moving into full swing. Anarchy reigned in several heavily Republican parishes well past election day.

---

[26]Ibid.

[27]Henry Adams to William Coppinger, Shreveport, Louisiana, August 5, 1878, ibid., 232: 120.

8

Henry Adams in Exile

The election campaign of 1878 was the first held in Redeemed Louisiana, the first of the so-called New Departure era. In the parishes of Tensas and Natchitoches, the canvass proved especially violent; Caddo Parish was far from peaceful from well before until well after the election. The campaign radically altered Henry Adams's life.

When the Colonization Council rescinded its 1876 boycott resolution, Adams made another supreme effort to get out the Republican vote. He entered the canvass, in his words, "like unto a roving lion," but his efforts met frustration. White Leaguers and obstreperous Democrats broke up Republican meetings, changed polling places at the last minute, pretended that the names of Republican voters were not on the registration lists, used three ballot boxes instead of one per poll, and stuffed ballot boxes to be absolutely sure that only "ultra" Democrats were elected. This last technique was known as "counting out." Thanks to these illegal measures, Democratic nominees won the election, but the flagrant and widespread outrages surrounding the contest triggered federal action. A United States grand jury in New Orleans heard testimony on breaches of federal election statutes; Henry Adams was one of its witnesses. Subpoenaed to testify before the grand jury, he left Shreveport for New Orleans on December 4, 1878.

Adams addressed one of his last letters from Shreveport to the United States attorney general, describing the violence and fraud that pervaded the 1878 election in Caddo Parish. He insisted that the Democratic victory gave no indication of a wholesale conversion of Black voters to the Democracy—as many Southern whites claimed. The victory was due entirely to terrorism and election chicanery:

. . . the colored [voted] the Rep[ublican] ticket [more] than ever before in the History of this country and on the day of election Nov. 5th the democrats had three ballot boxes at every poll in this parish one for the Congressman and one for the State and parish and one for the Ward and we had our tickets whole and Numbers of us voted our tickets whole. . . .

The three-ballot-box strategy seriously diminished Republican voting strength, because

if we put our tickets in the Ward box they counted nothing only for the Ward and the Parish & Congressional boxes they counted them for one Side or the others. and part of the Col[ored] people tore their tickets into [three parts] and put them in all three of the boxes—and the democrats found out that we were beating them, and so they hunted and swore that they could not find our names on the list of Registration.

When neither ruse succeeded in neutralizing the heavy Republican plurality, the White Leaguers resorted to violence and barred Black voters from the polls:

[At] about ten or eleven o'clock in the day we all found out that they aimed for the Col[ored] man's vote to count nothing and so there were orders given for them all to stop voting and so we did so and in the other parts of the parish where they did not stop they were driven from the polls with Sticks and guns. in the Campobella Ward which is Called the 8th the white league have killed or wounded and ran off 200 Col[ored] people—out of that Ward—and even killed three Col[ored] women and children about their husbands. . . .

Enumerating several instances of intimidation in neighboring parishes, Adams showed why he wanted the government to set aside a place for Blacks outside the South. White opposition was aimed at one ironclad goal—the negation of Black suffrage. And whites vowed to continue killing and beating Blacks until that goal was reached. Adams bolstered his argument by pointing to white as well as Black victims of the White League:

Some of the Democrats tells me just so long as we Colored people fools with politics, and try to vote here in the South, So long as the white man of the South are going to kill us and from what I can see it seem so—and they have threatened about a hundred of our lives now and many are scared to stay in their houses at night and the White League have made some of them leave the State and my life is threatened . . . I trust God that the United States will give us some Territory to our selves—and let us leave these Slave holders to work their own land, for they are killing our race by the hundreds every day and night. . . .

the white Southern Republicans are not allowed any more showing about political matters than the poor Colored people and we pray God that the Northern people will take this in Consideration and do something for our poor race.[1]

Henry Adams was not the only Black man protesting the election outrages to Washington from Shreveport. R. J. Cromwell, the president of the Negro Union Cooperative Aid Association, sent a letter to President Hayes on November 10, 1878. Cromwell asked that Black United States troops be sent to Louisiana to protect the colored people, not only from the election depredations but also from the unrelenting, everyday outrages that the Black population had suffered for years on end at the hands of Louisiana whites. According to Cromwell, the freedpeople had long been denied the right merely to exist in peace. Prefacing his discussion of conditions of life in general, he described the 1878 election:

I write to you my dear Sir amid a terror stricken and distressed people —and I do it solely for the purpose of showing you the condition of my race (the Negro people in this State). On the 5th Inst, our Election was held, on that day Republicans and Unionists who wished to vote a Republican ticket was driven from the Poll murdered, or intimidated. This morning five days since the so called election I am told the Rebels are still Killing *freedmen* the news are that the bodies are lying in the wood unburried and eaten by the hogs—our town is full of refugees, our most industrious men are hunted down like they were wild beasts of prey. . . .

Nor was this deplorable state of affairs an isolated occurrence:

The History of Louisiana for the last twelve years reveals nothing more interesting than prosecutions, murders, Etc. Etc. of the negro citizens of this state—It has been an exterminating and intimidating war—yes, Churches burned, Ignorant defenseless negroes Killed, innocent women, that were pregnant had the child rifled from the *womb,* of a living mother —Our young women subjected to treatment too horrible to mention.[2]

---

[1] Henry Adams to U.S. Attorney General Charles Devens, Shreveport, Louisiana, November 11, 1878, Record Group 60, Department of Justice Source-Chronological Files, Louisiana, box 434.

[2] R. G. Cromwell to President R. B. Hayes, Shreveport, Louisiana, November 10, 1878, Record Group 60, Department of Justice Source-Chronological Files, President, box 6.

Unlike the whites, who were secure in their homes, and the Indians, who roamed freely across broad prairies, poor Blacks were "without lands, homes or friends." Cromwell called for the strong, *Black* arm of the United States Army: "To remedy all these misfortunes, you have an army composed of black and white Soldiers, fill the south with Negro Soldiers to protect the freedmen and you will do the freedmen justice."[3]

Cromwell differed from Adams in specifically requesting Black soldiers, but he agreed on the need for resettlement, although he favored colonization of Southern Blacks within the South. In June 1878 he had sent a petition to the House of Representatives via General Benjamin F. Butler, asking that Congress "set a part the public lands in the Southern states for freedmen— for an act of Congress fixing the quantity to which each head of family shall be entitled—and for [the] establishement of a colonizing bureau."[4] The Negro Union Cooperative Aid Association, although separate from Adams's Colonization Council, worked alongside the older body. Cromwell was simply open to Southern solutions to race problems.

Adams, by contrast, adamantly insisted on leaving the South altogether if no "protection" (that is, United States troops) was forthcoming. And by 1878 he had relinquished hope that this protection could be secured without Grant's election. While the Grant movement was not entirely dead in 1879, it was a long shot, a kind of vain but fondly held hope for many Southern Blacks and Northern Stalwarts. For all intents and purposes, then, Adams envisioned emigration out of the South, preferably all the way to Liberia, as the best assurance of security for the colored people of the South. He therefore continued to work toward emigration to Liberia through the auspices of the American Colonization Society after he left Caddo Parish to testify before the United States grand jury in New Orleans.

Henry Adams came to New Orleans on December 11, 1878. In reaching New Orleans safely, he was already more fortunate than two other Black men who had been similarly subpoenaed but who had been kidnaped and murdered en route. Some fifty or sixty

---

[3]Ibid.

[4]Ibid. Cromwell later showed interest in migration to Kansas and wrote to the governor of Kansas for information about Kansas.

Black men like Adams were now in New Orleans to testify against whites in election cases, and for that reason they could not return home with any certainty that their lives would be safe. For Adams it was a trying time. He was an exile in New Orleans, his mother had died in DeSoto Parish shortly before his departure, and he was sick for some time after his arrival in the city. With the other witnesses, who were, in effect, refugees by the spring of 1879, Adams shared the hardship of having been unexpectedly and permanently removed from his source of income. To tide them over, he and several other political refugees sought federal employment in an interview with Senator William Kellogg in New Orleans in March 1879. Kellogg agreed to speak to the president about the possibility of work for the exiles. Meanwhile, the refugees buttressed Kellogg's approach to Hayes with a petition to the president:

We poor men summoned from our homes as witnesses against these murderers dare not return home to our Families, for to do so would be but to be murdered there and by the verry men Against whome we were summoned to testify before the U.S. Court now sitting in the Custome House in this City.

And now that the trials of these men are going on we the witnesses are threatened with death should we dare return home and only because we have told the truth before the U.S. Court. these threats have evin been made within the walls of the Custome House where the court is sitting and trying men who have murdered colord men in north La. on account of their politics.

Nevertheless the Stars and stripes that emblem ever honored by the brave and true while floating over the U.S. Custome House seems to us a hollow mockery yet as an Emblem of Freedom where it waves.[5]

The first of the fifty-four signatures appended to the petition was Henry Adams's; others who signed it testified before the Teller committee, a United States Senate committee investigating 1878 election abuses. Among them were Lafayette Thorp, John Young, and Fleming Branch. During that spring, Adams worked for the New Orleans Customs House for about three months.[6]

.   .   .

[5]Henry Adams to President Hayes, New Orleans, Louisiana, March 13, 1879, Record Group 60, Department of Justice Source-Chronological Files, President, box 7.

[6]Henry Adams, *Senate Report 693,* II: 126.

Benjamin "Pap" Singleton *(Kansas State Historical Society)*

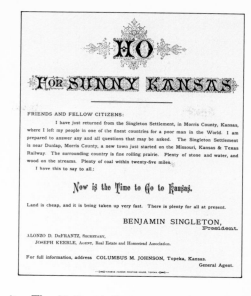

HO
FOR SUNNY KANSAS

FRIENDS AND FELLOW CITIZENS:

I have just returned from the Singleton Settlement, in Morris County, Kansas, where I left my people in one of the finest countries for a poor man in the World. I am prepared to answer any and all questions that may be asked. The Singleton Settlement is near Dunlap, Morris County, a new town just started on the Missouri, Kansas & Texas Railway. The surrounding country is fine rolling prairie. Plenty of stone and water, and wood on the streams. Plenty of coal within twenty-five miles.

I have this to say to all;

Now is the Time to Go to Kansas.

Land is cheap, and it is being taken up very fast. There is plenty for all at present.

BENJAMIN SINGLETON,
President.

ALONZO D. DeFRANTZ, Secretary,
JOSEPH KEEBLE, Agent, Real Estate and Homestead Association.

For full information, address COLUMBUS M. JOHNSON, Topeka, Kansas.
General Agent.

Opposite: The National Convention of Colored Men in Nashville, April 1876 (*Library of Congress*)
Ex-slaves en route to Kansas (*Harper's Weekly*)

Below: Exodusters preparing to leave Nashville for Kansas, 1879 (*Kansas State Historical Society*)

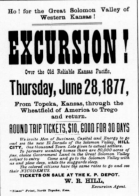

Emigrants waiting for
a Mississippi River boat
(Library of Congress)

Various handbills that
appeared in the 1870s
and 1880s *(Kansas State
Historical Society,
Union Pacific
Railroad Company)*

Opposite: Outside and inside Floral Hall,
Topeka, 1879 *(Kansas State Historical Society)*

Edward P. McCabe, Kansas State Auditor,
1883–87 *(Kansas State Historical Society)*

A cartoon of Garfield during the 1880 campaign:
"Now that we have made them free, we will stand by these black allies!
We will stand by them until the sun of liberty shall shine with equal ray
upon every man, black or white, throughout the Union." *(Harper's Weekly)*

In New Orleans, Adams continued to address emigration meetings. But in April 1879 his Liberia work was overwhelmed by the Kansas Fever Exodus. Initially taken by surprise by the sudden and massive move toward Kansas, Adams and the Colonization Council wisely worked along with the tremendously popular Kansas movement. The Council downplayed its ultimate goal of emigration to Africa, advising Blacks to leave the South while it was still possible. The Colonization Council did not modify its line out of mere political opportunism. Many of its members, perhaps including Adams himself, honestly feared that the New Departure would reimpose the conditions of 1865–66, including restriction of Blacks' freedom of movement.

The apprehension was neither foolish nor groundless. Already in 1878 certain parishes in Louisiana had begun to require Blacks to carry passes in order to move about on the public roads. In addition, protection papers—membership cards in fictitious Democratic clubs—served the same purpose elsewhere. If a Black man refused to "join" such a Democratic club, he made himself fair game for White Leaguers or mercenaries, on the roads or in his own home. Membership in these Democratic clubs indicated that the individual in question had promised to vote Democratic (and could be held to that promise).

The need for passes and protection papers effectively abridged Blacks' freedom to come and go as they wished. For them, this circumscription recalled slavery and the Black Code regimes. To Henry Adams and his fellows, it was a warning sign presaging their future in the Redeemed South. If a Democrat was elected president, his inauguration in 1881 would spell doomsday for Blacks still in the South. "So," wrote Henry Adams, "we know that we all could not get to Liberia without a mighty Hand of God within 2 years. So our Council thought it best to advise our People to leave the South and get Somewhere we could Be able to Leave for Liberia in the time to come." He now planned to leave for Liberia early in 1881.[7]

In spite of his work and his plans, however, Adams gradually lost contact with the Colonization Council members who were still

---

[7]Henry Adams to William Coppinger, New Orleans, Louisiana, April 28, 1879, *Am. Col. Soc. Papers,* Ser. IA, 234: 78. Both houses of Congress had Democratic majorities already.

in its area of greatest strength, rural north Louisiana. Opposition to the return home of the United States grand jury witnesses continued unabated throughout 1879, and the witnesses' emigrationist activities in New Orleans did nothing to reconcile their white enemies to their return to the parishes. Adams could not return for the important general Council meeting of December 1879, and, in addition, he worked at the quarantine station on the Mississippi River, isolated some seventy-five miles below New Orleans. For a month in the middle of the year he received no mail. Nonetheless, in October 1879 Adams was able to submit a list of seventy-two people who were ready to leave for Liberia on January 1, 1880. This was the last enumerated list he sent to the American Colonization Society.

In March 1880 the United States Senate Committee on the Negro Exodus subpoenaed Adams to appear as a witness in Washington, D.C. On his return to New Orleans, he found work in the Customs House again, aided this time by Senators William Windom and Henry Blair, the two Republicans on the Senate Committee. Adams held the Customs House job for over a year, and during that time he continued to speak and write for the emigrationist cause. Cut off from the Colonization Council and in precarious financial straits, he missed the 1881 boat for Liberia.

During the early 1880s a shift occurred in the Liberia lobby's emphasis in New Orleans. Adams and the Colonization Council had consistently worked to transfer massive numbers of rural working-class Blacks, primarily farmers, to Liberia, in hopes of finding a home for them where they could freely exercise their citizenship rights. His was neither a missionary nor a philanthropic movement. Adams and the Council saw Liberia as a haven for Afro-Americans where they could realize their potential, which had been frustrated by white racism in the United States. When the Colonization Council requested transportation funds from Congress, it viewed the appropriation as a trade-off for the federal government's refusal to guarantee Black constitutional rights in the South, rights to which Southern Blacks felt they were entitled as United States citizens. In this sense, Liberia was an American frontier for Americans of African descent.

Hoping to encourage Afro-American emigration to Liberia, Adams published a letter that had been sent to him by a Negro immigrant to Liberia:

All we want is men who believe they have something in the world to do, and can do something—men who believe that they ought to make a nation; men who believe that they are not the white man's inferior. Come to Liberia. . . . We are a free people here, make our own laws, not subject to any class of men, north or south; we are a Sovereign and Independent Nation. . . . You come to this country, and should you be elected to an office, you will get it. Let me ask you how many black men you have in the United States Senate now? and how many black men have you in the United States House of Representatives?[8]

This was an appeal for hard-working, independent, sensible, but nonetheless ordinary people willing to live and struggle in pioneer surroundings. It addressed the hardy, self-reliant, farming freed-people seeking their land, freedom, and recognition—Henry Adams's constitutents, "laboring men and women," as he called them.

In 1882, however, Henry Adams was working at collecting signatures for a new petition, which differed radically from those he had sent to President Hayes during the 1870s. Instead of seeking protection or aid for expatriation to Liberia, the 1882 petition called for a government subsidy for a direct mail steamer between the United States and Liberia. In place of the moving of people, it supported business communications.[9] This shift of interest, from transferring people to freedom to transferring commercial mail, signaled the emergence of new influences in the New Orleans faction of the Liberia movement. By this time, Adams was not only out of touch with his north Louisiana Council, he was out of step with the leadership of the Liberia interest group in New Orleans.

This new group of men, with whom Adams worked in the spring of 1882, had no connection with the old Colonization Council. They were strangers to the ranks of Adams's "hard laboring men" in the rural parishes. These men, particularly John W. Pierce and the Reverend C. H. Thompson, were "representative colored men" of Western education and progressive outlook, more in tune with the preoccupations of the New South than with slavery and oppression. While in March 1882 Adams served on a

---

[8]Charles W. Bryant to Henry Adams, Grand Bassa County, Liberia, September 18, 1879, *Southwestern Christian Advocate*, January 1, 1880. The *Southwestern* was the organ of the Methodist Episcopal Church, which Henry Adams had recently joined in New Orleans.

[9]Henry Adams to William Coppinger, New Orleans, Louisiana, February 16, 1882, *Am. Col. Soc. Papers*, Ser. IA, 246: 134.

committee of seven or eight preparing a memorial service for the recently deceased Henry Highland Garnet, by September of the same year he was eased out of the Liberia field by the "representative colored men." Pierce and Thompson were frankly embarrassed by Henry Adams. They feared that he would beg the American Colonization Society for money and degrade their unsentimental approach. In fact, Adams had not asked the Society for money, but over the years he had often recited his difficulties in raising funds to send delegates or emigrants to Liberia. Adams's whole style clashed with that of Pierce and Thompson, who declared baldly, "We mean business."[10]

Pierce and Thompson opened regular correspondence with the American Colonization Society in the spring of 1882—Adams had been writing the Society since the summer of 1877. But the two "leading colored men" resented Adams's continuing correspondence. Adams, in turn, complained of their attitude in a letter of April 1882:

i was much surprised at Mr. J. W. Pearces and Rev. Dr. C. H. Thompson it seem to me that [the two] of them dide not like it becase i was writing to you a Bout the affairs and our workes. I know that I am in good faith with this work, and i must say that i have done more for the work than any of the members of the committeemen i have got as many if not more men to signe the petition than all of the others members of the committee together and all know it is facts. . . .[11]

Thompson sent a petition to Congress for a direct mail service to Liberia early in May 1882 without Henry Adams's knowledge and despite the four thousand signatures that Adams held. Thompson and Pierce cut Adams out of the ad hoc committee formed to lobby for the steamship line, and they aimed to form a permanent society without his participation. The African Trade Society included the "better class" of colored people in New Orleans who were not themselves interested in emigrating to Liberia (unless it was as United States minister to that country, a post Pierce coveted). This group of New Orleans "representative colored men" saw themselves as philanthropists aiding the poor, benighted Africans, not as refugees. Instead of contacting Liberi-

---

[10]J. W. Pierce to William Coppinger, New Orleans, Louisiana, April 5, 1882, ibid., 247: 11.

[11]Henry Adams to William Coppinger, New Orleans, Louisiana, April 5, 1882, ibid., p. 12.

ans or Afro-Americans in Liberia for information on that country as a haven for exiles, they planned to entertain prominent Liberians such as Dr. Edward W. Blyden. When Blyden visited the United States early in 1883, members of the African Trade Society planned gala social events around his projected visit, and they were hurt and resentful when Blyden did not come to New Orleans. They had prepared to welcome the famous Liberian statesman "in grand style." Henry Adams expressed regret that ordinary people lost the chance to hear Blyden, for "he would have created some enthusiasm here in favor of Africa. Our people were desirous of seeing and hearing him." Pierce, on the other hand, was personally crushed, and thought the "the Rev. Dr. Blyden has treated me and not only myself but the members of the Trade Society very bad in not telling us that he could not come."[12]

In succeeding years, Adams slipped further from the mainstream of New Orleans Blacks' attitudes toward Africa. Advocating the New South values of commerce and industry, they turned their attention to the Commercial Exposition in New York in 1883 and toward sending funds to uplift and modernize Liberia. Adams, however, continued to think of Liberia as the home for the persecuted Black masses. In his last letter to the American Colonization Society he nostalgically recalled 1877–79, the halcyon days of the Liberia movement in Louisiana. He reported renewed interest among the working people in emigration to Liberia, fed by the prospect of the approaching presidential election of 1884. But the movement was played out for the time being.[13]

Last heard from in 1884, Henry Adams serves as an example —by no means unique—of an intelligent though unschooled freedman who experienced slavery, military life, and the first

---

[12]Henry Adams to William Coppinger, New Orleans, Louisiana, May 2, 1883, ibid., 251: 115; J. W. Pierce to Coppinger, New Orleans, Louisiana, January 4, 1883, ibid., 250: 21. Blyden evidently was unaware of the preparations made in New Orleans.

[13]Henry Adams to William Coppinger, New Orleans, Louisiana, August 27, 1884, ibid., 256: 123. Interest in emigration subsided in Louisiana in the 1880s. However, the movement periodically cropped up across the South well into the twentieth century. The Garvey movement was the last popularly based Black movement supporting emigration. See Redkey, *Black Exodus*, for back-to-Africa movements between 1890 and 1910, and William Bittle and Gilbert Geis, *The Longest Way Home: Chief Alfred C. Sam's Back-to-Africa Movement* (Detroit, 1964). Chief Sam was active around 1915 in Oklahoma especially.

wave of political activity among his fellows during Reconstruction. His view of Southern society was particular to rural, working-class Black people who had endured slavery. Like many of his peers, he looked to a new frontier to solve problems of politics and survival, and Adams's favorite solution, that of migration from the South, was a popular one. Sadly, it exceeded the material reach of the vast majority of Black working people. For many others with some money, like Adams himself, the solution of migration was attractive, yet, for one reason or another, they never migrated.

Adams had lived his most prestigious and powerful days before 1880. He was at his best with his basic constituency of north Louisianian agricultural workers. In New Departure New Orleans, Adams was a misplaced rustic among "representative colored men" of more "modern" ideas. Whereas in Caddo Parish he embodied the best of the mother-wit and solid common sense of an unschooled people, in New Orleans he was a country bumpkin. In the eyes of the more sophisticated and educated men of New Orleans, he embodied the freedman-ward-of-the-state, helpless, complaining of his rights, and hopelessly muddled in his forty-acres-and-a-mule claims. This embarrassing stereotype recalled the bygone and discredited era of Reconstruction, for by the early 1880s Radical Reconstruction was already being denigrated as a worthless era of "Negro mis-rule," during which the real "wealth and intelligence of the South" was overrun by ignorant Blacks and unscrupulous carpetbaggers. In short, the "representative colored men" of the New South rendered Henry Adams obsolete.

Adams continued to benefit from his contacts with national Republicans down through the mid-1880s. Although he was unable to find steady employment in New Orleans, he often worked in the Customs House and the United States mint for periods of a few weeks or months. And while his work was primarily in New Orleans, he continued to travel in Texas, Arkansas, Mississippi, and Louisiana, and thus to receive firsthand the opinions of rural Black people. Liberia, for Adams, promised in the long run the best solution to the ills besetting Blacks in the South. Just as he reported during the first half of the 1880s that interest in Liberia and Africa in general rose and fell, so the 1890s would see several movements toward emigration to Africa on the part of working-class Blacks.

In the late 1880s and the 1890s Black voices like Henry Adams's, relating the concerns of everyday Black people, received little hearing, for articulate and prestigious Southern Blacks monopolized whatever little attention Gilded America accorded Black opinion. White Americans showed progressively less interest in what Blacks had to say about Black life. With few exceptions, they preferred either to ridicule Blacks through stereotyped monstrosities or, at best, to take the words of white experts on Black life, such as George Washington Cable or Bishop Atticus G. Haygood.

"Representative colored men" shouldered the white man's burden vis-à-vis Africa, and the most heeded Black opinions were clearly culturally imperialist in tone. Edward W. Blyden and Alexander Crummell were both well-respected Black authorities on Africa; while they disagreed on the value of autochthonous African cultures, neither of them favored unrestricted Afro-American immigration. Nor did they consider Africa a haven for the masses of oppressed Negro Americans. Only among the people who continued to suffer the insecurity and violence of everyday life in the nineteenth-century South did the vision of Africa as an asylum for the Negro race persist. Among these last, Henry Adams originally hoped Southern Blacks might remain at home, in the South. The force of circumstances made him a Liberia immigrationist, and circumstances caught and momentarily swept him onto the Kansas bandwagon in 1879. By then, Benjamin Singleton had been taking Negroes to Kansas for several years.

9

Benjamin "Pap" Singleton and Migration to Kansas

Benjamin Singleton and Henry Adams amazed the American public in 1879–80; Adams told of ninety-eight thousand Blacks organized to emigrate, and staggered Northern imaginations, and Singleton asserted flat out, *"I am the whole cause of the Kansas immigration!"*[1] Since 1880, secondary literature on the Exodus has mentioned Adams and Singleton in the same breath. Yet the two men never knew each other and never collaborated, not even by mail.

Benjamin Singleton, like Henry Adams, took enormous interest in the welfare of the race, and, like Adams, he grew convinced that Blacks could prosper only outside the old slave states. Also like Adams, Singleton unequivocally divorced himself from "politicians." He, too, thought himself the possessor of certain extraordinary, God-given talents. But, whereas Adams's gift was the power of healing, Singleton was an instrument expressing the will of God, more precisely, the will of the "God of Daniel."

Although both Singleton and Adams had been slaves before the Civil War, and both favored migration out of the South, they were otherwise very dissimilar men. Much of the difference between them stemmed from the vast disparity in their ages; Adams was thirty-six in 1879, Singleton, seventy. Singleton had grown up

---

[1] Benjamin Singleton, *Senate Report 693*, III: 382. (Emphasis in original.) Singleton claimed to have "fetched out" from the South 7,432 people. (Ibid, p. 379.)

and grown old in slavery, while Adams was still a young man when he was freed at the end of the war. Adams came to maturity amid Radical Reconstruction in one of the most radically reconstructed states of all, Louisiana. He also served in the United States Army. Like Black veterans in other periods, Adams emerged from the Army stiffened with a resolve to see Blacks secure their citizens' rights. Singleton, too old for the Union Army, lived most of his life in Tennessee, where the changes wrought by Reconstruction were superficial and ephemeral.

Little is known of Singleton's life before the mid-1870s. He spent his young manhood as a cabinetmaker in Nashville, where he was born and raised. Sold to owners in the Gulf States several times, he repeatedly escaped back to Nashville, until finally he fled to Canada. He stayed only briefly in Canada, soon returning to Detroit, where he worked as a scavenger and ran a boarding house that often harbored other fugitive slaves. After the war, he returned to Nashville and began to fulfill his "mission," as he saw it, to see Black people safe and secure, whether within or outside Tennessee. With the passage of time, he came to view his God-given mission as the removal of Blacks from the former slave states.[2]

During the late 1860s and the 1870s, Singleton lived in Edgefield, across the Cumberland River from Nashville. In his work as a carpenter and coffinmaker in the country around Nashville, he fashioned coffins for many of the victims of racially motivated murders and heard stories of their untimely deaths. The magnitude of the carnage convinced him that "the Southern country is out of joint." He was moved by the unending violence of whites against Blacks that typified conditions in the postwar South generally. Black men in Tennessee might risk their lives or lose them trying to shield their wives or daughters from the attentions of "trashy" white men:

Our people in times of their little social gatherings at nights—quilting, perhaps, and weddings, throughout the country, you will see a dirty, low-lived, trashy [white] man out in the town, and he will send some weak-minded one there to tell some colored man's daughter or wife he loves to come out, he wants a word with them. He will stop along the road and have some talk with them, and then that poor black man

---

[2]St. Louis *Globe-Democrat*, April 21, 1879.

daren't say nothing, or there will go to his house, a lot of them scoundrels—I am not talking of Democrats only—a lot of them scoundrels will
go in there and take that negro out and kill him. I know lots of folks
they took out.

Two cases stuck in Singleton's memory:

Julia Haven; I made the outside box and her coffin, in Smith County,
Tennessee. And another young colored lady I know, about my color, they
committed an outrage on her and then shot her, and I helped myself to
make the outside box.[3]

For both historic and personal reasons, Singleton placed less
importance on Black people's right to vote and run for office
than did Henry Adams. The United States Army, including
Black soldiers, had occupied Louisiana over a period of years;
Tennessee had had no postwar occupation and only a brief
Reconstruction. Tennessee's whites far outnumbered its Blacks,
and the state's politics divided on differences between various
groups of whites. Its Republican regime reflected the concerns
of men like Andrew Johnson, who reserved their real passion
for large planters in the southwestern portion of the state,
whom they opposed on economic and regional grounds. They
cared little for erecting a political base for the Republican
party among new Black voters. Reconstruction in Tennessee,
such as it was, had ended in 1870. Singleton not only lived in a
state where the Black masses played a less active political role,
he was also of a generation that had matured well before Black
emancipation and enfranchisement were even topics for discussion. In Singleton's view, proper public action sprang from divine revelation, not from the democratic process.

Adams lived and traveled among the people whose opinions
and interests he articulated, and he stressed the importance of
listening to what they said. Singleton, in contrast, claimed knowledge of the Black situation from experience, and its solutions from
the advice of God. Adams tried his best to express the wishes of
the people. Singleton presented them with divinely inspired solutions and attempted to lead them to receive his truths. Thus, for
Singleton, voting and running for office were mere diversions,
sometimes dangerous pastimes not necessarily intended for the
colored people. Here he found ready agreement with Southern

---

[3]Benjamin Singleton, *Senate Report 693*, III: 382–83.

whites where Adams could not. Not surprisingly, Singleton pointed with pride at the approval his ideas received from prominent Tennessee whites:

The white people said, "you are right; take your people away." And let me tell you, it was the white people—the ex-governor of the State, felt like I did. And they said to me, "You have tooken a great deal on to yourself, but if these negroes, instead of deceiving one another and running for office, would take the same idea that you have in your head, you will be a people."[4]

Singleton had voted several times and called himself a Grant man, but he was not immersed in political organizing in the way that Adams was.

Just as there was a certain disingenuousness in Adams's distinction between himself and "politicians," Singleton was less than candid when he insisted that there were no "political men" in his migration movement in Tennessee. Columbus M. Johnson, for instance, was associated with Singleton perhaps longer than any other man, having explored farm purchase in Tennessee in 1869. Johnson accompanied Singleton to Kansas, gathering information on homesteading there. Singleton returned to Nashville, and Johnson remained in Topeka as the Kansas-based agent of the Edgefield Real Estate Association. But Johnson had not avoided politics; he was a delegate to the Republican National Conventions of 1872 and 1874.[5]

W. A. Sizemore also worked with Singleton over several years.[6] Although he was not a full-time politician, Sizemore was elected a member of the Davidson County Republican Central Committee in 1874. Another of Singleton's associates, A. W. McConnell, served on the same committee that year. Both Sizemore and McConnell were elected delegates from Davidson

---

[4]Ibid., p. 381.

[5]Chicago Daily *Tribune,* March 27, 1879.

[6]Singleton and Sizemore had collaborated from the incorporation of the Edgefield Real Estate Association in September 1874 to the incorporation of the Singleton Colony at Dunlap, Kansas, in June 1879. Sizemore, a carpenter, may have actually been more important in the movement in Tennessee than was Singleton. In any case, his was the first name of the association's memorandum of incorporation. Further, in Singleton's first letter to Kansas, he requested his answer through either the Second Baptist Church or W. A. Sizemore. (Benjamin Singleton to Governor Thomas A. Osborn, Nashville, Tennessee, August 7, 1876, CRSF, Osborn, box 2, KSHS.)

County to the State Convention of Colored Men.[7] (Singleton came into more prominence the following year, when he, too, was elected to the Tennessee Convention of Colored Men.)

Sizemore chaired the State Convention of Colored Men in 1875, in which Singleton and McConnell participated prominently. All three men gave major speeches advocating migration out of the state, which convinced one white Nashville newspaper that interest in migration was not limited to the "most ignorant grades of the colored population."[8] (Another paper found the meeting devoid of significance, noting that it was neither representative nor statewide, and that "outside of some windy harrangues against Grangers and office-holding and office-seeking Republicans, the preceedings were without point or coherence."[9]) The *Union and American* distinguished the migrationist movement now "controlled by the more sagacious of [the colored] race," from the Kansas Fever "sensation," but admitted that the two might be confused.[10] Singleton clearly belonged to the former group, and by spring 1875 he gained prominence in this growing migration movement in middle Tennessee, as did several other very respectable and politically active Black men in Nashville and Edgefield.

Singleton was most visible in Nashville between 1875 and 1877, although during 1876 his activities were briefly overshadowed by the National Convention of Colored Men. This Nashville convention brought together the most illustrious Black men on the national scene, and none of the delegates from Tennessee was of the Sizemore-Singleton-McConnell circle. Instead of the craftsmen of the Singleton group, the Tennessee delegates to the convention were "representative colored men," lawyers, schoolteachers, civil servants, and doctors.[11] While the nation's "leading colored men" debated the desirability of migrating, Singleton was taking steps

[7]Nashville *Union and American,* May 2, 1874.

[8]Ibid., May 16, 1875.

[9]Nashville *Republican Banner,* May 20, 1875.

[10]Nashville *Union and American,* May 20, 1875.

[11]*Nashville and Edgefield City Directory* (Nashville; 1876, 1877, 1878, 1879). Several Tennessee delegates held (or would hold) local offices. One delegate, W. F. Yardley of Knoxville, ran for governor in 1876. (Mingo Scott, Jr., *The Negro in Tennessee Politics and Governmental Affairs* [Nashville, 1964], pp. 50–57.) See also Joseph Howard Cartwright, "The Negro in Tennessee Politics," unpublished M.A. thesis, Vanderbilt University, 1963.

to fulfill his own mission of conducting Tennessee Blacks to the free land in the West.

Since the late 1860s Singleton had attempted to convince his fellow Blacks of the feasibility of investing in their own farms. Lack of capital, as ever, posed the great stumbling block. Even though in this early period Singleton favored Kansas, a combination of circumstances persuaded him to pursue the purchase of farms in Tennessee.

First of all, Blacks in Tennessee were reluctant to forsake their old homes. In an 1877 migration meeting, Stokely Walton said, "We feel sorry to think that we have to leave our fathers, mothers, wives and children's dust and flee into other States to make a living."[12] In Tennessee this sense of continuity and proximity to one's parents' graves waxed stronger than in the Gulf States for immediately comprehensible reasons. In Mississippi, Louisiana, and Texas, adults of the postwar years were very likely to have been born in the southeastern states, especially in South Carolina and Georgia. Having traveled to the Gulf States as youngsters, they knew long-distance migration and hesitated less than Tennesseans to move again. But in Tennessee, the postwar adult generation most likely shared Tennessee nativity with both parents. The initial inertia of the native Black population corresponded with advice Singleton received from other quarters. "My white friends," he said, advised him to "make a trial and see if we could not buy land in Tennessee. So we did. We made one or two selections, but the land in Tennessee was sixty dollars an acre."[13]

Once it was apparent that finding accessible land in Tennessee would prove exceedingly difficult, Singleton's Kansas alternative prevailed. In 1870 a handful of men went to Kansas and returned a favorable report of homesteading possibilities. Several families migrated, and their assessments were also positive. In 1873 Singleton himself visited southeastern Kansas and discovered that the lands that had formerly been the Cherokee reservation would serve well as homesteads for Tennessee Blacks. By his account, he began conveying families to the Singleton Colony in Cherokee County in the early 1870s, but it is not at all clear that this move-

---

[12]Singleton Scrapbook, p. 50.
[13]Benjamin Singleton, *Senate Report 693*, III: 389.

ment had actually progressed beyond the talking stage before the middle of the decade.[14] Singleton's 1880 version of the Kansas beginnings explained that

my people, for the want of land—we needed land for our children—and their disadvantages—that caused my heart to grieve and sorrow; pity for my race, sir, that was coming down, instead of going up—that caused me to go to work for them. I sent out [to Kansas] perhaps in '66—perhaps so; or in '65, any way—my memory don't recollect which; and they brought back tolerable favorable reports; then I jacked up three or four hundred, and went into Southern Kansas, and found it was a good country, and I thought Southern Kansas was congenial to our nature, sir; and I formed a colony there, and bought about a thousand acres of ground—the colony did—my people.[15]

Singleton's own letters, circulars, and interviews between 1875 and 1880 confirm this summary but situate it in a somewhat later period.

While Singleton doubtless visited Kansas in 1873, he did not begin making serious inquiries of the state government until 1876. In August of the latter year he wrote to the governor, explaining that the Black people of Tennessee wanted to purchase land over a long period, as they lacked the liquid capital to purchase farms outright. He asked whether any aid was available for their transportation or settlement.[16] Citing hard times as their main reason for wanting to go to Kansas, he said that thousands were ready to leave Tennessee: "Will you pleas to Write to me all about it and the turms that it can be had and I will no What to do we are bound to leve this State fast as Soon as we can get a Way for Starvation is Staring us in the face. . . . I think that we can Rais about from one to three thousand people that will leve this fall. . . ."[17]

---

[14]St. Louis *Globe-Democrat*, April 21, 1879.

[15]Benjamin Singleton, *Senate Report 693*, III: 380.

[16]This is of interest because during the Kansas Fever Exodus, which set in motion a national charity drive, Singleton pointed with pride to "his" migrants, none of whom had ever needed or asked for any outside help. "My people that I carried to Kansas ever since 1879 have generally, sir, come on our own resources, and generally went on our own workings. We have tried to make a people of ourselves. I tell you to-day, sir, this [Freedman's Aid] committee is outside of me, for I don't know nothing about it hardly; my people depends on their own resources." (Ibid., p. 390.)

[17]Benjamin Singleton to Governor Osborn, Nashville, Tennessee, August 7, 1876, CRSF, Osborn, box 2, KSHS. The governor's office gave the standard response to such inquiries: guarded encouragement emphasizing the need for a minimum of money.

In the following year, 1877, Singleton and Columbus Johnson visited Kansas on a tour of inspection. On his return, Singleton inserted a notice in a Nashville newspaper indicating his willingness to supply information about Kansas to interested people, free of charge. A year later he issued a circular notifying potential migrants that he would conduct them to the Cherokee County colony. During the intervening period he worked to build interest in migration to Kansas, especially through the Edgefield Real Estate and Homestead Association.[18]

During 1877 and 1878 the Edgefield Real Estate Association sponsored mass meetings and maintained an office to drum up support for its migrationist cause. The officers of the real estate association issued a call for an investigative meeting on May 30, 1877, emphasizing the need for a spirit of peace, for race unity, and for divine approval (rather than the material gains to be realized through migration). Singleton, chairman of the meeting, wanted to awaken the race "to a sense of their duty." Stressing peace and goodwill to all mankind, he said that "peace and time have met together and kissed each other, and it is now high time to be looking after the interest of our downtrodden race." Huston Soloman, the superintendent of the meeting, underlined the need for racial unity on both secular and spiritual grounds:

There are a great number of our people that don't heed to any advice of their own color, and I say that is just the reason we are in the condition that we are to-day, so let us wake up to the sense of our duty, and begin to look after our downtrodden race. Let us come together like the family of Israel, that we may inherit eternal life, for I believe in Daniel's God, the inheritor of eternal life. . . .[19]

Open to "the State of Tennessee," not just to Blacks, the meeting was held on July 31 and August 1, 1877, in Nashville. Although it was a great success, Singleton took "representative colored men" to task for their notable absence: "I am now compelled to say something to our leading men of our race that sit in high places and get their living off of our poor laboring class, and then point the finger of scorn at us for calling together a meeting for our future welfare, when white men praise us for so doing. Such men as this should not be leaders of our race any longer."[20] By Sin-

---

[18]Singleton Scrapbook, unpaginated fliers.

[19]Ibid., p. 21.

[20]Ibid., p. 24.

gleton's reckoning, about five hundred people "of the laboring class" attended the two-day meeting. They took twelve hundred of Singleton's notices back home with them, to areas in and around Nashville and elsewhere in Tennessee.

The Edgefield Real Estate and Homestead Association shifted into high gear after the summer meeting. It publicized its migration activities at festivals and picnics, earning enough money to cover its expenses. In 1878 the association regularly conducted working-class Blacks to Kansas and incorporated the Singleton Colony in Dunlap, Morris County, Kansas, in 1879.[21] Singleton, W. A. Sizemore, and Alonzo DeFrantz lived there from the middle of 1879 to the early part of 1880; Singleton's temporary residence in this colony marked the end of his most active period of conducting settlers from Tennessee to Kansas. Nonetheless, the sense of mission he developed in this work in the 1870s continued to pervade his life.

Benjamin "Pap" Singleton interpreted his role as an instrument of God in a broad sense, transcending the single question of migration. Meetings of the Edgefield Real Estate and Homestead Association spoke of peace and goodwill toward all mankind, and after 1879 Singleton saw himself as a vessel to shower these blessings on his people at large. He would bring peace to the South, he said, by teaching the Southern white people a lesson. By taking the Black people out of the South, he would show Southern whites that they must live with their Black neighbors in tranquillity. He had tried to show the whites that they must change their ways, he said; he had prayed for peace with his people: "I have talked about this, and called a convention, and tried to harmonize things and promote the spirit of conciliation, and to do everything that could be done in the name of God. Why, I have prayed to the Almighty when it appeared to me an imposition before heaven to pray for them." Reaching beyond the tools of secular organization and of the Christian churches, beyond meetings in Liberty Hall, Singleton tapped the living sources of Black folk religion: "I have taken my people out in the roads and in the dark places, and looked to the stars of heaven and prayed for the Southern man to turn his heart."[22]

---

[21]Benjamin Singleton, *Senate Report 693*, III: 387–88.
[22]Ibid., pp. 383–84.

When the concerted will and soul of his community together would not "turn" the heart of white Southerners, the only other divinely acceptable alternative was for Blacks to forsake the South. Yet, once the lesson had been well learned, Singleton said he would lead the people *back* to the land most suited to them, back to the South. "We don't want to leave the South," he said, "and just as soon as we have confidence in the South I am going to be an instrument in the hands of God to persuade every man to go back, because that is the best country; that is genial to our nature, we love that country, and it is the best country in the world for us; but we are going to learn the South a lesson."[23]

White Southerners did not learn Singleton's lesson, at least not during his lifetime. He had called himself the "Father of the Kansas emigration" from Tennessee as early as 1877, and it was as the father of migration that he was known in 1879. His work for race betterment continued well into the decade that followed.

---

[23]Ibid., p. 383. Singleton reasoned that creating a labor shortage in the cotton states would drive the price of cotton intolerably high and thereby teach the white South not to mistreat its Blacks.

10
Solving the Race Problem

"Pap" Singleton and Emigration after 1880

"I am now getting too old," "Pap" Singleton wrote in 1880, "and I think it would be better to send some one more competent that is identified with the emigration and has the interest of his race at heart, and not his own pocket; some one that has heretofore directed and established colonies in the state and is known in the South." Among the men Singleton recommended to take his place were A. D. DeFrantz and Columbus Johnson, both of them longtime colleagues from Tennessee who had moved to Kansas with him.[1] But toward the end of 1880 he reconsidered the wisdom of leaving migration to others. Singleton wrote an open letter from Topeka in November to the "prospective Exodites," in which he said that he would not retire, that he had had second thoughts, and "I see that it behooves me to lend a helping hand yet."[2] Shortly thereafter, he began organizing what he called the United Colored Links. A Topeka convention of colored people in January 1881 voiced the need for a new organization; by March the United Colored Links had organized in Tennessee Town (the Black section of northern Topeka, to which many migrants from Tennessee had moved). The Links

---

[1] Topeka Daily *Blade*, March 8, 1880, in Singleton Scrapbook, p. 32. In 1880 Singleton petitioned Governor St. John for a position on behalf of Alonzo DeFrantz because "when I was out of door[s] he took me in & no one to care for me he taken me as one of the family." (Benjamin Singleton to Governor St. John, Topeka, Kansas, November 10, 1880. Correspondence Received, Negro Exodus Folder, April–December 1880, Kansas State Historical Society.)

[2] No source, November 18, 1880, in Singleton Scrapbook, p. 30.

held a large, public convention in Topeka on August 1 and 2, 1881, which attempted to do several things at once: first, to convince Topeka Blacks that Singleton was a divinely designated leader; second, that they should join forces with white Greenbackers; and third, that they should come together in a movement of racial solidarity, without which the race could never progress.

The Links showed willingness to make noteworthy concessions to the nascent working men's Greenback party. The 1880 Greenback candidate for president, General J. B. Weaver, was advertised to speak at the August 1881 meeting of the Links, although the advertisement indicated more a disposition to hear out his point of view than the certainty that he would actually appear. (The Greenbackers were, in fact, meeting in Topeka at the same time, but the two groups did not achieve fusion. They held a joint barbecue, however, on one of the August meeting days.)[3] The attempted rapprochement was not without significance, for white laborers resented Black workers taking jobs for less than whites in the 1880s, and while whites generally hesitated to bar Black workers from the new labor organizations on naked color grounds, they readily used the wage differential and Black scabbing to justify exclusionary policies. The whole question of interracial labor problems would prove a persistent one, but in August 1881, the United Colored Links prepared to meet white labor at least halfway. The Links promised not to undercut white labor or pursue its aims at the expense of organized white workers or farmers, solemnly declaring its intention to avoid "any strife or conflict among the people in the way of regulating prices of work" and to promote "labor at all regularly arranged prices which govern the masses."[4] However, these concessions to the organized white working class were incidental to the Links' central preoccupation.

The main goal of the United Colored Links was to unite all colored people in order to improve the lot of the race. Assuming that amelioration could be accomplished only through race unity, the Links' concept of race unity bore a distinctive, transcendent character. It in no way resembled a dynamic process of political unification of a widespread, heterogeneous people numbering about six and one half million in 1880. Although this population

---

[3]Walter L. Fleming, " 'Pap' Singleton, the Moses of the Colored Exodus," *American Journal of Sociology* XV, no. 1 (July 1909): 76.

[4]Singleton Scrapbook, p. 33.

was heavily Southern and rural, it was hardly of one mind. Unification of a significant part of these millions for more than momentary action would impose an enormous task; not surprisingly, the undertaking proved impossible. Unity could have been realized only by balancing various interest groups and working out conflicts through continual adjustment and compromise. However, this was not the Links' view of race unity; for them, the "consolidation of the race" was attainable, and once achieved would, like the New Jerusalem, last forever. Instead of an ongoing, dynamic set of coalitions across space and time, bridging class and regional cleavages, the Links considered race unity a higher, permanent state of the collective mind.

For the Links, the process of building toward a coexisting but physically distinct Black society was to move through a series of chronologically discrete steps. First, all Blacks must come together, "to unite and consolidate as a band of brethren." Once this step was accomplished, "peace and harmony will reign among them." In the second stage of peace and harmony, separate institutions would be erected enabling Blacks to achieve material and moral equality with American whites. This uplift would be automatically sustained over succeeding generations. In the words of a Links circular, "It behooves us as a race of color to harmonize ourselves together and consolidate as a band of brethren good, not only for ourselves alone, but for our children yet unborn." Now was the chosen time, and the chosen person had been sent to the colored people to help them realize the unity that had hitherto eluded them: "It seems that this is an age of reason, and the time and person has at last arrived that we are to dissipate the errors that have overspread our race for the past generations of ignorance. . . ."[5]

With this racially exclusive future before them, the Links easily accorded concessions to white working men's parties. In the Links' view of the race unity to come, Black workers only temporarily acquiesced to white labor's demands. Ultimately the races would not compete for the same jobs. The Links envisioned the establishment of Black industries that would employ all Black workers. The goal of race unity was to

build manufactories and other institutions of industries, which will enable

---

[5]No source, April 8, 1881, in ibid., pp. 10, 33.

us to make men and women of our sons and daughters. . . .

As we now stand divided, we are a hundred years behind, and if we unite, we drop off ninety years, and then we will be within ten years of the distance.[6]

These ideals of race unity and uplift were general and innocuous, but their realization stumbled on the realities of class differences among Blacks. In Topeka the Links had not closed the distance between "representative colored men" and working-class Negro Kansans. The organizers of the Links' convention and its executive committee omitted three of the best-known and most respected Black citizens, John L. Waller, a rising Republican (and an earlier migrant), the Reverend John Lynch of the Methodist Episcopal Church, who had been sent by his church to look after the Exodusters, and the Reverend T. W. Henderson of the African Methodist Episcopal Church. These "leading colored men" were accepted by both Blacks and whites in Topeka and were already well assimilated into the very life, material and cultural, that the Links sought to attain. Taking nineteenth-century Euro-American respectability as its model, the Links set out to duplicate it as closely as possible. Success, in its view, would come with material wealth and cultural assimilation. While the organization ultimately aimed at closing the gap between Blacks and whites, it was doomed to failure because it neither redefined the terms of success (especially culturally) nor attracted individuals who were already successful. Respectability and membership in the Links were mutually exclusive.

From the beginning the United Colored Links was led by Benjamin Singleton, preeminently a man of the people. The active members were also Southern transplants from Tennessee, Mississippi, and Louisiana. Lynch, Waller, Henderson, and other "representative colored men" in Topeka felt little attraction to this group, growing as it had from a small-time mutual-aid society, so the United Colored Links never brought together Black Kansans across class lines. Years later, Singleton spoke of the Links with pride; yet in the months immediately following the August 1881 convention, his certainty faltered perceptibly.

As early as January 1881 the Topeka *Commonwealth* published a short article on "Pap" Singleton, calling its readers' attention to

---

[6]Ibid., p. 33.

his past dedication to the betterment of his race. The paper noted that Singleton was "now old and poor, and [was] deserving not only of good wishes but financial aid from his race and from the Republican party."[7] It said he was setting out on a trip to raise money to support him for the rest of his days. While the ultimate results of the proposed trip are unknown, it is likely that the United Colored Links helped Singleton keep body and soul together before it withered away. In September Singleton wrote a cryptic but forlorn letter indicating his sense of abandonment. He indirectly rebuked his people as neglectful ingrates, but his stance as a disinterested sage was at once familiar and striking. He spoke from on high to his "FRIENDS & FELLOW CITIZENS":

The old sign was that when a craft was going to be lost the rats would take the stage plank. That was a token and then the sailors would begin to leave. I have been looking at the sign and the mice are leaving and now and then a half grown rat. I am yet upon the old vessel but discontented. I have been slighted, all of my work prevaileth nothing. I seek no more honor from man. I have got all the honor I want and what I have got would not pay my burial expenses. I am now in my seventy-third year, and if I was to die sooner or later I would have to be lowered in a pauper's grave. My colored friends it is wise to seek wisdom. No more at present.[8]

In letters to President Chester A. Arthur, Singleton complained that he had been "slighted" and that all his work for the race was for naught. Writing to Washington, however, he stressed his "loyalty and perseverance to the Party," saying that he had "been overlooked and it prevaileth me nothing. I am now an old man born in 1809 almost 73 years of age, and I have as true a record an any man in America and I think that the Republicans should look after me and assistance extended to me if it was ever so little." Singleton asked Arthur to read his letter to his Cabinet, not to forget him, and to send him a "consoling letter." "Give my love to Robert Lincoln and tell him that I am his friend until Death," he wrote in closing, indicating the unbridgeable chasm between the official, Gilded Age Washington of the early 1880s and the intimate world of the old Black supplicant in Topeka.[9] Singleton's

---

[7]Topeka *Commonwealth*, January 27, 1881, in ibid., p. 39.

[8]Daily *Kansas State Journal*, n.d. [about September 23, 1881], in ibid., p. 39.

[9]Benjamin Singleton to President Arthur, Topeka, Kansas, November 16, 1881, Record Group 56, Personnel Applications Files of U.S. Department of Treasury. Singleton considered himself a friend of Robert Lincoln's because he had invited him to a celebration in Topeka and Lincoln had sent regrets. The president's

letters lay submerged in the files of the Treasury Department, and nothing came of his pleas, although he renewed his request early the following year.

The United Colored Links grew moribund after its first big convention in the summer of 1881, but Singleton, propelled by his God-given mission, did not fade from the public scene. He continued to heed the dictates of his Old Testament God. Years before, in Nashville, he had spoken of his mission, calling upon the God of Daniel by name to hear the cries of His children in their time of especial need: "Let us come together like the family of Isreal, that we may inherit eternal life, for I believe in Daniel's God, the inheritor of eternal life, and He says He will be with us in every time of need, and I feel that this is a needy time, so pray for our condition."[10] Singleton's personal sense of divine appointment intensified in the 1880s. Even the short-lived United Colored Links appeared to him as evidence of his having been "instructed by the spirit of the 'Lord' to call his people together to unite them from their divided condition."[11] Throughout the decade, he continued to communicate with his people in the South through the Topeka, St. Louis, and Kansas City newspapers. "I still pray to Daniel's God for you," he wrote, offering them guidance and reassurance.[12] Daniel's God was the God of the children of Israel entrapped in an alien and hostile land; Daniel, a Jew, would not forsake his God, though plied with goods and honors and menaced by wild beasts. Daniel's God was the God of the Apocalypse, who rewarded the faithful in the end and punished the evil, even as they seemed to rule the earth. It appeared to Singleton in the late 1880s that the unity of the colored people —like the unity of the people of Israel—would bring the final Day of Judgment. Time was fleeting, he urged, and soon the colored people, like "all other nationalities," would unite and "the Caucasian will drop to a level with the freed slaves."[13]

In expectation of the millennium, Singleton continued his

---

private secretary merely acknowledged receipt of Singleton's letter and passed it on to the Treasury Department, where no action was taken on it. Singleton wrote again in February 1882 and received no reply.

[10]Singleton Scrapbook, p. 50.

[11]North Topeka *Benevolent Banner*, September 10, 1887, in ibid., p. 39.

[12]North Topeka *Times*, September 28, n.d. [1883?], in ibid., p. 20.

[13]Singleton Scrapbook, p. 39. My thanks to Preston Williams for helping me through the theology.

work for the salvation of the race. In return, the Black communities in which he lived, whether in Topeka, St. Louis, or Kansas City, did their best to see that he did not starve. Every year after 1882 Singleton's friends and neighbors had a birthday party for the old man, at which they collected a purse, usually amounting to about two hundred dollars, and presented it to "Old Pap." Meanwhile, Singleton kept vigil on the fate of the race.

Sensing a renewed interest in migration and emigration in 1883–84 (as, indeed, did Henry Adams), Singleton wrote an open letter to the "freedslaves of the South" in which he warned his "dear friends" never to cast another vote in the South, for "it is just getting you all murdered up and slaughtered in a brutal manner." His letter exhibited a new receptivity to the concept of overseas migration, which in time grew central to his views. "Seek a government, and [do] that soon or go to British North America, where you can be protected as a people." He recalled the long, pathetic past of Blacks in America, who "for nearly three hundred years . . . were captured and brought to this country and worked for the white man and got nothing for it." Unless the freedpeople left this country, the future would prove equally bleak:

When we were delivered from slavery we were delivered with nothing and have since been trying to rise up and have some protection and be respected and yet they still try to hold us down but we can't stand to be treated in this manner. They must not think their vessels are the only ones that sail the briny waters. I still pray to Daniel's God for you.[14]

This time, however, Singleton received an encouraging response.

As though in answer to Singleton's prayer, a white man in St. Louis named Joseph E. Ware wrote a lengthy, open letter suggesting that Afro-Americans emigrate to Cyprus. There they might enjoy a limited measure of self-government under the benevolent umbrella of a British protectorate, and an Afro-American nation might establish itself and take root. He thought that the combination of the British government's kindly hegemony, the "bone and sinew of the colored people of America" (not its politicians), the "millions of acres of land [in Cyprus] and its thousand miles of sea, teeming with fish," would provide a happy solution to the prob-

---

[14]North Topeka *Times,* September 28, n.d. [1883?], in ibid., p. 20. Henry Adams, too, sensed a renewed interest among Blacks in leaving the South in 1884.

lems of Black Americans seeking "a new home and better sympathies."[15]

Ware thought the solution tailor-made from several points of view. First, it was futile for Blacks in the United States to look forward to a government of their own anywhere in North America. While race prejudice was not as strong in Canada, it nonetheless existed. Second, Canada's weather reduced the growing season to half that of the South. Negroes, he said, needed a place with a mild climate, like Cyprus, "that great and early cradle of civilization, agriculture, commerce and ancient greatness," crying out for regeneration at the hands of the deserving colored people of America. Third, Cyprus was doubly in need of the modernizing influences of American Blacks with Anglo-Saxon virtues, having been ruined by the "misgovernment and rapacity of the Turkish Government" and now threatened with Russian Jewish immigration if it were not given over to Afro-Americans.

Like many other white Americans and not a few Blacks, Ware was appalled by Eastern and Southern Europeans and immigrant groups from non-Anglo-Saxon cultures. (Singleton, too, inveighed against the "Hungarians, Bohemians, Germans, Bosnians, Wallachians, Italians and others who can work and live where you'd starve [and who] crowd in every day." Hundreds of thousands of Black women and children who had once been gainfully and honorably employed in washing and ironing were now "forced into idleness, and hundreds of them into base prostitution," their former occupations taken over by "steam laundries and Chinamen."[16]) Ware preferred that a valuable land such as Cyprus be made an American Negro homeland to its further ruination by Eastern Europeans, "the worthlessness of whom we have found out to our cost." Since the genius of modern technology, combined with British administration, assured the island's "future restoration and destiny . . . through the wonderful agencies of modern agriculture, art and science," Ware suggested that Singleton apply to the British government for the opportunity to settle American Blacks there, to the mutual benefit of all.[17]

Singleton generally preferred segregated settlement within or

---

[15]Topeka *Commonwealth*, October 21, 1883, in ibid., p. 49. Ware evidently had some experience with British imperialism, but no more is known of him.

[16]St. Louis *Post-Dispatch*, n.d. [about 1883], in ibid., p. 32.

[17]Topeka *Commonwealth*, October 21, 1883, in ibid., p. 49.

near United States territory, but that solution was no more feasible
in 1884 than in earlier years. He therefore embraced the Cyprus
suggestion with enthusiasm, at least until mid-1885. He and his
assistant, John Williamson, began organizing what they termed a
"Chief League" to promote and rationalize emigration to Cyprus
from St. Louis, where Singleton now lived with his nephew. Singleton spoke of an "offer from the English to go to Cyprus" and
"a committee to examine the places and find a good one where we
can settle and live" as though the trans-Atlantic exodus were a
move across the Mississippi, uncomplicated by diplomatic, linguis-
tic, or cultural considerations.[18] But the "offer from the British"
was no more than Joseph Ware's well-intentioned, suggestive letter; the money and the administration necessary to carry out a
long-range international venture were still lacking. The Cyprus
bubble burst in 1884, and the "unmerited lot" of Afro-Americans
in the South continued to be, in Singleton's words, "storms of
sorrow and whirlwinds filled with fire."[19]

The United Trans-Atlantic Society, not the stillborn Cyprus
enterprise, was Singleton's last salvationist undertaking. Its rhetoric carried to a new pitch the racial exclusivity that had increasingly marked Singleton's 1880s endeavors. In thundering Old Testament language, the Trans-Atlantic Society called for the
salvation of the Africans in America.

Singleton had opened a Nashville migration meeting back in
1877 in pacific tones: "We are glad now and do thank our Heavenly
Father that the banner of peace blows over our land and country
once more. . . ."[20] But nearly a decade later, the circulars of the
United Trans-Atlantic Society echoed the church militant and prepared Afro-Americans for a holy struggle for expatriation. Although Singleton still lived, his was no longer the sole beckoning
voice; like a founding father, he served to legitimate the Society
from on high. The stated objectives of the United Trans-Atlantic
Society recaptured Singleton's mission to care for the poor, downtrodden race. Invoking his name, the Society's circular proclaimed
that it was organized "by Pap Singleton, June 16th, 1885, for the
purpose of arranging and inducing emigrators among the people
of African descent from this country to Africa. . . ." The goals of

---

[18]St. Louis *Post-Dispatch*, n.d. [about 1884], in ibid., p. 54.
[19]Ibid.
[20]Benjamin Singleton and Washington Anthony, in ibid., p. 50.

the Society were as fatherly as Singleton's concern for his people: "The object of this society is as the Master's eye, to hold a commanding view over the race; its rising progress; its present dilemma; its future necessities, and it exerts an influence on the political and social world to establish the true social equality which justice demands wherever the foot of an African treads the soil."[21]

Yet the race-unifying, conciliatory tone of the United Colored Links was foreign to the circulars of the United Trans-Atlantic Society. Where the migrationist Edgefield Real Estate and Homestead Association and the Links spoke of embracing all members of the race, the constitution of the United Trans-Atlantic Society reached out only to a special segment of Blacks for membership:

None but males of the African race who have attained at least 18 years of age, and shall be of good moral character before he can become [a] member of this society.
Each individual shall take the obligation of the order.
Any member may be suspended or expelled from this society for any breach of the obligations or neglect of duty.[22]

Other fliers of the Society were no more aimed at omnibus membership than was the constitution. An invitation to the public to the National Annual Convention in 1886 just outside Kansas City, Missouri, sought "All Colored Men who are interested in their race . . ." while it frankly anticipated opposition from several other Black organizations: "This society expects to meet great opposition from ignorance,—in the pulpit, in politics, and in older established societies. . . ." Older organizations would oppose the Trans-Atlantic when they realized the superiority of the new Society and its transcendent aims "because there is more merit in this object than they comprehend in their department." Rendering all pre-existing associations obsolete, the Trans-Atlantic would sweep aside their ashes in triumph, because it was right. The Society would care for the entire membership of its fraternity, "anticipat[ing] its necessities individually and collectively wherever an African exists to open the doors of the world before him and remove the obstacles to his speedy arrival to the acme of illustrious manhood."[23] Merely uniting the colored

---

[21]Constitution of the United Trans-Atlantic Society, March 29, 1886, in ibid., p. 56.
[22]Ibid.
[23]Ibid.

people no longer sufficed to insure their salvation.

Based on "Pap" Singleton's analysis of the condition of the people whom the Trans-Atlantic now referred to as African, the Society called for the removal of Blacks from white America to Africa. This new insistence on Africa sets the Trans-Atlantic apart from Singleton's earlier organizations, in which removal was most important, destination secondary. In Trans-Atlantic statements, Africa meant more than the site of the future Black nation, it was the Fatherland, where "our children and our children's children" would be able to grow and prosper, "protected by the God of Battles and [the] God of Freedom."[24] Early on, Singleton had seen the condition of Blacks among their former owners as reason enough for their leaving the old slave states. Later, in the movement toward Cyprus, he frequently cited the need for Blacks to free themselves from the yoke of white oppression. In this sense, the Trans-Atlantic's call for a separate Black nation in Africa merely hardened these earlier positions. In addition to the grievances of slavery ("the fruits of cruelty, as inflicted upon the downtrodden race, is a terror"), Singleton's complaints of immigrant competition found place in Trans-Atlantic material:

We find ourselves daily serving under cloudy frowns of distinction. The scum of the foreign powers emigrate to America and put their feet on our necks. They are schooled to count a negro as the last of creation from their earliest infancy. So goes the wailings of old Pap Singleton, a lover of his race. My friends! My people! The emigrants—the hungry-footed fragments are up-rooting us. We cannot feed, clothe and school our children on starvation wages, and when we have attained an education, of what use it is to them here? None whatever. Their ambition can only reach the school teacher or preacher,—for anything else they are no good.[25]

New here was the Trans-Atlantic's alarm at the crowding out of Blacks by the "hungry-footed fragments," the "scum of foreign powers." To remedy the hopelessness of Blacks' present condition, the Trans-Atlantic Society posed a transcendent and militant solution, the regeneration of the African race through emigration to the Fatherland:

We shall! We will, bridge the ocean, that the sons and daughters of Ham may return to their God-given inheritance, and Ethiopia regain her an-

---

[24]North Topeka *Benevolent Banner*, September 24, 1887, in ibid., p. 57.
[25]Singleton Scrapbook, p. 56.

cient renown, and be enhanced with modern splendor. We shall not die out! We shall not wear out. The God of heaven marches with us and will manifest his power. The waters of adversity will tumble as did the walls of Jerico at the approach of Israel.[26]

Along with Singleton's sense of divine inspiration, his 1870s circulars had spoken of the "pursuit of Homes in the Southwestern Lands of America" and of a real-estate association led by "square-headed, honest men."[27] The special songs of the migration meetings, such as "The Land That Gives Birth to Freedom," also included verses attesting to Singleton's divine guidance:

We have Mr. Singleton for our President, he will go on before us, and lead us through. (Repeat.)
Chorus.—Marching along, yes we are marching along, To Kansas City we are bound. (Repeat.)
Surely this must be the Lord that has gone before him, and opened the way. (Repeat.)

But this song ended with a verse citing the aims of the pilgrims who were forsaking their homes to "flee into a Strange land unknown":

We want peaceful homes and quiet firesides; no one to disturb us or turn us out. (Repeat.)

Another song, "Extending Our Voices to Heaven," recognized the uniqueness of the time of the Exodus with a sense of special mission:

It seems to me like the year of jubilee has come; surely this is the time that is spoken of in history, Farewell, dear friends, farewell.[28]

Yet none of this material from the Kansas migration approaches the grandiose, sweeping tone of a destiny fulfilled that marked the 1885–87 salvationist aims of the Trans-Atlantic Society: "A movement has been inaugurated by Father Singleton and his co-workers which fills the emergency and meets our necessities, know[n] as the National Transatlantic society. A movement which in its grand conception and ultimate consummation reaches across the mighty Atlantic to the original Fatherland of the colored race . . ." Here, then, was the great, ultimate solution of the

---

[26]Ibid.
[27]Ibid., unpaginated circulars.
[28]Ibid.

American racial problem, the establishment of a Black nation where Afro-Americans could live and prosper, generation after generation, protected by the "God of Battles and [the] God of Freedom."

Benjamin "Pap" Singleton ended his career as the father of an organization calling upon its people to "Come Brother Sailor and Don't Fall Asleep." The Trans-Atlantic Society's aims far surpassed the mundane goals of Singleton's migration movement from Tennessee. Between his early, conciliatory activities and the militant Trans-Atlantic Society lay the United Links and the Cyprus movement, each straining toward an increasingly transcendent salvation.

Between the mid-1870s and the mid-1880s, Singleton's migrationist solutions hardened as the difficulties arising from racial issues grew more pervasive. In 1876 it seemed as though leaving the land of slavery would mitigate racial tensions (especially in their economic manifestations) sufficiently for Blacks at least to survive. Ten years later, even with the migration to Kansas, racial problems had multiplied to the extent that they no longer seemed solvable within the bounds of this country. The elaboration of the solutions matched the increasing obstinacy of the problem. But a people whose resources were unequal to the more modest tasks of the 1870s were even less able to come to terms with the racism of the 1880s. The chronic lack of money, which had complicated the move to Kansas, blocked a move across the ocean, and all the back-to-Africa movements of the nineteenth and twentieth centuries would finally founder on this material stumbling block.

Adams, Singleton, and the Politics of Assassination

Both Henry Adams and Benjamin Singleton participated prominently in migrationist activities in the late 1870s and early 1880s. Both were public figures, political leaders in the broadest sense of the term. If one remembers that during the nineteenth century a Black man identified by the wider society as a "leader" of the colored people would actually function more like their employee, then Singleton and Adams provide useful examples of two domi-

nant types of "leadership."[29] There is no confusing these men of
the people with the nationally known and assimilated officeholders such as Hiram Revels or P. B. S. Pinchback. Having been slaves
in the South during the antebellum period, neither man could
hope to reign like George T. Downing or Frederick Douglass,
whose renown rested on their abolitionist past. Again, Adams and
Singleton did not possess enough Western education to allow them
to function as "respectable colored men," taking their reputation
from their ability to manipulate Western culture, as did John Mercer Langston or Richard T. Greener. Adams was a political organizer, and Singleton originated several public-action groups.

Both Singleton and Adams were anxious to divorce themselves
from "politicians" (presumably, men who ran for office) despite
their associations and activities in the public realm.[30] Whereas
Adams stressed the unreliability of colored politicians—they were
likely to place partisan interests above those of the race and tell
white politicians what no white person should know of Black
thinking—Singleton cited their money-grubbing aspect: "They
would want to pilfer and rob at the cents before they got the
dollars. O, no, it was the muscle of the arm, the men that worked
that we wanted." No political men ever participated in the movement, he said: "This thing was got up by an ignorant class of men,
and I will prove it to you. I am the leader of it, and have been at
[it] for thirteen years, and I am the smartest man in it, and I am
only an ignorant man."[31] Both Singleton and Adams underscored
their absolute equality with the people with perfect justice, for
neither man was a manipulator or a demagogue.

---

[29]"Leaders" functioned as employees in the sense that they served at the
pleasure of their employers, the people they supposedly "led." They could be
dismissed from positions of "leadership" whenever they failed to pursue the aims
of the people they served, either as spokesmen or organizers. I am grateful to
Nancy Farriss for suggesting the very appropriate term "employee."

[30]Henry Adams, *Senate Report 693*, II: 105.

[31]Benjamin Singleton, ibid., III: 380, 385. We must take the political import
of the testimony before the Senate committee on the Exodus into account—both
Singleton and Adams were trying to counter the stereotyped opinion that the
Exodus was the fruit of rascally Black and white politicians who had misled the
colored people for their own gain. But even then, the extent to which both men
insisted that they and their constituents were hard-laboring men and women is
noteworthy. Their insistence on their absolute equality with the people was the
only thing that could clear them of the charge of manipulating other, ordinary
colored people.

Had the political fortunes of Blacks in this country not been uniquely distorted by racism in the late nineteenth century, Singleton's concept of leadership soon would have been rendered archaic. Adams's voice should have been the voice of the future, because he worked within the framework of electoral politics. Early on, Singleton's divine inspiration and sweeping truisms would have been thrust aside in the bustle of concrete political realities, were it not for the political assassinations, exiles, and the utter intractability of race problems in America. Instead, as Black suffrage was continually interfered with and political organizers murdered or exiled, democratic solutions grew less and less useful. The ordinary, democratic channels to which most Americans turned to redress their grievances did not function for Negro citizens. With the perversion of the electoral process in the states where most Blacks lived, the foundation for democratic action laid during Reconstruction crumbled. Divinely inspired leaders, it seemed, offered the most attractive and transcendent solutions to real material and legal problems among Blacks, problems they could not correct through elective politics.

Although some Blacks continued to vote during the remainder of the nineteenth century, the constituency-representative relationship suffered inalterable perversion. Extralegal intimidation of their natural constituencies of rural Blacks neutralized grass roots organizers like Henry Adams. The instruments of distortion and manipulation of Black votes were first political violence (bulldozing), then later disfranchising legislation. As Southern life grew progressively more feudal, men such as Adams, who worked squarely within the American tradition of representative democracy, became anachronisms. Thinking Black men were favorite targets for bulldozing, since their influence stirred special resentment among violent whites. An "Address of the Louisiana Colored Citizens' Convention" cited a typical example of politically motivated terrorism:

On the 21st of last September, 1878, an organization of white men, known as the 298 of the parish of Natchitoches, drove the leaders of the colored people from the parish, after hunting them down like dogs, for no other reason than being influential and popular with their people; drove them from their homes, their families, and property, and all that is dear to the heart of the freemen, because they thought and dared to put that thought into execution.[32]

The speech stated further that this sort of activity occurred in several Louisiana parishes during the electoral campaign of 1878, and abundant testimony shows that selective terrorism was fairly common in other years. As a result, men who would have functioned as political organizers or candidates for office were continually murdered or hounded off the land. Exiled in New Orleans, Henry Adams encountered scores of other Black men in similar circumstances.

Coercion was not reserved solely for organizers and thinking men. It became a tool to control the suffrage of ordinary Black voters, who were menaced with death or beating if they did not "vote right." Not protected by the U.S. Army, or by state or local militia after 1877, Black voters faced a choice between personal and chattel security on the one hand, and elective autonomy on the other, their lives and livelihoods held ransom for their votes. Lacking any other recourse, Blacks had to think first of insuring their own survival. In such situations, protection, not representation, loomed most crucial. The address cited above described the protective badges issued to Black voters who had voted Democratic in the 1878 campaign in Natchitoches Parish, Louisiana:

[The 298 of Natchitoches] herded the colored people together and made them vote contrary to their wishes, under the threat and peril of being exiled from their homes, if not murdered on the spot, should they refuse to obey them. Badges were pinned on the lappel of their coats, after voting, as a source of protection from the ruthless mobocrats patrolling the streets and public highways of the parish. One of these badges marked *voted the Democratic ticket* is far more potent than the arm of the law.[33]

In this state of siege, Adams and his counterparts could offer no practical measure of protection to the rural Black masses—they could give only the advice to flee.

In the United States, where there has been a general tendency toward secularization of political action, one would expect divine inspiration to carry progressively less weight in the formulation of

---

[32]George T. Ruby, ibid., II: 78.
[33]Ibid. (Emphasis in original.)

policies of public action. Yet, the modernization and assimilation of American Blacks appears at first glance to confound that expectation. Modernization seems to have occurred uniquely on the level of educational assimilation. This apparent lack of political modernization is directly traceable to the door of Southern violence used as a tool of political coercion. Institutionalization of violence in politics—politics of assassination—deracinated elective politics, modern politics, among rural Blacks, not just once but again and again, each time political organizers surfaced. Throughout the rest of the nineteenth century, with few exceptions, each generation of modern political activists, such as John Kemp, Henry Adams, Rayford Blount, and Alfred Fairfax, was forcibly exiled or assassinated. Black educational modernization was not, therefore, accompanied by sustained political modernization.

In the political realm, Benjamin Singleton and his divinely inspired peers continued to hold sway with their salvationist or other-worldly solutions to race problems, right down through the nineteenth century. (In fact, it may be argued that the prevalence of ministers among Black leaders even today is a legacy of the tradition to which Singleton belonged.) This more conservative, less concrete, apolitical tradition endured mainly because of the barriers Black people faced time and again when they attempted to express their desires as political persons at the polls and through democratic action. Rather than exemplifying a waning tradition of public action, Singleton represented a flourishing mode of leadership. Any resemblance to the give and take of normal, electoral political action among Blacks in the South had to wait until well into the second half of the present century, when Black political organizers might be tolerated in their work among ordinary Black people.

Part III
Emigration

11
Liberia Fever

Benjamin Singleton and Henry Adams were only two among thousands of Southern Blacks who saw migration as the most obvious remedy to their plight. But most Blacks envisioned less sweeping improvements. When they migrated, they moved locally, aiming for better contracts, lower rents, and perhaps the opportunity to save a little money. Throughout the entire nineteenth century, the Black population drifted southwest, and the pace quickened in the 1870s. Migrating Blacks attracted newspaper attention, particularly as they left Georgia and Alabama for Mississippi and Louisiana, and Tennessee for northern Mississippi and Arkansas. Texas, too, received large numbers of Blacks from the nearby states of Louisiana and Mississippi.[1] Families moving across county lines or men traveling across state lines with labor contractors were the basic units of this overall southwesterly trend. Although most migrants stayed within the South, the prospect of leaving the region entirely for truly free soil fired the imaginations of Blacks who realized that their oppression was inextricably bound up with Southern or perhaps American life. Since short-range moves were far more easily accomplished, interstate or trans-Atlantic

---

[1] *Negro Population, 1790–1915*, p. 41; Nashville *Union and American*, March 19, 1874; Nashville Weekly *American*, January 13, 1876; Fort Scott (Kan.) *Colored Citizen*, May 10, 1878; New Orleans Daily *Picayune*, November 14, 1878; *Statistics of the Population of the United States at the Tenth Census* [1880] (Washington, 1883), pp. 488–91.

During the nineteenth century the word "emigration" applied to emigration to Africa and migration out of the South. In keeping with that usage, Part III includes organizations favoring both ranges of movement.

emigration remained a dream for the great majority of Southern emigrationists.

Liberia Fever followed fast on the heels of Reconstruction in the Carolinas, Mississippi, and Louisiana, as Blacks perceived clearly and cheerlessly that they stood alone. In the aftermath of the violence surrounding the campaign of 1876, many Afro-Americans admitted that they would never be first-class citizens in this country; they might as well relinquish their American identity and emphasize their African descent. Turning to the most American part of Africa—Liberia—they envisioned building a perfected America, free from racial hatred and color disabilities. Unfortunately, in their quest for safe harbor from injustices suffered on Southern soil, Afro-Americans gave little thought to the native Liberians.

For all too many emigrants, their own American troubles obliterated their ideals of fairness toward African Liberians. Like Harrison Bouey of South Carolina, prospective emigrants looked to Liberia convinced "that the colored man has no home in America" and certain that whites "believe that my race have no more right to any of the profits of their labor than one of their mules. . . ."[2] But unlike Bouey, few of them served as teachers and missionaries in Liberia. (Americo-Liberians tyrannized native Liberians for years. During the nineteenth century, Liberians of American Negro descent formed a social and economic elite which rigorously excluded any but the most assimilated Africans.)

The first half of 1877 saw a rising tide of what Richard H. Cain called "a deep and growing interest taken by the Colored people . . . in the subject of Emigration."[3] In the spring of that year, Harrison Bouey joined George Curtis, a resident of Beaufort, South Carolina, and they persuaded the Reverend B. F. Porter of Charleston to join them in organizing Black emigration to Liberia. Shortly after Porter had addressed a receptive Charleston crowd on the thirtieth anniversary of Liberia's independence, the Liberian Exodus Joint-Stock Steamship Company incorporated,

---

[2]Harrison N. Bouey to the Reverend Henry M. Turner, Edgefield, South Carolina, May 23, 1877, *Am. Col. Soc. Papers,* Ser. IA, 227: 142.

[3]Quoted in George B. Tindall, "The Liberian Exodus of 1878," *South Carolina Historical Magazine* LIII, no. 3 (July 1952): 139. The Reverend Richard H. Cain, "Daddy" Cain, was a U.S. congressman in 1877.

with Porter as its president. The Charleston-based company was to issue thirty thousand shares for ten thousand dollars, meant to pay the initial costs of transportation and settlement in Liberia.[4]

At the same time, mounting interest in emigration among Blacks also affected the American Colonization Society. Since the new enthusiasm for expatriation far exceeded the Society's capabilities, it welcomed the formation of the Liberian Exodus Joint-Stock Steamship Company and furnished it with moral support and advice. But even the two associations working together could not transfer and settle the masses poised for emigration.

In August 1877 B. F. Porter sanguinely wrote that "our people are paying up their shares rapidly, and as soon as fall puts in, and crops are harvested, you will see a mighty moving here among our people."[5] But the company was financially insecure. Its board of directors lacked managerial expertise; none of its politicians, teachers, and ministers had naval or colonizing experience. And the six thousand dollars in the company's coffers fell short of covering the purchase and outfitting of a ship, food for the emigrants, and unforeseen expenses.

Yet, word of the Black emigration company spread throughout South Carolina, and in January 1878 hundreds of emigrants converged on Charleston. Although the company was not yet ready to operate, the pressure for departure exerted by hundreds of propsective passengers forced Porter hastily to acquire a ship. The *Azor* was consecrated on March 21, 1878, and it sailed from Charleston a month later, carrying 206 emigrants to Liberia.[6]

The apparent success of the *Azor*'s departure soon faded in delays, deaths, and unexpected expenses incurred in Sierra Leone. After a passage of forty-two days, the emigrants arrived in Liberia, short of money and supplies. The disastrous crossing devastated the hundreds still waiting to leave for Liberia, for the debt-ridden *Azor* made just one trip. Unplanned costs of the first sailing exhausted the company's revenues. A projected commercial voyage

---

[4]Ibid., pp. 134–35. Martin Delany also played a central role in the Liberian Exodus Joint-Stock Steamship Company.

[5]The Reverend B. F. Porter to Edward S. Morris, Charleston, South Carolina, August 22, 1877, *Am. Col. Soc. Papers*, Ser. IA, 228:157. Morris was a Philadelphia trader to Liberia and an associate of the American Colonization Society.

[6]Tindall, "The Liberian Exodus," pp. 138–39. A number of the immigrants ultimately returned to this country, but some stuck it out, including the ancestor of the Tolbert family.

for February 1879 never materialized, and the ship was sold for debt at auction in November.[7] However, the demise of the Liberian Exodus Joint-Stock Steamship Company did not turn Blacks against emigration or stem Liberia Fever. Their interest now focused entirely on the American Colonization Society, at least for the next few years.

Between 1877 and 1879 the American Colonization Society received an ever-increasing volume of mail indicating burgeoning interest in Liberia. Correspondence to the Society was especially heavy from North Carolina, particularly the eastern counties, between mid-1877 and the end of 1879. During 1878 and 1879, however, mail from Mississippi, Louisiana, Texas, and Arkansas increased dramatically.[8] A Pennsylvania Colonization Society report of 1878 said that letters to the Society came from several states and represented some fifty thousand people.[9] Yet the Society sent only one or two ships a year, each carrying fifty to one hundred settlers. Further, most of the aspiring emigrants were so discouragingly poor that the trip to New York to join the American Colonization Society's boats would in itself exhaust their finances. The Society could neither afford to send boats from New Orleans and Galveston (the Gulf ports nearest to many of the prospective emigrants) nor transport and settle them in Liberia. In the end, emigration to Liberia remained an unfulfilled dream for the great masses of Blacks desiring to leave the South. For these poor people, migration to Kansas offered a more feasible alternative. As interest in migration to Kansas swept over Mississippi and Louisiana, some who had favored Liberia asked themselves whether Kansas might not provide an acceptable substitute. But even at the height of the Kansas Fever in 1879, interest in a Black nation remained high. "Thire is a greate many wants to go to Libeara but cant get in for mation," wrote a Black Mississippian, "i had much rather see them going to our own country But they says they will only [go to] Kansas till they can get to go [to] Liberar."[10]

[7]Ibid., pp. 141–42.

[8]*Am. Col. Soc. Papers,* Ser. IA, 228–37: passim.

[9]New York Daily *Herald,* quoted in Nashville Weekly *American,* March 28, 1878.

[10]Abraham Cashaw to William Coppinger, Vicksburg, Mississippi, March 23, 1879, *Am. Col. Soc. Papers,* Ser. IA, 234: 307.

. . .

Interest in emigration to Liberia was current in Louisiana and Mississippi by early 1878. Like the Kansas Fever that followed it, Liberia Fever reached Texas some six months after its appearance in the two states to the east. In mid-1878, while Liberia clubs flourished in Mississippi and the Colonization Council held regular Liberia meetings in north Louisiana, Blacks in Texas were just beginning to cast about for information on Liberia. Lacking precise data, James Green of Houston wrote to the editor of the Philadelphia *Christian Recorder*. The editor published the notice and sent a copy to the American Colonization Society, whose secretary answered Green's inquiries.

In Texas, emigration attracted a considerable following. Green and several other Black men called a convention on Liberia emigration in Houston in July 1879. Delegates were divided on whether to leave Texas for the Northwest or for Liberia. The Green faction, holding out for Liberia, formed the Liberian Emigration Association at the convention.[11]

They reasoned that any part of America, this "white man's country," was subject to the same criticism that Blacks made of the South. Proponents of Liberia emigration pointed to Copperhead Democrats and prejudiced Northern Republicans as evidence that Negrophobia haunted them everywhere. Green saw it as an inextricable part of the white American character: "I want the negroes to go back to their own country, which is Africa. I want no Kansas and no white man's country in mine. Let the negro go where he will in a white man's country he will find it all the same. He will have no more chance than a cat in hell without claws."[12] For Green and those who thought like him, any migration had to reach beyond the United States. But all Blacks did not share this desire to leave the country or the South.

A significant body of Afro-American opinion opposed any emigration whatever. This point of view was most prevalent among "representative colored men" who were well off financially, and their position received widespread publicity. Opponents of the Liberia and Kansas movements were articulate, and they enjoyed

---

[11]James Green to William Coppinger, Houston, Texas, n.d. [April 1879], ibid., 235: 64 and 237: 210.

[12]Galveston Weekly *News,* July 10, 1879.

far greater access to newspapers edited by other anti-migrationists and whites. Since the Liberia idea circulated longer and seemed unthinkably radical, it stirred up considerable opposition. The editor of the Philadelphia *Christian Recorder,* the Reverend B. T. Tanner, condemned the Liberia idea "in so far as it partakes of anything like a wholesale egress from the country."[13] But Tanner bravely attempted to straddle the issue, as did Senator Blanche K. Bruce of Mississippi. While the *Christian Recorder* published articles and letters from pro-Liberia writers, it counseled caution and stressed the formidable obstacles that massive emigration entailed.

The Liberia question entangled Senator Bruce in late 1877. A body of his Mississippi constituents requested him to submit a petition to Congress asking for an appropriation of one hundred thousand dollars toward emigration to Liberia. Bruce presented the petition, but he discreetly divorced himself from its goal.[14] As the furor over Liberia grew in Mississippi and throughout the South, Bruce felt pressed to clarify his attitude toward the movement; he did so in March 1878. He based his opposition on three convictions, the first of which he shared with many Southern whites and conservative, "representative colored men" such as Frederick Douglass. Overlooking the enormous difficulties Blacks faced in the South, Bruce focused on the good of the entire region, much as the planters at the Vicksburg Labor Convention would do in 1879. (They quite naturally identified the good of the whole South with their own prosperity.) Bruce was also a landowner, but this does not completely explain his position. Many "representative colored men" took a planter's-eye view of the interests of the South, not because they themselves were proprietors or employers, but because the ideals of this "better sort" were the most respectable in the South. Respectability, not self-interest, motivated Bruce when he argued that the Liberia movement was "of such magnitude and subject to such conditions as, in my judgement, to threaten mischievous consequences, not only to my race, but to the section generally in which they live."[15]

Secondly, Bruce argued, in common with Tanner and many

---

[13]Philadelphia *Christian Recorder,* April 18, 1878. The *Christian Recorder* was the organ of the African Methodist Episcopal Church and the most respected Black newspaper of the time.

[14]Nashville Weekly *American,* November 22, 1877.

[15]Cincinnati *Commercial,* n.d., quoted in Philadelphia *Christian Recorder,* March 17, 1878.

other Blacks—both respectable anti-migrationists and Kansas migrationists—Blacks in America were not Africans, but Americans. Just as African emigrationists stressed pan-Blackness or the similarity of Afro-Americans to their African brothers in their statements about "our own country," Bruce stressed the American-ness of Afro-Americans:

The negro of America is not African, but American—in his physical qualities and aptitudes, in his mental developments and biases, in his religious beliefs and hopes, and in his political conception and conviction he is an American.

He is not a parasite, but a branch, drawing its life from the great American vine, taking on the type of American civilization and adapting himself to the genius of her institutions, as readily and unreservedly as his Caucasian brother.[16]

Finally, Bruce took the position later shared by the New South's Liberia lobbyists such as John Pierce in New Orleans. Rejecting benighted Liberia as a haven for the oppressed Afro-American masses, Bruce looked toward its modernization:

What Liberia needs to-day from America is not a hundred thousand dependent, uneducated emigrants, but the money and effort required to move them to her shores should be expended in institutions that shall educate her native sons, and in establishing a commerce that shall bring her people in contact with the thoughts and industries of the enlightened nations of the world.[17]

Blanche K. Bruce opposed Liberia emigration for Southern Blacks for the good of the South, for the good of Blacks themselves, and for the good of Liberia. His view of the relationship of Americans to Africans dominated respectable philanthropic circles in the 1880s and 1890s.

One might well argue that Bruce's position was not entirely a disinterested one. After all, these were his constituents threatening to desert Mississippi. Many Southern Blacks accused politicians of opposing emigration out of self-interest. In Bruce's case, however, it is doubtful that political self-interest dictated his stance toward the Liberia movement. He had left Mississippi for the Senate, and he simply remained in Washington at the expiration of his term in 1881.[18] Since he knew in the late 1870s that his

---

[16]Ibid.

[17]Ibid.

[18]President Garfield appointed Bruce register of the Treasury in 1881. Be-

chances of reelection to high office in the Redeemed South were extremely slim, he expressed what he thought were entirely disinterested, enlightened views. In fact, he only regurgitated conservative, respectable clichés.

Another opponent of emigration, Louis Stubblefield, attacked it at the source. Stubblefield, a Black planter in Bolivar County, Mississippi, owned property and belonged to the county board of supervisors, serving his fifth term. In 1880 he owned 160 acres of "very good" land, nine horses and mules, about forty head of cattle, and some hogs. Stubblefield was a paternalist, too, and he said that he acted for the good of his people when an agitator named Dr. Collins, from Helena, Arkansas, came talking of Liberian breadfruit and oil-palm trees:

[Collins] came down there in '78, and he got it into the minds of the people there that they could go to Liberia; that there was one tree there that bore the bread and another tree that bore the lard, and they had nothing at all to do but to go to one tree and dry the fruit and that gave the bread, and to the other tree and cut it and set a bucket under it and catch the lard. It was the most outrageous thing ever perpetrated on an ignorant race in the world.[19]

Collins organized Liberia clubs that only pro-Liberia people could join, and Stubblefield grew suspicious when he was excluded:

I saw the man and I didn't like his face. I told the boys that was down on the place I had rented, when I saw him sitting there in my engineers's house—they were talking to me about the meeting. I looked at the man, and I said to the boys, "Boys, you had better let that man alone; he is a swindler, and we can't carry so many people, it is all we can do to carry ourselves, and it is best to take a man from amongst ourselves to transact our own business, and not depend so much on strangers and foreigners."

He prevented some laborers on his plantations from attending the first secret meeting: "I didn't let anybody in my employment at home that I had the full control of go there," he said.[20] But the Liberia idea took root.

Stubblefield worried. It "hurt my feelings to do it very much

---

tween 1891 and 1893 he served as recorder of deeds of Washington, and between 1897 and his death in 1898 he was again Register of the Treasury. All were appointive positions.

[19]Louis Stubblefield, *Senate Report 693*, III: 520–21. Except for a measure of exaggeration, Collins was right.

[20]Ibid.

at the time," he said, but "I had some very near and dear friends to do it there, and men that was worth as much as I am, and they were getting carried away with it, and they were ready to throw down everything they had in the world and go off and leave it." Swallowing their guilt pangs, he and some friends infiltrated the Liberia movement:

So I made up my mind I would urge upon the best men in our county, to fall in and join these clubs, and get inside in some way or other, in order that we might have a combination against this thing, as I saw where it was going to lead to. So consequently I got into it too. . . . I knew that would be the ruin of them, and I was ready to go into it, to get at the head that I might have some chance to break it up.[21]

Although Stubblefield subverted the movement by exposing Collins as an imposter, it was too late to reverse the harm that had already been done. Having once considered leaving, Blacks in Bolivar County entertained the idea again when the Kansas migration swept across Mississippi. Stubblefield struck again: "Then this Kansas movement was the next thing that sprang up. We got into that, too, and managed to keep our people at home."[22] As a planter, he enjoyed the unique advantage of participating in the movements of working-class Blacks, for no white owners could ever hope to know the Liberia or Kansas clubs firsthand.[23]

It is difficult to determine whether interest in Kansas migration grew out of the ground already prepared by Liberia Fever or it was the fruit of the same desire of Southern Blacks to escape oppression. Certainly in the late 1870s in Mississippi and Louisiana (and, to a certain extent, Texas), Liberia Fever and Kansas Fever flourished in the same fields. Many of the organizational characteristics of planned migration to Kansas were common to the Liberia emigrationists.

---

[21]Ibid.

[22]Ibid.

[23]Other Black planters were unwilling or perhaps unable to infiltrate with Stubblefield's success. Isaiah T. Montgomery, for instance, a Black planter in Warren County, Mississippi, lost a significant portion of his work force to the Kansas Exodus. Montgomery actually visited Kansas in an attempt to retrieve some of the tenants from his Hurricane Bend Plantation. While he was there, he invested in Kansas lands with the Freedmen's Aid Association. For Montgomery's version of these experiences, as told to Booker T. Washington, see Washington's *The Negro in Business* (n.p., 1907), pp. 87–88.

12
Migration to Kansas Preceding the Exodus

While Blacks in the Deep South set their sights on Liberia, a steady stream of migrants flowed from three border states to Kansas. Instead of entertaining thoughts of Liberia, Blacks in Kentucky, Missouri, and Tennessee established small colonies on the western prairies or in Kansas cities and towns. The movement was gradual, and little is known of its progress, particularly from the neighboring state of Missouri. Black migrants from Kentucky and Tennessee attracted attention in Kansas, however, and it is possible to trace their settlement before 1879.

During the 1870s, the total population of Kansas grew enormously. Although many Blacks moved there, the percentage of Blacks actually dropped during that period. In 1870 there were about 16,250 Afro-Americans in Kansas, about 5,925 of whom were born in the neighboring state of Missouri.[1] About 3,800 were born in Kansas, many of them the young children of migrants. Of the remainder, 2,360 were born in Kentucky, about 1,140 in Virginia and West Virginia, about 890 in Arkansas, about 700 in Tennessee, about 180 in Texas, 130 in Mississippi, and 100 in Louisiana.[2]

After ten years of migration and colonization, the Black population of Kansas had grown to about 43,110, an increase of some 26,000 people. In addition to the large increase in numbers of

---

[1] *Statistics of the Population* [1880], p. xxxviii.

[2] *Compendium of the Ninth United States Census* [1870] (Washington, 1872), p. 388. The census of 1870 is not very reliable, unfortunately.

Blacks in Kansas, a shift in proportional representation by state of nativity occurred. By 1880 the largest group was Kansas born (some 10,920).[3] Whereas in 1870, the largest group of Blacks were Missouri born, in 1880, 6,490 were of Missouri birth, 6,990 were Kentucky born, and 5,420 were from Tennessee. In 1880, 2,780 Blacks in Kansas had been born in Mississippi; 2,460 in Texas; 1,300 in Louisiana; 1,840 in Virginia and West Virginia; and 770 in Arkansas.[4]

In short, the sustained migration of some 9,500 Blacks from Tennessee and Kentucky to Kansas during the decade far exceeded the much publicized migration of 1879, which netted no more than about 4,000 people from Mississippi and Louisiana. After 1870, Missouri no longer contributed the major portion of colored migrants to Kansas. It is important to keep these relative figures in mind, since the Kansas Fever Exodus attracted attention completely out of proportion to its actual numbers.

The beginnings of the heavy Black migration to Kansas from Kentucky and Tennessee in the mid-1870s are easier to trace in Tennessee than Kentucky. A spontaneous, popular movement sprang up in the winter of 1874–75, resembling the Kansas Fever Exodus of 1879. In 1874 and 1875, the rumor of free transportation, land, and supplies circulated in middle Tennessee, and concern for people affected with Kansas Fever led to the colored people's convention in Nashville in May 1875. The convention sought to rationalize the movement and lay false rumors to rest. Pointing to the "unsettled condition of the colored people of Tennessee," and the "excitement" among them, several migrationists, including W. A. Sizemore, Benjamin Singleton, and A. W. McConnell, issued a call "To the Colored People of Tennessee" in April 1875:

We . . . do hereby call the attention of every colored man to the convention of the colored people of the State of Tennessee, to be held at the city of Nashville on the 19th day of May next, for the purpose of looking after

---

[3]Naturally, many newborns of Exoduster families were counted in that total, but they belonged to the Exoduster (1879 migrant) population socially.

[4]*Compendium of the Tenth United States Census* [1880] (Washington, 1883), pp. 476–78. Only about 2,390 of the colored population born in Kansas were one year of age or younger. The absolute changes between 1870 and 1880 of the colored population by state of nativity were: Missouri, +560; Kentucky, +4,630; Tennessee, +4,720; Mississippi, +2,640; Texas, +2,290; Louisiana, +1,200; Virginia and West Virginia, +730; and Arkansas, −130.

the interests of the colored people. Seeing that there is so much imposition practiced upon the people, day by day, in regard to emigrating, by some unknown persons, that has caused a great deal of excitement among the colored people, and a great meny have sold out and left their homes with the purpose of going to Kansas free.[5]

At the same time that the Sizemore and Singleton group called the convention, the Nashville *Republican Banner* reported a "considerable and continual" exodus of Blacks from Tennessee. The paper also noted that "some foolish ones" were convinced that they were eligible for free government transportation, a mule, and provisions for a year. "Sensible ones," said the *Banner,* "are better posted up."[6]

Events unfolded in Nashville in 1875 very much as they later did around the Exodus of the spring of 1879: the massive, spontaneous, popular action of one group of Blacks triggered deliberate consideration of the same course among others in conventions, meetings, and investigations. The 1875 Nashville meeting designated a board of commissioners to encourage migration from Tennessee. The board, in turn, appointed several delegates to visit the West and report on the conditions of settlement. One of them, N. A. Napier, visited Kansas during the early summer of 1875 and reported his findings at a meeting held in mid-August.[7]

Napier reported that a prospective settler would need money and tools worth about a thousand dollars to relocate in Kansas. This sum included the cost of a pair of good mules and two plows, and five hundred dollars for expenses and transportation. B. F. Frierson reiterated the migrants' need for capital, but he estimated that about two hundred dollars would stand settlers in good stead. Had a thousand dollars been necessary for migration, few Tennessee Blacks could have afforded to move. But Napier's report notwithstanding, migration from Tennessee to Kansas grew increasingly attractive in the following year.[8]

Soon migration "conductors" like Benjamin Singleton were regularly steering Black families to Kansas. One of them was a white man from Williamson County, William Griffin, who claimed

---

[5]Nashville *Republican Banner,* April 25, 1875.

[6]Ibid., May 1 and 8, 1875.

[7]Ibid., May 21, 1875; Nashville *Union and American,* May 20, 1875.

[8]Ibid. B. F. Frierson later migrated to Kansas and, in the 1880s, showed interest in emigrating to Liberia.

to have taken several families to Kansas City at his own cost in October 1875.[9] A Negro, George Brown, acted as travel agent for a large number of families, collecting their money and buying their steamboat tickets. Brown transported people to Kansas City from Nashville for about $10.00 each—$2.50 from Nashville to Cairo, Illinois; $1.50 from Cairo to St. Louis; and $5.00 to $6.00 from St. Louis to Kansas City.

Migration moved along briskly after early 1876. In the same fortnight in March 1876 that Griffin took several families to Kansas and Brown conducted several more, some fifty additional Blacks left Nashville for Kansas by rail.[10] In August, Benjamin Singleton wrote to the governor of Kansas saying that he expected one to three thousand Blacks to leave middle Tennessee for Kansas during the fall.[11] The following spring, Columbus Johnson and Benjamin Singleton began to take people from Tennessee to Topeka and thence to the Singleton Colony in Cherokee County.[12] In 1877 as well, two Black colonies were formed in Kentucky.

The first well-known settlement of Black Kentuckians in Kansas was Nicodemus, located well out on the prairie, on the Solomon River in Graham County. (Nicodemus was and still is the most famous Black settlement in Kansas.[13]) It was founded by Black

---

[9]Nashville Weekly *American,* March 16, 1876.

[10]Ibid., March 23, 1876, p. 16.

[11]Benjamin Singleton to Governor Osborn, Nashville, Tennessee, August 7, 1876, CRSF, Osborn, box 2, KSHS.

[12]Chicago Daily *Tribune,* March 27, 1879.

[13]Singleton's colonizing activities inspired the founders of Nicodemus, and Nicodemus, in turn, stimulated the formation of another Black colony by Kentuckians in Hodgeman County, on the prairie, not far from what is now Jetmore, Kansas. Organized by Blacks in Harrodsburg and Lexington in 1877, the Hodgeman colony sent delegates to investigate Kansas and Nicodemus. Their report recommended settlement somewhat to the south of Nicodemus. The colony arrived at Kinsley, Kansas, in March 1878, and they initially attempted to found a city, which they called "Morton City," after Oliver P. Morton. But the double task of opening homesteads and building a town overburdened the hundred or so settlers, and they abandoned the town. Fifty more settlers joined the colony later, and in 1879 about fifty homesteads had been taken, as well as a few timber claims. During the first season of settlement, only the settlers equipped with teams succeeded in making crops; the others had to get by with gardens and hiring themselves out by the day or month to established farmers. The Moore brothers, Thomas and Benjamin, were carpenters and had businesses in Kinsley, about thirty miles southeast of the colony. Another Kentuckian, Robert Johnson, owned a livery stable. In 1879 all three

colonists from Lexington, Kentucky, who arrived in five groups in 1877 and 1878; W. J. Niles and W. R. Hill had recruited the settlers for Nicodemus in Kentucky and Kansas during the summer of 1877. Niles was a Black businessman, Hill a white minister and speculator attempting to drum up settlers for the area around his Hill City. Hill acted as agent for two groups of Lexington Blacks seeking to relocate in Kansas. The Nicodemus Town Company of Graham County was the first on the ground, with the April 1877 arrival of the Reverend S. P. Roundtree, the town company's secretary. Shortly after the planting of the town company's standard, a second group, the Nicodemus Colony, merged with the town company. M. M. Bell and W. J. Niles were the most prominent officers of the colony. Alcoholic beverages were prohibited in Nicodemus because both the colony and the town company were dry.

The first group of 30 colonists arrived at Nicodemus from Topeka in July 1877. They were originally from Kentucky and were associated with the Nicodemus Town Company. In September 1877 the second and largest addition, 350 settlers, came to Nicodemus with the Reverend M. M. Bell of the Nicodemus Colony, under the aegis of W. R. Hill. Hill also conducted the third contingent, 150 people from Scott County, Kentucky, which arrived in March 1878. The fourth group, from Missouri, numbered only about 50. The last early arrivals came from Kentucky under Roundtree's guidance. In addition, small family groups joined the colony from time to time. A native of Holly Springs, Mississippi, Samuel Garland had lived in Kansas since the early 1870s and had married there. Garland joined Nicodemus in 1878 along with three other families from Wyandotte who were associated with his wife's father and originally from Kentucky. In 1880 the total colored population of Nicodemus was about 700.[14] Before Nicodemus fell

---

of them were doing well. In addition to the Morton City colony in Hodgeman County, there was another called the David City colony. In addition to a short-lived colony in Marion County, Black colonies grew up in Barton and Rice counties. (Ibid., May 8, 1879; St. Louis *Globe-Democrat*, April 21, 1879; Nell B. Waldron, "Colonization in Kansas, 1861–1890," unpublished typescript, KSHS, n.d., pp. 125–26; Frank Doster, *Senate Report 693*, III: 106; Singleton Scrapbook, unpaginated circular.)

[14]Orval L. McDaniel, "A History of Nicodemus," unpublished typescript, KSHS, 1950, p. 42; A. T. Hall, Jr., Fort Scott *Colored Citizen*, May 10, 1878; Roy Garvin, "Benjamin, or 'Pap,' Singleton and His Followers," *Journal of Negro History* XXXIII, no. 1 (January 1948): 16; Glen Schwendemann, "Nicodemus: Negro

upon hard times, the settlers cooperated well with one another and with Hill. But difficulty fissured the settlement into its two largest original components, the colony and the town company.

Problems began when the largest group of settlers arrived too late in the season to start crops. They were also short of teams, and the settlement fared very poorly during the winter of 1877–78. Men worked for the farmers scattered across the area, as Niles and Roundtree solicited aid throughout Kansas and Colorado. In attempting to relieve the Nicodemus colonists they exposed Kansas to needy Black migrants for the first time. While Niles collected aid from Kansans in the longer-settled eastern portions of the state, Roundtree tried to work through the governor.

Niles met reasonable success in Kansas and Colorado, and he was credited in mid-1878 by one Black settler in Nicodemus with "keeping the wolf from the door."[15] But by March 1878, Roundtree (Nicodemus Town Company) denounced Niles (Nicodemus Colony) as "an imposter" who was "gathering aid and not making an honest return of it to the sufferers." Roundtree had conceived a more sweeping plan for saving Nicodemus.[16]

Roundtree proposed going to Congress with the governor's endorsement to solicit aid for Blacks in Kansas, until Governor George T. Anthony nipped the proposition in the bud. Recalling with shame Kansas's nationwide appeal for aid in 1874 when grasshoppers invaded the state, Anthony wrote, "We cannot afford to send beggars out of Kansas at this time, when ten thousand are seeking homes here expecting [it] to be the granary of the West."[17] To forestall Roundtree's Washington appeal, Governor Anthony sent his private secretary to survey conditions at Nicodemus. Fortunately, the situation rapidly improved later in March, when nearby Methodist ministers organized the loan of several teams. In addition, a new group of settlers arrived from Scott County, Kentucky, well furnished with teams and farming implements. With a sigh of relief, W. R. Hill sent word to the governor of the new

---

Haven on the Solomon," *Kansas Historical Quarterly* XXXIV, no. 1 (Spring 1968): 14–15. Wyandotte is now Kansas City, Kansas.

[15]A. T. Hall, Jr., Fort Scott *Colored Citizen*, May 10, 1878.

[16]William P. Tomlinson to Governor George T. Anthony, Ellis, Kansas, March 14, 1878, CRSF, Anthony, box 1, KSHS; Governor Anthony to John H. Edwards, Topeka, Kansas, March 13, 1878, Letters, II (1878): 9–11, KSHS.

[17]Governor Anthony to John H. Edwards, Topeka, Kansas, March 13, 1878, ibid.

arrivals: "The Nicodemus Colony from Scott Co. Ky all leave here [Ellis, Kansas, about 30 miles south of Nicodemus] this morning for Nicodemus and Graham Co   all in good spirits with teams stock farming implements provisions & so and do not look like a begardly set as has been represented."[18] New settlers and a fresh growing season saved the Nicodemus colonists from the worst of their wants. By the next harvest they were on their feet again.

Out on the prairie in unorganized territory, the Nicodemus settlers faced difficulties with their two sets of white neighbors. Nearby white farmers watched the Black colony's rapid growth with increasing alarm. They attempted to delay organization of Graham County until there were not merely fifteen hundred people in the territory (as stipulated by state law), but fifteen hundred *white* people. One white settler feared that if the county was organized as soon as it numbered fifteen hundred people of any color, the white settlers would be saddled with debts. She blamed Hill for "rushing a lot of colored men in," just so he could speculate on school bonds. The sixty white families would bear the brunt of financing Hill's school bonds, she thought, because the Black settlers were so poor. On behalf of the white farmers, she asked that Graham County not be formally organized "untill we can have it with out bonds or debt if we can only get a long with the cattle men."[19] In the end, white settlement advanced by leaps and bounds, and Graham County was organized in 1880 with a large white majority. But all the settlers, Black and white, confronted the cattlemen on the prairie.

Nicodemus's other neighbors, the ranchers, plagued the farmers for several years. In March 1878 the Reverend Roundtree wrote to Governor Anthony asking if he could control the cattlemen's herds, which were trampling the farmers' plowed fields: "Govner Dear ser   we would ask you plese to get rede of the Catel we ar so rounded with the hured [herders] do not care for us."[20] The governor could offer the settlers no relief from the

---

[18]W. R. Hill to Governor Anthony, Ellis, Kansas, March 23, 1878, CRSF, Anthony, box 1, KSHS.

[19]Mrs. Marie L. Stanley to Governor Anthony, Nicodemus, April 7, 1878, CRSF, Anthony, box 1, KSHS.

[20]The Reverend S. P. Roundtree to Governor Anthony, Nicodemus, Kansas, March 26, 1878, CRSF, Anthony, box 1, KSHS. Barbed wire was not invented until the following year.

ranchers, and all the Graham County farmers waged a long struggle with gun-carrying cattlemen and their wide-ranging herds.

By the end of 1878 Nicodemus was growing, if not yet prospering. Educated, ambitious young men such as Edward McCabe and A. T. Hall, Jr., of Chicago also joined the colony. They received two of Graham County's first political appointments, and in the 1880s McCabe was elected state auditor, the highest office in Kansas held by a Black man in the nineteenth century.[21]

Nicodemus was the most important Black settlement in Kansas before the Exodus of 1879. For most migrants, taking up a homestead was a toilsome process that often included their first working for wages in eastern Kansas as laborers. Men held odd jobs by the day or month, on farms, on the railroads, or in the mines; women worked as washerwomen or domestics. The most fortunate gradually accumulated enough money to rent or buy farms. The less fortunate—and in 1880 these outnumbered the former—remained in the towns. When the agricultural boom of the 1880s collapsed, many who had taken up land on the prairie were forced to seek work in the towns of eastern Kansas or to move to Colorado or Missouri. Nicodemus, for instance, had its flush times in the mid-1880s and slowly declined thereafter. But on the eve of the 1879 Exodus, the Black colonies of Kansas (the two Singleton colonies, Nicodemus, and the Hodgeman, Barton, Rice, and Marion County settlements) were doing reasonably well.

In Mississippi and Louisiana, interest in Kansas gradually increased after the mid-1870s. Small groups of rural Blacks—fami-

---

[21]E. P. McCabe was born in Troy, New York, in 1850 and grew up in New England. As a young man he worked as a clerk to Potter Palmer in Chicago and held a Cook County clerkship in the early 1870s. He moved to Kansas and was engaged in a real estate business with Abram T. Hall, Jr., who in the mid-1880s was city editor of Ferdinand Barnett's Chicago *Conservator*. In the 1880s McCabe was considered very much an up-and-coming young man: "Mr. McCabe's career is illustrative of the possibilities of self-made men, who make their impressions upon our times by sheer force of character. Mr. McCabe is still a very young man, and the successes which are possible in his life appear to us to be vast and honorable to himself and to his race. We can only hope to conquer by those qualities of head and heart by which all other men conquer." (New York *Globe* [T. Thomas Fortune's paper], February 17, 1883.)

lies, individuals, small colonies—left the South with the end of Reconstruction, and by 1877–78, particularly in Mississippi, large numbers of Blacks were sending letters of inquiry to the governor of Kansas. The response was a standard, encouraging reply along with the Kansas Agricultural Report, which described farming opportunities, types and prices of land. If the Kansas material suited their possibilities, the prospective settlers formed emigration clubs to organize for movement to the West.

Mississippi Blacks seriously questioned their future after Reconstruction ended in 1875. J. C. Embry, for instance, who had moved from the Vicksburg area to Leavenworth, Kansas, expressed his doubts about the future to Senator Blanche K. Bruce:

I shall return to the south in a few days. Whether I stay there till after the campaign & election will depend upon the attitude of the administration towards us in that section. If those fellows are to be allowed to arm and persecute us at pleasure as they have done the past season [1875, when Mississippi was "Redeemed"], we must all of necessity soon abandon the state & the south entirely.[22]

The campaign of 1875 had not entirely wiped out Republicanism in Mississippi, but it convinced Embry that Blacks must seriously consider migration. During the mid-1870s he wrote letters to several journals, including the Chicago *Inter-Ocean* and the Leavenworth *Times,* and published a pamphlet entitled *Thoughts for To-day upon the Past, Present and Future of Colored Americans.* He spoke to Bruce about the possibility of securing a Congressional appropriation to help poor Blacks quit the South, and Bruce put him in touch with Senator William Windom of Minnesota. This, according to Embry, was the genesis of the 1879 Windom Resolution to study the feasibility of government-aided resettlement of Southern Blacks.[23]

Kansas appeared increasingly attractive to Black Mississippians in 1877. S. M. Cole of Chickasaw County in north-central Mississippi wrote to Governor Anthony of Kansas, asking for information to clear up confusion about homesteading: ". . . theire is many people here who would leave here and go to your part of the Country ef they only had the meanes to carry them, and there is some who have meanes, but the reports that we have conflict so,

---

[22]J. C. Embry to Senator B. K. Bruce, Leavenworth, Kansas, February 21, 1876, Bruce Papers, Moorland-Spingarn Collection, Howard University.

[23]St. Louis *Globe-Democrat,* March 28, 1879.

that a person hardley knowes what to think."[24] In the fall and winter of 1877, newspapers in Mississippi and Kansas reported widespread interest in Kansas throughout southern Mississippi, and several families migrated from the riverine areas that later spawned the Kansas Fever Exodus.[25] Looking back from 1879, a migrant traced the roots of the Exodus to the migration of families from Washington, Issaquena, and Warren counties: "Well, about eighteen months ago [in the fall of 1877] a few families from my section, near Delta, and between Greenville and Vicksburg, went to Kansas and wrote back to their friends of the glorious country, and how easy it was to make a living out there. This news got around among the people. . . ."[26]

In New Orleans, a committee of Black women organized to combat infringements on Blacks' civil rights. In late 1877 this "Committee of Five Hundred Women," headed by Mary Jane Garrett, wrote Ben Butler of the plight of Black people in Louisiana. According to a hostile white Nashville weekly, the letter was in the "old bloody-shirt style, altered, to suit the present, and terribly denunciatory of Mr. Hayes and the Southern people. These sable workwomen claim that they are exposed to robbery, murder, swindling and all the other foibles and pleasantries. They have organized an emigration society, and say they propose to move."[27] But a Black politician in New Orleans praised the women for demanding "every right and privilege that the Constitution guarantees to their race," and for insisting they would "use every power in their hands to get it."[28]

Signs of an impending massive migration to Kansas appeared with increasing frequency in November and December 1878. In November the Hinds County *Gazette* twice sounded the alarm, claiming on good authority that there were emigration agents working in Hinds County to encourage migration to Kansas, "offering to pay all transportation charges, and guaranteeing 'the best of homes' and good wages to all who go." In December the paper

[24]S. M. Cole to Governor Anthony, Atlanta, Mississippi, May 8, 1877, CRSF, Anthony, box 3, KSHS.

[25]Raymond (Miss.) *Hinds County Gazette,* December 26, 1877; Fort Scott *Colored Citizen,* April 19, 1878; T. W. Henderson of Topeka, Kansas, Philadelphia *Christian Recorder,* April 18, 1878.

[26]St. Louis *Globe-Democrat,* March 17, 1879.

[27]Nashville Weekly *American,* November 8, 1877.

[28]J. Henri Burch, *Senate Report 693,* II: 232–33.

reported that it had the names of the "parties" said to be enrolling emigrants to Kansas.[29] At the same time, in Topeka, the *Colored Citizen* reported the arrival of several families from Mississippi: they complained of the high cost of living and lack of freedom in their home state. The *Colored Citizen* by this time received such a volume of inquiries about conditions in Kansas that the paper answered in its columns. It gave advice about how and where to settle, exhorting its Southern brethren to "COME WEST. COME TO KANSAS."[30] In late 1878 and early 1879, several newspapers in Mississippi carried the same small article exulting over the impending departure of the Blacks:

One thousand negroes will emigrate this season from Hinds and Madison counties, Miss., to Kansas. We hope they will better their condition, and send back so favorable a report from the "land of promise" that thousands will be induced to follow them; and the emigration will go on till the whites will have a numerical majority in every county in Mississippi.[31]

Indeed, emigration clubs dotted southern Mississippi, and the people were ready to go.

Blacks had obtained information about Kansas through several channels: letters from migrants, circulars, mass meetings, on-the-spot investigators, and letters to Kansas—either to the governor or to the *Colored Citizen*. Letters back home sustained interest in Kansas and encouraged friends and neighbors to migrate, too. Many of the Kentuckians who settled Nicodemus in different waves had been friends at home.[32] Letters from Kansas were often read in church, where the information could reach the largest number of people. But not all prospective migrants were fortunate enough to have contacts in Kansas. Conductors and colonies aimed circulars at this audience in their attempt to attract settlers.

Both W. R. Hill and Benjamin Singleton printed exhortations to visit or settle in Kansas. One of Singleton's fliers cried:

HO FOR KANSAS!

---

[29]Raymond *Hinds County Gazette,* November 27 and December 11, 1878.

[30]Topeka *Colored Citizen,* December 7 and November 30, 1878. The *Colored Citizen* moved from Fort Scott to Topeka in late 1878.

[31]Columbus (Miss.) *Democrat,* quoted in New Orleans Daily *Picayune,* December 20, 1878; Summit (Miss.) *Sentinel,* quoted in Raymond *Hinds County Gazette,* January 15, 1879.

[32]Topeka *Capital,* August 29, 1877, quoted in "Negro Clippings," vol. 7, KSHS.

and informed "Brethren, Friends, & Fellow Citizens" that the Edgefield Real Estate and Homestead Association would be taking a group of settlers "in pursuit of Homes in the Southwestern Lands of America, at Transportation Rates, cheaper than ever was known before," on April 15, 1878. With the aid of this circular, Singleton assembled 120 people and conducted them to Kansas. Hill, in Topeka, ran excursions to Hill City and the Solomon Valley, luring prospective settlers with the rallying cry "Ho! for the Great Solomon Valley of Western Kansas!"[33]

The Black colonies also used broadsides to attract newcomers. The Hodgeman settlement issued a handbill headed "COME!" It encouraged colored people to come to settle in Hodgeman County, the "best place for climate and for soil for the smallest capital."[34] And the Nicodemus Town Company invited colored people to its "beautifully located" town site, and printed the words of the song "Nicodemus" at the foot of the circular:

NICODEMUS

Nicodemus was a slave of African birth,
    And was bought for a bag full of gold;
He was reckoned a part of the salt of the earth,
    But he died years ago, very old.
Nicodemus was a prophet, at least he was as wise,
    For he told of the battles to come;
How we trembled with fear, when he rolled up his eyes,
    And we heeded the shake of his thumb.

Chorus:
Good time coming, good time coming,
    Long, long time on the way;
Run and tell Elija to hurry up Pomp,
    To meet us under the cottonwood tree,
In the Great Solomon Valley
    At the first break of day.[35]

Railroad placards, meant for America at large, doubtless found their way into Black hands as well.

At mass meetings, such as the 1875 Emigration Convention in

---

[33]Singleton Scrapbook, unpaginated circulars; Topeka Daily *Blade*, April 23, 1878.

[34]Singleton Scrapbook, unpaginated circulars.

[35]Ibid.

Nashville, railroad agents, labor contractors, migration conductors, and migration polemicists addressed large numbers of people. Meetings often delegated one of their number to travel to Kansas to survey the situation for the rest, as N. A. Napier had done after the Nashville convocation. The delegates would report back their findings, which, of course, were not always heeded. Later, after the Exodus had generated enormous controversy, a whole trainful of people visited Kansas to see for themselves and report back.

Sending delegates entailed expenditures that often surpassed the capabilities of many Black groups. In such cases, letters to Kansas sufficed. The *Colored Citizen* filled the gaps, furnishing information addressed particularly to other Blacks. The *Colored Citizen* encouraged industrious, hard-working settlers to come to Kansas and live in a free land, but reminded them that they must be willing to work and be able to bring enough money to tide them over the first year. It also published the notices of conductors, such as Turner Stevenson of Lexington, Kentucky. Stevenson warned colored people to "be careful of any scheme which has for its object a settlement in uninhabited counties on the frontiers, remote from railroads," a warning against the promoters of Nicodemus. He advised migrants to "select your location in a well-settled country, where those that have not sufficient money to purchase land can rent farms or find other employment." He particularly recommended Cherokee County, in the extreme southeastern corner of the state.[36]

Many families set out on their own, fed up with life in the South. The ten-member family of Joe Hartwell left Pulaski, Tennessee, for Kansas in 1876, saying simply that Tennessee was "no place for colored people."[37]

Well before 1879, thousands of Southern Blacks migrated to Kansas seeking to better their economic and political conditions by leaving the land of the slave, the master, and the bulldozer. They went to Kansas because it was known for its ample homesteading lands and abundant crops, the "Garden Spot of the Earth." (In fact, the state attracted a tremendous migration of

[36]Fort Scott *Colored Citizen*, October 17, 1878.
[37]Pulaski (Tenn.) *Citizen*, quoted in Nashville Weekly *American*, April 13, 1876.

whites, especially from Ohio, Indiana, and Illinois in these years, for those same reasons.) But for Afro-American migrants, Kansas represented something that Nebraska and the Dakotas did not. To make Kansas a Free State, blood flowed freely during the 1850s. It was the quintessential Free State, the land of John Brown, "a free state in which a colored man can enjoy his freedom."[38] He could prosper under his own vine and fig tree and watch his children grow up free and educated. "I am anxious to reach your state," a Black Louisianian wrote to the governor of Kansas, "not because of the great race now made for it but because of the sacredness of her soil washed by the blood of humanitarians for the cause of freedom."[39] Now, Kansas made no special appeal to attract Black migrants; it offered them no special inducements. But old abolitionist, temperance Republicans ruled the state, and they held out precisely the same welcome to Black settlers as to white. This even-handed sense of fair play amounted to an open-armed welcome, in comparison to much of the rest of the country at the time.

The gradual, planned migration of Blacks from Kentucky, Tennessee, and Mississippi in the second half of the 1870s scattered Afro-Americans throughout Kansas, from Nicodemus to Dodge City, from Parsons and Fort Scott to Topeka, Leavenworth, and Atchison. That long-lived movement sketched out the routes of migration from the Southern states. The Kansas Fever Exodus etched those lines indelibly. On the most fundamental level, the Kansas Fever Exodus shared the motivations of the more gradual migrations that preceded it and continued after it. In 1878, the violence surrounding the election left frightened Blacks in the Gulf States convinced that they must leave the South then or never.

---

[38]S. L. Johnson to Governor St. John, Centreville, Leon County, Texas, August 21, 1879, CRSF, St. John, box 10, KSHS.

[39]G. R. M. Newman to Governor St. John, n.d. [about September 13, 1879], CRSF, St. John, box 10, KSHS.

13

The Campaign of 1878 in Louisiana

The Compromise of 1877 recognized the Democratic administration of Francis T. Nicholls in Louisiana and sealed the doom of Republicanism on the state level. Locally, however, the process unfolded more gradually. In the first elections after Redemption, in 1878, Republicans maneuvered to their best advantage whatever power they still wielded. In parishes with Black majorities they were relatively well situated and attempted to parlay numerical strength into political currency. Republicans sought to forge working coalitions with disaffected or conservative Democrats against the "ultra" Democrats. Faced with the threat of fusionist opposition, Democrats mounted all-out campaigns of destruction.

Democrats intended first to isolate Black Republicans, then paralyze them politically. Through intimidation and inducement, they lured white Republicans into the Democratic ranks; nightriding and assassination effectively eliminated Black Republican opposition. Tensas, Natchitoches, Caddo, St. Mary, Ouachita, Concordia, and Pointe Coupée parishes all witnessed lawlessness and election irregularities in 1878.

When the Nicholls administration inaugurated the New Departure Democratic state government in early 1877, the Louisiana Senate and House of Representatives promised to accept in good faith the Thirteenth, Fourteenth, and Fifteenth amendments to the United States Constitution. These pious resolves were little more than a year old when north Louisiana newspapers began exhorting white voters to maintain their vigilance. The Shreveport Evening *Standard* cautioned that the "Democratic party of Louisiana is in danger of being lulled into a sense of security by the idea that the Republican party is dead," for Republicans harbored a diabolical hatred for Democrats, which led them to organize "quietly and secretly, but vigorously in Caddo Parish." Blacks were registering in greater numbers than were whites, and, according to the *Standard*, "the colored voter will doubtless take the same interest in this matter [registration], as we know from observation, that he has always taken in it."[1] (Across the Mississippi River in Natchez, the *Democrat* advised that "the most persistent, active and ceaseless work will be required to prevent the district again falling into the hands of the Radicals." Only through united support of its candidate, General J. R. Chalmers, the *Democrat* warned, would the "shoestring district" remain safely Democratic.)[2]

By the end of the summer, prominent Black men in New Orleans also began issuing statements calculated to strengthen the hand of Blacks in New Departure Louisiana politics. The Colored Men's Protective Union, organized in mid-1878, aimed at securing political unity of Lousiana Blacks in cooperation with conservative white Democrats. Early in August, the union issued an "Address to the Colored People of Louisiana," appealing "to all colored men to consider our situation and do his upmost to secure unity among our people in the present crisis. If prudent counsels prevail," the address continued, "our people may profitably accept the situation, and so pass through the ordeal that, as a race, we may reasonably expect to enter on a new and higher plane both of observation and of action."[3] Counseling adjustment to the Nicholls regime and Democratic rule, this address differed markedly from those issued after the election. Perhaps at the behest of the Protective Union, Black Republicans began to sound out the Democratic ranks for defectors early in the fall.

In Caddo Parish, meanwhile, Democrats shrilly denounced the embryonic "Independent" party, a coalition of Black Republicans and disaffected Democrats:

---

[1] Shreveport Evening *Standard*, July 30, 1878.

[2] Natchez Daily *Democrat*, June 27, 1878. The *Democrat* served as the local paper for the entire Natchez region, on both sides of the Mississippi River, in Mississippi and Louisiana.

[3] Ibid., August 13, 1878.

In point of fact, they have no political tenents—are governed by no fixed principles of governmental policy, and stand midway between the two parties to attract the disaffected soreheads of Democrats, the camp-followers of the Republican party, whose rapacity and greed for plunder have been disappointed, and the unthinking and irresolute men whom the glittering generality of "good men for office" can allure with its specious bait.[4]

Democrats in other parishes, particularly Natchitoches and Tensas, reacted similarly to incipient fusion slates. While in Natchitoches cooperation never reached the stage of nominating a working men's ticket—Democratic bulldozers forced the Republican executive committee of the parish into exile before any hard bargaining could get under way with the poor whites—in Tensas the opposition was not disposed of so neatly.

Tensas, like its neighbors Madison and Concordia, was a heavily Black cotton parish, and therefore solidly Republican. The great highway of the Mississippi River linked these three intensely rural parishes with the Mississippi counties between Vicksburg and Natchez: Adams, Jefferson, Claiborne, and Warren. Waterproof and St. Joseph, the two towns of Tensas Parish, lay on the river about halfway between Natchez and Vicksburg. In 1878 Tensas was less securely Republican than the parishes above and below it. Madison Parish suffered little or no violence in 1878 (although it would in 1879); Concordia was not the prime target of bulldozers in 1878, but there was some spill-over violence from the Tensas troubles, as there was also in Adams County, Mississippi.

In September and early October, Republicans in Tensas Parish opened the nomination process. Republican tickets were usually racially mixed, and in 1878 two leading incumbents standing for reelection were white, the parish judge and the sheriff. Before the October 5 convention, J. Ross Stewart, a Black aspirant to the office of sheriff, solicited support from various Republican clubs. Although several important Black Republicans disliked Stewart, he counted on this appeal to racial solidarity to win him the nomination:

We, the undersigned, do hereby agree to support a colored man for the office of sheriff at the convention to be held at Saint Joseph, October, 1878.[5]

---

[4]Shreveport Evening *Standard,* August 30, 1878.

[5]J. Ross Stewart, *Senate Report 855,* I: 343.

The pledge was signed by twelve prominent Black Republicans, including Stewart himself, and Robert J. Walker. Yet, the most influential Black Republican in the parish, the Reverend Alfred Fairfax, did not sign, probably because he intended to support the white incumbent in return for support for his Congressional bid.

On October 5, the day of the Republican parish convention, a white Democrat telegraphed the Natchez *Democrat* that the Blacks were drawing the color line, determined that only colored men should be nominated for *all* the offices. Stewart knew full well that such a charge portended violence, and he showed the actual agreement to leading Democrats to appease their anger. The Democrats merely repeated their earlier threats that the Republicans invited violence if they fielded any ticket whatever.

None of the parish's white Republicans attended the convention, and when he inquired after their whereabouts, Alfred Fairfax found the parish judge and the sheriff with members of the Democratic executive committee. One white Republican informed Fairfax that he would no longer work with the Blacks: "All I have is here and what the Democrats have done in other parishes they propose to do here. . . . You know how the Democrats have carried other parishes, and I know that if I run on the Republican ticket here I will be killed and I don't propose to put my self up as a target to be shot at."[6] Lacking white Republican candidates, the Blacks rejected the alternative of an all-Black ticket as too provocative. Instead, Fairfax drafted a resolution to the effect that Black Republicans wanted to choose a slate "that will be satisfactory to

---

[6]Alfred Fairfax to President Hayes, n.d., n.p. [New Orleans, late December 1878], Record Group 60, Department of Justice Source-Chronological Files, President, box 6. Fairfax was born a slave in Virginia in 1840. Sold to Louisiana, he remained in bondage until he organized a band of slaves to flee to the Union lines in 1862. They enlisted in the Army's Pioneer Corps, and there Fairfax, like Henry Adams, learned to read. Fairfax was discharged in 1864 and returned to Tensas Parish. Between 1870 and 1874 he served as Tensas Parish commissioner, member of the educational board, and assistant appraiser of the port of New Orleans. Following his exile in 1878, he returned home briefly in 1879 only to take several families to Chatauqua County, Kansas, late in the year. In Kansas he grew cotton and pastored the New Hope Baptist Church in Parsons. Elected to the Kansas legislature in the late 1880s, he was the first Black man to serve there. During the same period he earned a premium citation at the New Orleans exposition for his Kansas-grown upland cotton. (This material comes from an article in the Topeka *American Citizen*, February 1, 1889. I am indebted to Luther P. Jackson, Jr., for bringing this article to my attention.)

all parties," that is, one with some whites on it. They would appoint a committee to meet with the Democrats in hopes of agreeing on an acceptable ticket. The Republican convention was set to reconvene after the committee met with the Democratic executive committee on October 7.[7]

Although most of the Black Republicans backed the resolution, one group that shared the cautious sentiments of R. J. Walker felt that the committee's action would prove futile, or worse, dangerous. Walker suggested instead that each colored man speak privately to his white friends after the Democrats nominated their candidates. In this way, Walker said, they could recruit disaffected Democrats:

I was one of those who believed that when the Democratic party had their convention on the 7th there would be a great many disaffected men, and possibly we could get enough to make up a ticket that would give satisfaction, and I advised my friends that we had better go home and wait, and in the mean time each member of the party would visit every white man of his acquaintance in the parish, to see how many we could get that would go on and help make up a ticket to satisfy the colored people and the white people in general. I was satisfied that the committee would do no good at that time.[8]

Walker correctly counted on a good deal of opposition within Democratic ranks to the executive committee's offer of leading nominations, in the name of white solidarity, to former Republican incumbents.

Meanwhile, on October 7, the Fairfax committee met with the Democratic executive committee, which ignored the Republicans entirely and proceeded to make a straight-out white ticket including newly converted ex-Republicans. After the nomination of the lily-white slate, according to Fairfax, the chairman of the Democratic executive committee said: ". . . The ticket [this] day nominated by the Democrats [is] a good ticket and we must and shall elect it cost what it will. We must elect it though we go through fire to do it—I make no declaration of war, we dont mean to hurt anybody unless there is opposition made to the election of this ticket and if there is we will quietly wipe it out or move it aside."[9] The chairman then stepped out from behind his desk, asked what

---

[7] New Orleans *Observer,* October 28, 1878, quoted in *Senate Report 855,* I: 598–99.

[8] Robert J. Walker, ibid., pp. 240–41.

[9] Alfred Fairfax to President Hayes, n.d., n.p. [New Orleans, late December

man would dare oppose the ticket, and, pointing to Fairfax, said, "There stands the great Ajax of the colored race I *know* that he will not oppose it. . . ."[10]

After the Democratic convention, white opinion split, and one faction announced their willingness to cooperate with the Blacks in a coalition ticket. This was later known as the Bland-Douglass ticket, which passed through a series of modifications before finally emerging all-white, and all-Democratic. Bland, Douglass, and their associates opposed the nomination of ex-Republicans for the plum positions of state representative and sheriff, but the Democratic executive committee accused them of drawing the color line and standing in readiness to "lead the negroes against our friends and neighbors to murder their women and children, to burn, pillage, and destroy."[11]

Several suspicious occurrences between Monday the seventh and Saturday the twelfth put Black Republicans on the alert: the sudden reimposition of the yellow fever quarantine between St. Joseph and Waterproof, rumors of impending violence, and insinuations that Fairfax invited trouble by insisting that the Republican convention meet and field a Republican slate. Fearing a late-night visitation, several of Fairfax's friends stayed at his house, armed, the night of Saturday, October 12. Walker Republicans met that same night in Fairfax's absence and decided to adopt the Bland-Douglass ticket, substituting Fairfax for its Congressional nominee. The Walker faction wanted to cancel the Republican convention set for the fourteenth, but the Fairfax faction remained adamant. A posse of armed whites from a neighboring parish visited Fairfax that night at about ten o'clock, to reason with him, they said:

. . . at Waterproof We found the [white] people of the town very much excited on account of the course pursued by Alfred Fairfax, the Radical nominee for Congress, and his followers, who had drawn the color line and were stirring up the passions of the negroes and threatening to come with five hundred armed men to override the quarantine in St. Joseph. . . .

1878], Record Group 60, Department of Justice Source-Chronological Files, President, box 6.

[10]Ibid. George T. Ruby described Fairfax as "a black man and a preacher— a man of very retiring disposition and very unobtrusive in his manners—and he never would have excited a war except for the fact that he had been nominated by the Republicans." (*Senate Report 693*, II: 48.)

[11]Lucien Bland, *Senate Report 855*, I: 200.

The Democrats of the parish had a few days before nominated their ticket, composed of two members of the legislature and a sheriff who had always acted with the Republican party, and in fact supported Hayes and Packard in 1876, but were good men and enjoy the confidence of the people. This course seemed to give umbrage to Fairfax and a few of the worst of the leaders, and they called a convention to meet in the town of St. Joseph to nominate a straight out black ticket. On account of fear of yellow fever, the town was strictly quarantined against all persons without and the authorities notified them that they would not be permitted to enter the corporate limits. To this they replied that they would come with five hundred armed men and ride down the quarantine guards. As the negroes of that parish outnumbered the whites ten to one, the white people were naturally alarmed. . . .[12]

According to this white version, Waterproof citizens feared being overrun by angry Blacks and called on the militia company under John Peck of Catahoula Parish, asking him to "come into the parish and visit Fairfax in person, and remonstrate with him and notify him that the State troops were prepared to sustain the authorities of Tensas parish." Peck agreed, and he reached Waterproof with "a few men" at about dark on Saturday evening:

He proceeded at once to the house of Fairfax, about one mile above the town, and dismounting from his horse, and suspecting no evil, walked up on the gallery for the purpose of knocking at the door. As he entered upon the gallery two shots were fired from the house, and he fell dead. The few men were naturally infuriated, and returning the shots, unfortunately wounded three negroes in the house, but immediately repented and spared their lives. They then immediately returned with the body of Captain Peck to his home in Catahoula.

The next day the lately Republican parish judge issued a warrant for Fairfax's arrest, but he lacked sufficient force to overcome possible resistance and waited for reinforcements: "The negroes are congregating about the town of Waterproof, from this parish [Concordia] and Tensas, with arms and threats to sack the town. State troops have been summoned from this and neighboring parishes, and it is hoped that a sufficient force will be assembled to overcome the negroes and disperse them without further bloodshed."[13]

---

[12]Natchez *Democrat*, October 15, 1878, quoted in New Orleans *Republican*, October 19, 1878, Record Group 60, Department of Justice Source-Chronological Files, Louisiana, box 434.

[13]Ibid.

The preceding white account of Peck's visit bears little in common with that of a Black witness who was inside Fairfax's house at the time:

I had been sick there all day Saturday [October 12] with a severe pain in my side. About four o'clock I got up and walked down town. After going down town—I didn't stay very long—I went back up to Mr. Fairfax's, where I very often staid. A friend of mine staid there. He was my brother-in-law. Between nine and eight o'clock Mrs. Ladd a friend who was spending the summer with the Fairfaxes was standing at the door, when she saw some gentlemen coming over the levee. She says to Mrs. Fairfax, "Who is them coming over the levee yonder?" I do not believe that Mrs. Fairfax returned any answer. Another girl came and said, "Here is a whole lot of men." Mrs. Fairfax looked and said, "There is, for a fact. I wonder what they want." When they got up to the hall-door they entered on the steps. They had guns with them till they looked like a small army. The captain—at least he seemed the leading one among them—he came up and inquired, "Is Mr. Fairfax at home?" Mrs. Fairfax said, "Yes; what do you want?" They returned no answer. Mr. Fairfax stood next to the kitchen-door, in the next room. The captain of the men said, "Yonder is the son of a bitch now," and then fired at him. Other firing followed. They called the man who fired the first time "Captain Peck." I thought they would shoot me next. I raised up a little in bed; the shot fired at Fairfax didn't hit him. Willie Singleton was standing by the side of the door next to a bureau. Peck said to him, "You son-of-a-bitch, what are you standing here for?" . . . They went up to him and shot him; he fell to the floor, and while he was lying there on the floor they emptied five or six more shots into him. Mr. Kemp was standing in the hall, and he said, "Look under the bed; maybe Fairfax has got under the bed." For as soon as the first shot was fired at him Fairfax had got out of the house, and in the confusion they didn't see where he had gone. They looked under the bed and they found me. Of course, I came right out partly, and partly they pulled me out. I was mighty scared, I tell you. I said, "O, no, boss; this isn't Mr. Fairfax." Then he grabbed at me here . . . and turned his face and shot me. It was Mr. Goldman that shot me. He wrestled with me, and wrestled until we got near the door; about turning the corner of the door I twisted his pistol out of his hand. . . . There was never a shot fired from the house; but from the outside of the house the shots just rained in. I tell you, sir, Peck was shot by his own party—by some of the men outside of the house. He was living when he went out of that house.[14]

At about eleven o'clock on Sunday the thirteenth, about twenty-five or thirty armed white men rode up to Fairfax's church

---

[14]Fleming Branch, *Senate Report 855*, I: 178–80.

to serve the warrant for his arrest. Their appearance alarmed the congregation, and men and women fled, crying, "They are after Mr. Fairfax again." Many of the Black men went home for their guns and stood guard over the church and Fairfax's house. They thought the vigil necessary, having recognized some of the posse attempting to arrest Fairfax on Sunday from the "little army" of the night before.[15]

Nonetheless, the Republican convention met as planned on Monday the fourteenth, outside St. Joseph on the "Miller place," whose manager was a particularly intrepid Black man named Ross. By now many Blacks were backing down from association with the Republican convention, but Ross dismissed the Democrats' "talking the same hard talk there as they were on the river." He had been threatened before, Ross said, "but it didn't work." The more cautious Walker faction gathered at the "Hard Bargain place," while the bitter-enders around Fairfax met at Ross's Miller place.[16]

Both meetings approved the Bland-Douglass ticket with certain modifications. The Fairfax meeting nominated Black Republicans for congressman—Fairfax was the Congressional candidate—justices of the peace, and constables. The Walker assemblage was less assertive and only nominated Fairfax for Congress, accepting the rest of the Bland-Douglass nominees, who were white Democrats. Then Fairfax went off to Vidalia to get his ballot printed. In his absence a vicious bulldozing campaign persuaded the Bland-Douglass men to remove all the Black nominees from their ticket. Once Fairfax had left, he did not return to Tensas (at least not until mid-1879), nor was his ballot used in the election.

During the interim between the issue of the warrant for Fairfax's arrest and the Republican convention, which most of the five or six hundred Black men attended armed, the whites of Waterproof and St. Joseph sent to neighboring parishes and to Mississippi for help. On Tuesday, October 15, armed whites came into Tensas from Mississippi with a cannon, which fortunately they did not use against people. Shotguns and pistols, however, had free rein. At "Bass place" a skirmish occurred when armed whites fired on a group of Blacks running away from them. In the disorder that followed, a cotton gin burned, for which the bulldozers hanged a

---

[15]New Orleans *Observer*, quoted in ibid., pp. 598–99.
[16]Alfred Fairfax, *Senate Report 855*, I: 773; Robert Walker, ibid., pp. 240–41.

Black man named Miller on the spot, even though the sheriff was present and could have taken the man into custody.

The first political consequences of the bulldozing were Fairfax's exile and his removal from the Bland-Douglass ticket. Walker and Stewart were enormously relieved, mistakenly assuming that Fairfax's absence would restore peace. But once the alarm had spread beyond the immediate environs of St. Joseph and Waterproof, rumors of bulldozing and Negro insurrection circulated wildly. Whites ignored the political origins of the crisis and resorted to arms in fear of a Black uprising.

Planters from outside Waterproof rallied to the aid of their fellow citizens whom they thought were endangered by rampaging Blacks. Whites from Natchez crossed the Mississippi to support whites in Tensas, but they soon returned, considerably annoyed at the grossly exaggerated hue and cry. (One Natchez man suffered a bruised nose—someone had stepped on his face when he fell asleep on the forward deck of the boat.) Justifying their alarm, a Tensas planter replied that Blacks all over the parish were arming in support of their beleaguered leader:

On the night of the 15th the negroes here on Lake St. Joseph received notice by courier that their chief, Fairfax, was surrounded by whites and all being butchered, and to come to his assistance at once. —The drum was beaten by the many clubs, and that night not less than one thousand men were armed on this lake, and ready to march, only awaiting a leader. Next morning they were riding up and down the road in squads of from twenty to fifty, threatening to burn and kill, and nothing but the want of a leader and the knowledge that the town was well filled with white troops, kept them away.[17]

Tensas whites also insisted that armed Blacks were entering Tensas from Mississippi and Concordia Parish.[18] It is extremely doubtful that any large body of armed Blacks was abroad after the Miller-place convention. They were woefully underarmed and very wary of furnishing bulldozers with even the semblance of a pretext for further retribution. Already on the night of Saturday the twelfth, the first large group of armed men had entered the parish with Peck and fired into Fairfax's house. Between October 12 and the election on November 5, some five hundred armed whites circulated throughout Tensas from Franklin, Cata-

---

[17]Natchez Daily *Democrat*, October 23, 1878.
[18]Ibid., October 19, 1878.

houla, Concordia, and other neighboring parishes.[19]

Once the fusionists adopted the Bland-Douglass ticket at the October 17 meeting—it was then known as the Country People's ticket—prominent Blacks in Tensas were warned that if they supported the ticket they would be killed. Despite the threats, a sizable number of fusionist voters turned out for the election. The Country People's ticket lost, its supporters charged, only because it had been "counted out." Their tickets were yellow, the Democrats' purple, and observers concluded that the ballot boxes, in which the top layer of ballots was solidly purple, had been illegally stuffed after the closing of the polls. The campaign ultimately resulted in a Democratic victory.[20]

Alfred Fairfax left Waterproof on October 19, smuggled onto a Mississippi River boat disguised as a woman. In New Orleans he joined the growing ranks of political refugees from the parishes. Their number increased steadily throughout the election campaign and was swollen by the witnesses subpoenaed to testify before the federal grand jury in December. These witnesses, too, became permanent exiles in New Orleans, where they soon constituted the core of Kansas-migration enthusiasts.

Blacks reacted immediately to the election "troubles" of 1878 by writing to Washington about the deplorable conditions in Louisiana. Fairfax sent a detailed account of the bulldozing in Tensas Parish to President Hayes. He listed the names of thirteen murdered Blacks and the circumstances surrounding their deaths. From Caddo Parish, R. J. Cromwell, president of the Negro Cooperative Aid Association, also wrote to Hayes. Five days after the election, he said, Blacks were still being killed, and Shreveport was full of refugees from the countryside.[21] Henry Adams described the outrages in Caddo and Bossier parishes to Attorney General Charles Devens, closing his letter with a plea for emigration: "I trust God that the United States will give us some territory to our

---

[19]*Senate Report 855*, I: xvi–xvii; Alfred Fairfax to President Hayes, n.d., n.p. [New Orleans, late December 1878], Record Group 60, Department of Justice Source-Chronological Files, President, box 6; Natchez Daily *Democrat*, October 19, 1878.

[20]J. Ross Stewart, *Senate Report 855*, I: 345; Elijah Warfield, ibid., p. 170.

[21]R. J. Cromwell to President Hayes, Shreveport, Louisiana, [about November 10, 1878], Record Group 60, Department of Justice Source-Chronological Files, President, box 6.

selves—and let us leave these Slave holders to work their own land, for they are killing our race by the hundred every day and night."[22] Adams earned a measure of vindication from the election troubles, for they reawoke Blacks to their precarious existence in the South; in the wake of the disorder, Adams wrote, "now we have thousands and thousands of colored people more anxious to go to Liberia."[23]

Whether or not they inclined toward migration, Blacks almost unanimously favored an appeal to the federal government for protection of their constitutional rights. In New Orleans, the Young Men's Protective Union (the *crème de la crème* of New Orleans Blacks) issued a ringing "Address to the People of the United States." The appeal listed the names of several men who had been killed in the campaign: Daniel Hill and Herman Bell of Ouachita Parish; Commodore Smallwood, Charles Carrol, John Higgins, and Washington Hill of Concordia Parish; Charles Bethel, Robert Williams, Munday Hill, James Stafford, Louis Postlewaite, and William Henry of Tensas Parish. It charged the Democratic regime with condoning their "extermination":

Our model State Government, in violation of law as well as good faith, has quietly acquiesced in these proceedings, and under that favor, the enemies of order have not been brought to justice, but allowed to roam at large, flaunting with impunity, their bloody standard in the face of civilization. The above summary is enough to show beyond controversy, that the corner stone of [the] Southern creed, consists in the gradual but relentless extermination of the negro race.[24]

The Address asked President Hayes to "rectify these unparallel outrages upon American citizens," Congress to "enact such laws as will remedy the present outrages upon the civil and political rights of Republican citizens of the South," and the courts to "punish without distinction of position, wealth or pedigree, these lawless men who dye their hands in innocent blood, or those who aid and abet the same." In short, it wanted "the plain and fearless

---

[22]Henry Adams to U.S. Attorney General Charles Devens, Shreveport, Louisiana, November 11, 1878, Record Group 60, Department of Justice Source-Chronological Files, Louisiana, box 434.

[23]Henry Adams to William Coppinger, Shreveport, Louisiana, November 16, 1878, *Am. Col. Soc. Papers*, Ser. IA, 233: 122–23.

[24]New Orleans Weekly *Louisianian*, December 28, 1878.

enforcement of the constitution and laws, considering that to be the most dignified and effective method of settling questions of violence which their provisions cover."[25]

Many Southern whites drew other conclusions; in light of the election outrages of 1878 in Louisiana and elsewhere in the South, they felt, Black voters must be disfranchised. Since Blacks were the primary support of the Republican party in the South, as well as the "inferior race," disfranchisement presumably would eliminate both racial and partisan conflict. Even so, warned the Natchez *Democrat,* a moderate Democratic newspaper, advocates of disfranchisement should be on their guard, since some Northern "radicals" eager to weaken the South's position in Congress were also ready to countenance the separation of Blacks from their votes. (James G. Blaine, in his December speech in the Senate on election irregularities in the South, remarked that the deeper question about de facto Black disfranchisement was "whether the white voter of the North shall be equal to the white voter of the South in shaping the policy and fixing the destiny of this country. . . ."[26] He showed how the vote of a former Rebel counted for more, with Blacks effectively disfranchised, than did the vote of a former Union soldier. This disparity, rather than Black disfranchisement, earned Blaine's concern.)

Wary of weakening Southern representation in Congress, the *Democrat* proposed an alternate plan that would assure political peace, full representation in Congress, and lily-white government. First, the Blacks must heed the lessons of the Louisiana election outrages

[which] we think, should be enough to determine the colored people to attend to their own business and to let the quarrels of politicians severely alone. If they are not aggressive they may rely upon the right thinking white men of the South to protect them in all their rights. If they allow themselves to be led by every aspiring politician into riots and outrages, they must expect the consequences.[27]

---

[25]Ibid.

[26]New York *Times,* December 12, 1878.

[27]Natchez Daily *Democrat,* October 19, 1878. The *Democrat* blamed the victims of bulldozing for perpetrating it in an exercise of inverted reasoning common among Southern whites. On October 18 the *Democrat* had written that "our conclusion, from what we have personally seen, is that while the colored people of Tensas and some of the adjoining parishes, have acted in such an imprudent and threatening manner as to cause serious apprehensions on the part of the white

Exhorting Blacks to forsake their false leaders, the *Democrat* then urged them to place their trust voluntarily in the "better class" of whites, whose interests they shared. Blacks could then continue to vote and the South would lose no representation in Congress. At best, the plan advocated nothing short of political serfdom for Black voters; yet, according to the *Democrat*, it was solidly based on the natural order of things, in which the "most vigorous" race must always rule. As for Blacks,

. . . let them lay aside for the present at least all political aspiration, and allow the united white men to do what it is utter folly for the negro to resist, and dictate the political complexion of the country. The history of the whole South since the emancipation of the negro has shown that the white man will be the controlling power in the country. —The resistance of the colored man to this fiat of nature has led to all the troubles between the races, and in one shape or another the conflict will continue just as long as the colored race aspire to be the governing power. It is all very well to preach up the abstract principles of equal rights, and the will of the majority, &c., but since the creation of the world the most vigorous have always governed, and the same will be the case until its end.[28]

The *Democrat* thus joined in one plan the two favorite themes of conventional wisdom, the Social Darwinists' survival-of-the-fittest and the New South's identity-of-interest.

Needless to say, Blacks unanimously rejected the *Democrat*'s reasoning. In mass meetings, conventions, petitions to Washington, and letters to newspaper editors, Blacks appealed for the protection rather than the abrogation of their suffrage. In one of the clearest and most succinct responses to specious arguments for Black disfranchisement, the "Address to the People of the United States" of the Young Men's Protective Union called for the enforcement of the laws:

We are uncompromisingly opposed to any scheme looking to the disfranchisement of our race. We indulge the conviction that the offenses committed against, and all assaults made upon American citizenship, can be checked in the South as they are in the North, if the laws are properly

---

people of the parish, there has been no probability at any time of a dangerous outbreak."

[28]Ibid., November 29, 1878.

enforced. The offenders should be brought to justice, and the duty of the Government in the premesis then, is unmistakable.[29]

The Protective Union spoke the mind of the race when it called disfranchisement a "damnable policy."

The outcry from Black and white Republicans over the elections of 1878 in Louisiana, Mississippi, and South Carolina bore fruit in the United States Senate in December, when Senator Blaine proposed an investigation of the election disorders. Senator Henry M. Teller chaired the committee. A subcommittee took testimony in New Orleans early in January 1879 from many of the United States grand jury witnesses, Black and white, who were intimately involved in the violence as victims and perpetrators.

The Teller committee recommended that Congress exercise powers given it by Article I of the Constitution, which allows it to make laws or alter state legislatures' regulations pertaining to the manner of holding Congressional elections. The committee also advised the mandating of provisions for enforcement of federal election laws, for it did not expect the states under review to comply voluntarily with such laws.[30] (Congress took no legislative action to this end until 1890 when the Senate killed the Lodge election law by filibuster.[31]) But the elections of 1878 affected nonlegislative activity in Washington and New Orleans with the Windom Resolution and the Louisiana constitutional convention. The campaign's unadulterated violence alerted Blacks in the lower Mississippi Valley that bulldozing would accompany politics as long as they pretended to any political autonomy, New Departure or no.

---

[29]New Orleans Weekly *Louisianian,* December 28, 1878.

[30]*Senate Report 855,* I: xlvi.

[31]The 1890 Federal Elections Bill of Congressman Henry Cabot Lodge of Massachusetts would have provided federal supervision of Congressional elections —and hence of any other contests occurring at the same time. Democrats in Louisiana foresaw that possibility in the 1870s and separated local and state elections from federal polls. The Lodge bill passed the House but was shunted aside and killed in the Senate by a combination of Southern filibusters, high tariff advocates, silver Republicans, merchant groups, and Mugwumps. Supported by Colored Farmers' Alliancemen and opposed by Southern (white) Farmers' Alliancemen, the issue split the agrarian movement in the South racially at the time when it was beginning to form a third party.

14

The Windom Resolution and the Louisiana Constitutional Convention

Thanks to their sweeping and largely illegitimate victories in the 1878 elections, Southern Democrats held the reins of government more securely than they had since before the war. Emboldened by their show of strength in Louisiana, the new, heavily Democratic state legislature voted early in 1879 to restore to political life its right order, by reshaping the state's constitution to expunge all traces of Radical Reconstruction. While Democrats exulted in their triumphs, a few Republicans in Washington remembered the Blacks, who faced a bleak future. In the United States Senate, Senator William Windom of Minnesota introduced a resolution encouraging Black migration out of the South. On the banks of the Mississippi River, Black millenarians acted on their faith.

When Senator Windom introduced his resolution on Black migration in the Senate on January 16, 1879, he had no idea of the potent emigration movement already existing on the grass roots level in the South. Moved by the apparent inability of the federal government to protect Black civil rights in the South, Windom read into the *Congressional Record:*

Resolved, That with a view to the peaceful adjustment of all questions relating to suffrage, to the effective enforcement of constitutional and natural rights, and to the promotion of the best interests of the whole country, by the elimination of sectionalism from politics, a committee of seven Senators be appointed by the Chair, and charged with the duty of inquiring as to the expediency and practicability of encouraging and promoting by all just and proper methods the partial migration of colored persons from those States and congressional districts where they are not allowed to freely and peacefully exercise and enjoy their constitutional rights as American citizens, into such States as may desire to receive them and will protect them in said rights, or into such Territory or Territories of the United States as may be provided for their use and occupation; and if said committee shall deem such migration expedient and practicable, that they report by bill or otherwise what in their judgment is the most effective method of accomplishing that objective; and that said committee have leave to sit during the recess.[1]

Newspapers gave the resolution considerable attention, some endorsing it, others denouncing it. In New Orleans, political refugees and "representative colored men" reacted immediately and positively.

The political refugees in New Orleans had already drawn up a petition to Congress by January 20, 1879, just a few days after the resolution was introduced in Washington. It was based in part on the Windom Resolution, and it delineated Black grievances and solicited Congressional aid in leaving Louisiana for the West—Kansas, in particular. Shortly afterward, J. Henri Burch held a meeting of colored "leading men" that warmly endorsed the Windom Resolution but did not mention Kansas.[2]

For their part, the "representative colored men" welcomed the scheme Burch presented. He was in close touch with their Washington counterparts who had attended a January 22 meeting with Senator Windom. With Howard University law professor Richard T. Greener as their spokesman, they explained their plan for a special but not legally exclusive Black territory. By filling the territorial offices with prominent Black men—former political figures and high office holders from the South—they expected to attract working-class Blacks from the South, for "the people thus encouraged would naturally follow their leaders."[3] The location of this territory remained indeterminate, although vague references in discussion and Senatorial debate mentioned Arizona or part of

---

[1] *Congressional Record*, United States Senate, 45th Congress, 3d session, p. 483

[2] New Orleans *Times*, January 20, 21, 25, 1879.

[3] New York *Times*, January 23, 1879.

the Indian Territory.[4] Neither the "leading men" nor Windom ever considered Kansas, for they envisioned a territory in which Blacks could be appointed to office from Washington. Indeed, Kansas, by virtue of its statehood, elected officers, and white majority, negated this central feature of the scheme. Respectable Blacks' interest in the Black territory, which emerged from the Windom Resolution, stood utterly distinct from the enthusiasm for Kansas prevalent among the New Orleans political refugees and its kindred movement in the rural parishes.

The Windom Resolution later bore considerable blame for the Kansas Fever Exodus that welled up from the rural parishes and counties of Louisiana and Mississippi. But in fact that Exodus grew from the Kansas Fever idea, which promised all Black people who wanted to go to Kansas free transportation, free land in Kansas, and free supplies and subsistence for the first year from the federal government. The movement surged up the Mississippi River in mid-March 1879, about a month after the Windom Resolution had been debated in the Senate. The relation between the Exodus and the resolution was not as direct as their chronological proximity seems to indicate, however. The provisions of the Kansas Fever idea stemmed from a predilection that freedpeople shared with most other Americans—soliciting Congress for aid.[5] Their readi-

---

[4] *Congressional Record,* Senate, 45th Cong., 3d sess., pp. 1077–82.

[5] I use the word "idea" in the phrase "Kansas Fever idea" as a synonym for myth, in the anthropological sense. It means a coherent and identifiable set of beliefs that interpreted the world and explained away unacceptable facts. The Kansas Fever myth allowed its adherents to avoid an unsatisfactory chain of reasoning: (1) that their being Black gave their white neighbors certain advantages over them and that they had, in the old Dred Scott phrase, no rights a white man need respect; (2) that because of their race, political affiliation, economic weakness, and non-Euro-American culture, their local and state governments felt no obligation to defend their legal rights—hence, the unpunished bulldozing; (3) that the federal government no longer intended to enforce their constitutional rights at the expense of whites; (4) that they were left to work out what arrangements they could with local whites. This entailed a sacrifice of life and liberty that large numbers of Blacks found excessive; (5) that while migration out of the South promised the only significant amelioration of their condition, the great majority of those who wished to leave were financially incapable of doing so; (6) that therefore they must remain in the South, dispossessed of their civil rights. This conclusion contradicted their interpretation of fair play and American citizenship, and to avoid it, millenarians believed it to be untrue. The Kansas Fever myth opened to the impoverished a way out of the South to a utopia where they would know true freedom. The federal government would usher in the millennium—a time and place where their lives

ness to seek Congressional assistance has already appeared several times in this discussion; for instance, the Reverend Roundtree's abortive plan to appeal to Congress for relief for the Nicodemus settlers in 1878, and J. C. Embry's pressuring Senator Bruce to secure federal aid for migration out of the South.[6]

In Tennessee during 1875, this tendency to look to the federal government for aid blossomed into belief when a movement much like the later (1879) Kansas Fever Exodus rose, creating expectations of free government transportation, land, and supplies. A Nashville paper wrote of that movement, as many others would in 1879, "The negroes themselves do not seem to know where they got the idea, but they refuse to be argued out of it."[7] Little is known about this Kansas Fever movement of 1875, but it most certainly arose independently of the Windom Resolution (introduced in 1879). A few years later, the bulldozing surrounding the elections of 1878 redoubled Black appeals to Washington, but the background discontent had *already* moved Blacks to seek federal aid for migration.

In early November 1878, J. T. Brewington, a Black schoolteacher who had moved to Kansas, wrote to President Hayes. Before his departure from Mississippi, he said, many of his neighbors had approached him, asking him to "seek aid for them if any could be found." Since his arrival in Kansas, he had received letters saying that hundreds of Black Mississippians were "waiting to hear of some relief." Already the people were organizing colonies, trying to accumulate enough money to migrate, but their finances were woefully inadequate. Nevertheless, they had begun to take what Brewington called "the first grand step." Now they turned

---

would be transformed—by offering them free transportation to Kansas, free land, and free subsistence for the first year there. The national government, in the terms of the myth, played a salvationist role. Not only had it freed them from slavery and made them citizens, but now it could, and would, put them in a position to enjoy full citizenship.

Southern Blacks were all the more likely to appeal to Congress because their state and local governments, run by Negrophobe Democrats, showed them little sympathy. In addition, recent tradition steered them toward Washington, for they had been, in effect, the wards of the federal government, their only source of protection from vindictive local whites after the Civil War.

[6]New Orleans Weekly *Louisianian*, March 22, 1879. Embry took credit for the Windom Resolution, saying that Bruce had put him in touch with Windom about Embry's plan.

[7]Nashville *Union and American*, May 25, 1875.

to Brewington, and Brewington turned to Washington: "This is the grand step now being taken by my people the colored race, but we are in the first place entirely unable, first to reach those lands, secondly to raise means to subsist the first year, thirdly to raise means to get implements with which to commence labor or get sheltering." These were, of course, the very same three needs that the Kansas Fever idea promised to fill and for which Brewington here petitioned the president:

Now since they that I have spoken of are looking to me to seek aid and I knowing no possible way to obtain it unless it be given by our National Government must as I have given a statement of our desire to you, appeal to you . . . being aided by the good members of political parties of Congress, we will soon be on a march to a land where we can be free and enjoy liberty, not having to send up cries as the people of Macedonia for we can take the gospel with us.[8]

In terms of the spread of the Kansas Fever idea among the plain, rural people of Mississippi, this letter is far more crucial and informative than is the introduction of Senator Windom's resolution far off in Washington. It confirms that well before the resolution was brought before the Senate in January 1879, and even before the elections of 1878, some Blacks were prepared for the Kansas Fever idea. Their expectation soon grew into the certainty that government assistance was forthcoming.

Senator Windom, too, recognized that his resolution had not unleashed the Kansas Fever idea or Exodus. (Windom only hazily distinguished the millenarian Exodus from the planned migration that grew out of Kansas clubs, noting that the Exodusters—millenarians arriving in St. Louis—"seem to regard themselves as refugees from some impending calamity rather than as emigrants seeking new homes.") But after the publicity accorded the resolution had stimulated many Kansas clubs to write to him, he learned that "those people were organized and ready to go long before the resolution was presented." Windom attributed the Exodus to political violence, not to his own influence: "Many of the leaders of the movement have been interviewed at St. Louis as to its cause, and they all say that it is on account of the denial of their political and personal rights, and the hardships and gross injustice they

---

[8] J. T. Brewington to President Hayes, Emporia, Kansas, November 6, 1878, Record Group 60, Department of Justice Source-Chronological Files, President, box 6.

have suffered.'"[9] And what is more important, none of the Exodusters ever mentioned Windom or gave any indication that they knew of the resolution.

Windom was right, in the larger sense, about the motives of the Kansas Fever Exodus. But the millenarian movement, an urgent attempt to leave the South, stemmed most immediately from apprehensions about the future. Blacks feared not only repetitions of the bulldozing that 1876 and 1878 had so vividly etched in their memories, but also the Louisiana constitutional convention, which threatened to reduce their status to little better than that of slaves. The anxiety spread across state lines, affecting Mississippi and Texas as well—panic was no respecter of state boundaries.

The constitutional convention bill passed the Louisiana legislature late in January 1879, over the adamant protests of Black state senators and representatives. Certain that it augured ill for their constituents, they denounced it in debate. Representative Hawkins of Madison Parish figured among the bill's opponents "because there are hundreds and thousands of our voters who were not permitted to vote, and who will not now be permitted. The vote for delegates will not be impartial, and *there is not a member on this floor but knows that I speak the truth.*"[10] Democratic fulminations in early 1879 put Hawkins and other Blacks doubly on their guard.

Immediately following the passage of the constitutional convention legislation, for instance, the Louisiana House and Senate passed and sent to Washington a joint resolution expressing annoyance at the federal government's interference—the federal grand jury and the attempted prosecution of the election cases of 1878, and the visit of the Teller subcommittee. The resolution tersely assured the federal government that Louisiana could take care of its own affairs:

Resolved by the Senate and House of Representatives of the State of Louisiana in General Assembly convened, That the State Government is fully equal to the discharge of the duties for which governments are organized, the protection of life, liberty, and property. That the interference of the General Government in our internal affairs is a reflection

---

[9] New York Daily *Herald*, April 12, 1879.

[10] New Orleans *Southwestern Christian Advocate*, January 23, 1879. (Emphasis in original.)

upon our civilization, a reproach to republican governments, and calculated to engender bitterness and strife by intermeddling with domestic affairs which can well be adjusted by the people interested, before constituted authorities of the State.[11]

A series of resolutions still less calculated to comfort Blacks completed the statement. While the resolutions closed with the pious assurance that Louisiana made no distinctions among her citizens according to race, color, or previous condition of servitude, the preamble boldly proclaimed the conditional nature of suffrage:

Whereas, The Constitution of the United States has not conferred the right of suffrage upon any one, and the United States have no voters of their own creation in the States, but the matter of suffrage is left entirely with the States themselves.[12]

Considering the tone of these remarks, it is hardly surprising that Blacks greeted the constitutional convention with trepidation.

Throughout north Louisiana, observers found rural Blacks exceedingly apprehensive and convinced that "the convention will not only deprive them of the right of franchise, but that they will not be allowed to sell their cotton or even to pass from one plantation to another—in fact, that they will be reduced to slavery again."[13] Re-enslavement incarnated the very worst fate former slaves could imagine, and to escape it, thousands believed the Kansas Fever idea, which promised a brighter future. P. B. S. Pinchback visited Madison Parish in mid-March and discovered Exodusters flocking to the riverbanks to flee to Kansas. Pinchback found the constitutional convention a tangible cause for their dread, for "they religiously believe that the constitutional convention bodes them no good; that it has been called for the express purpose of abridging their rights and liberties. . . . They are 'fleeing from the wrath to come.' They are absolutely panic stricken."[14]

The Kansas Fever Exodus that Pinchback witnessed reached massive proportions in March just as delegates were elected for the constitutional convention. Voter turnout was exceedingly light, and thirty-two Republicans, two Nationals, two Independ-

---

[11]*Appleton's Annual Cyclopaedia . . . 1879,* p. 561.
[12]Ibid.
[13]New York Daily *Herald,* April 5, 1879.
[14]New Orleans Weekly *Louisianian,* March 15, 1879. See also St. Joseph *North Louisiana Journal,* April 12, 1879.

ents, and ninety-eight Democrats were elected.[15] Although considerable Democratic saber-rattling about curbing the Fifteenth Amendment had accompanied the decision to revise the state constitution, by the time the convention actually met in late April, the Exodus had given rise to second thoughts. Planters now faced the loss of their entire labor supply. Accordingly, the convention immediately passed a resolution meant to reassure the fleeing Blacks and appease national opinion:

Resolved, That there is no intention whatever entertained by this body of impairing or restricting the political, civil, or religious rights of any class of citizens of this State on account of race, color, or previous condition of servitude, but on the contrary the intention is to defend and maintain the rights of the United States and of this State, under the new Constitution about to be formed.[16]

When the convention adjourned in July the most sensational part of the Exodus was over. Although the specter of the convention played a central role in the rise of the Kansas Fever Exodus, the Exodus itself posed the most important obstacle to the proposed interference with Black suffrage. It proved to planters and the rest of the country that Black people cared very much for their rights. By focusing national attention on Louisiana politics, the Exodus insured that the constitutional convention would not tamper—at least not blatantly—with Black suffrage. In fact, the new constitution appeared with a provision stating that there could be "no qualification of any kind for suffrage or office, nor any restraint upon the same, on account of race, color, or previous condition. . . ."[17] However, the constitution neither envisioned nor provided for enforcement machinery.

Nor was the new constitution an entirely innocent document. Republicans criticized two of its propositions, which they thought tended indirectly to dilute the strength of the Black vote. One provision gerrymandered the senatorial and representational districts; the second changed the date of local elections, staggering them with Congressional elections and thereby avoiding any future federal supervision of state and local contests. Despite these objections, the voters accepted the constitution in early December 1879.

---

[15]*Appleton's Annual Cyclopaedia . . . 1879,* p. 564.
[16]Ibid.
[17]Ibid., p. 570; St. Joseph *North Louisiana Journal,* July 26, 1879.

The December campaign continued the terrorist trend established in the mid-1870s. Bulldozers assassinated prominent Black political figures, this time in parishes that had previously been safely Republican—Concordia and Madison—and stirred new disorder in Tensas. In the Red River parishes of Caddo, Bossier, DeSoto, and Natchitoches, Republicans were unable to organize their campaigns. Some two hundred additional political refugees sought safety in New Orleans.[18]

The bulldozing accompanying the 1879 elections marked a further step toward solidified Democratic rule in Louisiana, a process that the Exodus ultimately affected very little. In the short run, nevertheless, the Exodus staved off disfranchisement for a few more years.

---

[18]New Orleans *Southwestern Christian Advocate,* November 20 and December 11, 1879. The new constitution also included a provision forbidding amendment until 1884.

15

The Kansas Fever Exodus
of 1879

The Kansas Fever Exodus—the most remarkable migration in the United States after the Civil War—took some six thousand Blacks from Louisiana, Mississippi, and Texas to Kansas in the space of a few months.[1] Rooted in faith and in fear, the movement in Louisiana fixed upon a particular object, the constitutional convention. The motivating fear in Mississippi and Texas was no less real, although it was not focused on any concrete event. In mid-1879 a Black Texan groped toward a description of this mood of alarm among the freedpeople:

There are no words which can fully express or explain the real condition of my people throughout the south, nor how deeply and keenly they feel the necessity of fleeing from the wrath and long pent-up hatred of their old masters which they feel assured will ere long burst loose like the pent-up fires of a volcano and crush them if they remain here many years longer.[2]

Pushed by fears of damnation and pulled by belief in the Kansas

---

[1] The actual number of Exodusters who passed through St. Louis and reached Kansas, however briefly, is exceedingly difficult to figure. Charleton H. Tandy of the Colored Relief Board in St. Louis estimated that 20,000 Exodusters reached the city in 1879–80. (*Senate Report 693*, III: 68.) According to the St. Louis *Globe-Democrat*'s figures, approximately 6,206 Exodusters arrived in St. Louis between mid-March and mid-April 1879. Not all the migrants to St. Louis made it from there to Kansas, and many reaching Kansas soon moved on, sometimes to Kansas City, Missouri.

[2] C. P. Hicks to Governor St. John, Brenham, Texas, July 30, 1879, CRSF, St. John, box 10, KSHS.

Fever idea, thousands left Mississippi and Louisiana between March and May 1879, and Texas in the latter part of the year.

Although the first large groups of Exodusters arrived in St. Louis in March, the movement had been building up since the end of 1878 in Madison, Tensas, and Concordia parishes in Louisiana, and in Hinds, Warren, and Madison counties in Mississippi. In late November and early December, the *Hinds County Gazette* drew attention to the local Blacks' vivid interest in migration. In late December a Columbus, Mississippi, newspaper reported that "one thousand negroes will emigrate this season from Hinds and Madison Counties to Kansas."[3]

By February the Exodus was under way, and the characteristics that marked the millenarian movement attracted comment: the Exodusters' unshakable faith in the Kansas Fever idea and their conviction that this faith was sufficient to assure their future. Early on, for instance, a white Mississippian tried to disabuse an Exoduster of his faith in the Kansas Fever idea:

We questioned him and discovered that he knew not to what particular point he was going, knew not the value or kind of land he was to occupy, knew not the conditions on which he was to take it, and in fact knew absolutely nothing. . . . [He was] most thoroughly in the dark as to hopes for the future. All that we said did not in the least waver his belief in that a fortune awaited him in Kansas, to be gotten by his making his home there.[4]

At the same time, Exodusters showed the tenacity of their faith, even as they discovered that free transportation to Kansas fell short of their expectations. Kansas Fever had already affected many Blacks in the Delta and Vicksburg area when this report appeared in February:

The African hegira continues. . . . We learn that quite a number of negroes left Madison parish yesterday [February 27], and others are expected to follow. A few days ago a number of would-be emigrants, about sixty of them, took passage on a passing steamer for St. Louis, intending to go thence by train to Kansas. When the clerk passed around among them he found they had just enough money to pay their way to the next landing, and at the next landing they were put off, less than twenty-five miles from

---

[3] *Hinds County Gazette*, November 27 and December 11, 1878; Columbus (Miss.) *Democrat* in the New Orleans Daily *Picayune*, December 20, 1878.

[4] *Hinds County Gazette*, February 26, 1879.

their starting place. This little incident is a sufficient illustration of the improvidence and want of sagacity of the negro.[5]

The "little incident" did not in the least slow the Exodus or diminish its allure. The idea of free transportation neatly accommodated hard fact, shifting to a promise of free transportation from St. Louis, after Exodusters paid their way there (about four dollars from the Vicksburg-Delta area).

When these Exodusters arrived in St. Louis about a week later, the peculiar nature of the movement, as well as its great numbers, began to provoke comment. During the first week of March, seventy-five migrants arrived in St. Louis on the packet boats *City of Vicksburg* and *Gold Dust,* and in the South thousands more anticipated a speedy departure. Planters estimated, with some hyperbole, that fifteen hundred Exodusters had already left for Kansas. At Delta, Louisiana, P. B. S. Pinchback was astonished by the fervor of the massive crowds on the river. Arriving on March 8, he found the banks of the Mississippi "literally covered with colored people and their little store of worldly goods." Within two days, the crowd increased from about three hundred to about five hundred people. Pinchback reported "every road leading to the river . . . filled with wagons loaded with plunder and families who seem to think anywhere is better than here."[6] At the same time, a rumor spread in Mississippi that on or about March 15 "a through train, or steamboat, (the best informed do not seem to know which,) will leave Vicksburg for Kansas City, conveying all colored people who wish to go to Kansas."[7] The Exodus had begun in earnest, and poor Black families flocked to the landings on both sides of the river around Vicksburg.

Between March 12 and 16 approximately eight hundred migrants arrived in St. Louis on the *Colorado,* the *Grand Tower* (the "government boat," as the Exodusters called this Anchor Line packet boat), and the *Joe Kinney.* They continued to arrive, almost without pause, until the middle of May. The overwhelming number of people of all ages in the Exodus astonished observers, but

---

[5]Vicksburg *Herald,* February 28, 1879, quoted in St. Joseph *North Louisiana Journal,* March 8, 1879.

[6]St. Louis *Globe-Democrat,* March 7, 13, 14, 16, 1879; New Orleans Weekly *Louisianian,* March 15, 1879; St. Joseph *North Louisiana Journal,* March 8, 1879. New Orleans *Louisianian,* March 15, 1879.

[7]*Hinds County Gazette,* March 5, 1879.

the Exodusters' apparent credulity surprised them most. Exodusters had set out knowing nothing of Kansas, trusting entirely in the Kansas Fever idea. Although eyewitness descriptions often cruelly ridiculed the Exodusters' faith, they caught the special character of the movement.

One observer found the second large group of Exodusters arriving in mid-March "as needy and ignorant as their predecessors. Most of them have not sufficient means to take them to their Mecca [Kansas]. . . . They have no recognized leader and no definite plans. They say they 'want to git dar, an' dat's all.' "[8] Another witness likened the Exodusters to livestock:

[The Exodus] started among the black people themselves, how or when nobody knows, and the negroes keep their own counsel about it. Persons of limited intelligence are often not unlike unreasoning animals in the way of following blindly on a given direction in which they have been started, like a flock of sheep jumping over a fence. The migration of the blacks having begun, it is not easy to tell where it will end. Something much like a panic seems to have set in.[9]

Other observers enjoyed little more success in discovering credible motivations for the Exodus. "As to the causes of the simultaneous stampede," wrote one witness, "no definite account can be obtained. It is one of those cases where the whole thing seemed to be in the air, a kind of migratory epidemic."[10] A Northern white noted that "the timid learned that they could escape what they have come to regard as a second bondage, and they flocked together to gain the moral support which comes from numbers."[11] For another witness, the Exodus seemed "a sort of religious exaltation, during which they had regarded Kansas as a modern Canaan and the God-appointed home of the negro race."[12]

As hundreds of millenarians arrived in St. Louis on nearly every boat from the South, reporters first sought the cause in some kind of trickery. Indeed, early headlines cried, "Duped Dark-

---

[8]St. Louis *Globe-Democrat,* March 18, 1879.

[9]Cincinnati *Commercial,* quoted in ibid., March 26, 1879.

[10]Chicago Daily *Tribune,* March 28, 1879.

[11]James B. Runnion, "The Negro Exodus," *Atlantic Monthly* XLIV, no. 262 (August 1879): 223. Runnion was also an Exodus correspondent in Louisiana and Mississippi for the Chicago Daily *Tribune.*

[12]F. R. Guernsey, "The Negro Exodus," *International Review* VII, no. 4 (October 1879): 375.

ies!"[13] At first it seemed that a circular had fooled the Blacks into believing the Kansas Fever idea, and the Exodusters' illiteracy aggravated the confusion around the elusive flier. Only one hand-bill actually turned up; it was issued by a Black labor contractor in Vicksburg, warning them not to be taken in by rumors of free transportation, land, and so forth. The circular only proved that it responded to an already pervasive Kansas Fever idea.

As the Exodus surged on, observers discovered and discarded a whole panoply of so-called causes, ranging from supposed rail-road promotional fliers to an obvious burlesque of a Kansas hand-bill by "Lycurgius P. Jones."[14] When the first apparent causes of the Exodus, "lying circulars," led to a dead end, Exodus-watchers turned to "rascally colored politicians," and "emigration agents" who supposedly misled the colored people with false promises about Kansas. According to these arguments, the Blacks naively believed them all, as they had a "childlike confidence in their chosen leaders, founded partly on their primitive character."[15] But false leaders were not the answer, and there was only one real emigration agent.

The Exodus had no anointed leader. Rather than being deluded by false leaders, the Exodusters rejected leadership alto-gether. "We have found no leader to trust but the God overhead of us," said a typical group of Exodusters.[16] In New Orleans, a prospective migrant summed up their position: "Every black man is his own Moses now."[17] Exodusters refused to hear out promi-nent Blacks who contradicted their beliefs. William Murrell, a popular political figure in Madison Parish, Louisiana, found that he could not reason with millenarians about their belief in the Kansas Fever myth, even though he had visited Kansas and could offer firsthand information. He opposed the movement, and the Ex-odusters ignored him.[18]

In Texas, millenarians regarded a "representative colored

---

[13]St. Louis *Globe-Democrat,* March 12, 1879.

[14]Natchez Daily *Democrat,* April 19, 1879.

[15]James B. Runnion, "The Negro Exodus," p. 228.

[16]Chicago Daily *Tribune,* March 27, 1879. Each little group had someone who organized the actions of the group, but there was no one leader of the whole Exodus.

[17]Ibid., March 23, 1879.

[18]*Senate Report 693,* II: 258; St. Joseph *North Louisiana Journal,* March 8, 1879.

man," C. P. Hicks, with extreme skepticism as he tried to disprove the Kansas Fever idea. A white friend of Hicks wrote Governor John P. St. John of Kansas:

When Mr. Hicks read your Excellency's letter—written some ten days ago —to a large meeting of the freedmen telling them Kansas had no free land, etc., it fell like a wet blanket upon the hopes of a large class of freedmen. Many declare the letter a forgery, while others think that Hicks' misrepresentations to you, induced you to write it. . . . Now there are not any of the leading colored men here who has more influence over the masses of their people than Mr. Hicks really has, but the very moment he or other colored leaders, throw themselves against the popular wishes and tide of sentiment of their people—right then their influence begins to ebb.[19]

Once the Kansas Fever idea gained a considerable following, ministers dared not express their own misgivings or convey the reservations of Exodusters who had gone to Kansas and now counseled others at home to wait. The Reverend Mr. Middleton of the Mount Hebron Baptist Church in Vicksburg would not read letters counseling patience from the pulpit, because "the members of his congregation would not like it. They were impatient and angry at everybody who tried to interfere with them."[20] And in New Orleans, an observer learned of a fruitless attempt to dampen Kansas Fever: "An influential colored man had tried at the last emigration meeting to temper the excitement of the people, and a motion to give him a vote of thanks for attending and addressing the meeting was denied . . . had the speaker been a less popular man, he would have been mobbed."[21] "When one tries to reason with and warn them against Kansas," wrote a Northern white who had tried to correct Exodusters' unreasonable expectations, "if they fail to excuse their act of leaving home in a matter-of-fact speech, they resort to religion and the laws of destiny. If you tell them they will die, they answer as a soldier who goes into battle, that they know some must die."[22] Millenarians still clung to their faith, despite well-intentioned advice and attempts at dissuasion.

---

[19]S. A. Hackworth to Governor St. John, Brenham, Texas, August 4, 1879, CRSF, St. John, box 10, KSHS. Hackworth pointed out the "suspicious ideas and character" of the millenarians.

[20]Chicago Daily *Tribune,* May 2, 1879.

[21]Ibid., May 23, 1879.

[22]Ibid.

Unscrupulous leadership was not at the heart of the Exodus, nor were "emigration agents," the favorite explanation of the Southern white press. Most often the "emigration agents" were merely local Blacks asking themselves why, indeed, they should stay in the South. But various Black men, and a Madame Walker in Texas, traveled about, lecturing on the Exodus.[23] James Caldwell even wrote to President Hayes for validation of his work:

I am well received by the Colored people. They have been hoping for such terms as I offer them to move to Kansas, for they are, many of them, in distress notwithstanding they have made the wealth of the South for which they now receive no thanks. They are treated by the white people as though they were under obligations to the whites.

I left the State of Louisiana the 1st of May where we were badly treated by the white people. Four of us, the writer one of them, was taken out of the Church and beaten until the blood ran down our backs. We did more good work in Mississippi. I ask you for authority over your own signature (if you deem such necessary) to continue to address the Colored people and advise them to go to Kansas.[24]

Caldwell's is a unique case, however, for he was an admitted emigration agent, offering "terms" for prospective migrants. Later on, in the summer and fall, when the Kansas Fever Exodus was widely known, swindlers and con men moved through areas where the fever prevailed, taking advantage of the interest and confusion surrounding the subject. Then, ill-informed Blacks were susceptible to hoaxes.

As an original stimulus to the Exodus, the role of drummers was negligible; at most, they may have helped keep the Exodus going. Terrorism and poverty lay at the root of the Exodus, and a Black Mississippian identified them as the reputed emigration agents: "The National government has stood idly by and refused to protect us against lawlessness, and to-day the blood of 5000 innocent colored martyrs calls from the ground and arouses us to action. These are the 'agents' and 'free homes.' "[25]

White observers of the Exodus finally came to realize what

---

[23]Denison Daily *News,* September 27, 1879.

[24]James Caldwell to President Hayes, Bowling Green, Kentucky, June 26, 1879, Record Group 60, Department of Justice Source-Chronological Files, President, box 7. Caldwell was probably a combination labor contractor and migration conductor.

[25]Samuel W. Winn, Enterprise, Mississippi, New Orleans *Southwestern Christian Advocate,* May 29, 1879.

Blacks had known all along: no frivolous motives propelled the phenomenon. The Exodusters' implacable determination not to return to the South, despite the cold and hunger, despite their discovery that there was no free transportation to Kansas and no free land, and despite offers of free transportation back to the South, etched a deep impression on witnesses. A St. Louis reporter, for instance, asked a woman with a child at her breast if she would consent to going back to the South. "What, go back!" she exclaimed. "Oh, no; I'd sooner starve here!"[26] The same firm refusal to return home marked a dialogue between an old man and the people who had come up with him, as they learned the empty reality of the Kansas Fever idea:

"Childer," addressed an aged darky to the rest of the company, "this genneman 'forms us what we have 'ready larned—that we've been fooled about that raillerd and land and mewl biz. And then this yar genneman asks us whether we'd not go back to Egypt. Childer, I've been gibben him de 'wing of old Missippi. I knows what you thinks, and I told him you'd rader jine hands and walk into Jordan's tide. And was I not right, childer?" And the "childer" all said "yes."[27]

They had, after all, escaped the South.

From the very beginning of the Exodus, Black onlookers pointed to political terrorism as the immediate cause, and they cast about very little for additional motives. In fact, bulldozing offered an entirely sufficient explanation. Most of the Exodusters interviewed by reporters and refugee-relief workers could provide firsthand accounts of blood-chilling violence within the last few years. At a mass meeting held on March 17 by St. Louis Blacks to collect money, food, and clothing for the Exodusters stranded there, the very first addresses were given by migrants from the South. A former state senator from Louisiana, Andrew Pollard, stressed that Exodusters were not migrants, but refugees "fleeing from oppression and bondage."[28] The Reverend J. D. Daniels, also from Louisiana, explained that Exodusters "were not emigrating because of inducements held out to them by parties in Kansas, but

---

[26]St. Louis *Globe-Democrat*, March 14, 1879.

[27]Ibid.

[28]Ibid., March 18, 1879. Pollard was helping Exodusters bring their household effects to the river landings when a group of whites blamed the Exodus on him and forced him to board the boat with the Exodusters.

because they were terrorized, robbed, and murdered by the bull-dozing desperadoes of Louisiana and Mississippi."[29] And Blacks persistently stressed this theme throughout the life of the movement.

Once they understood that Exodusters were not duped into leaving their homes by unprincipled leaders or emigration agents, some whites began listening to their stories of terrorism. But Exodusters' testimonies concerning bulldozing showed that the violence which had occurred in the immediate past—such as the hanging of two Black men in Vicksburg at the beginning of the movement—was a white response to the Exodus, not its cause; planters attempting to stop the Exodus assassinated men whom they suspected of encouraging the movement.[30] An Exoduster from Warren County, Mississippi, told of an incident in Grand Gulf in which a mob of thirty-five whites tried to stop Blacks from going to Kansas by seizing them at night and beating them.[31] Such Exodus-inspired crimes recurred as whites sought to halt the migration, but, as one might expect, the result was just the opposite of the perpetrators' intentions.

In addition to violence directly related to the Exodus, millenarians told of bulldozing incidents stretching back over several years. Of particular import was the violence that had occurred in the northern parishes of Louisiana and adjacent areas in Mississippi in 1878. Frederick Marshall, from Natchez, Mississippi (right across the river from Vidalia in Concordia Parish), told of being taken out of his house by nightriders:

Just before Christmas, 1878, three or four men came to my house to kill me, and I run out of the way; just before daylight they came there and wanted matches; after they came in the house I ran out doors and staid out the rest of the night; they went away; didn't know the men; they said they would kill me, and had a rope around my neck, and said they were going to kill all the smart men, and I told them I didn't know anything.[32]

Marshall arrived in St. Louis in mid-March 1879, and his fairly representative testimony merits closer scrutiny.

Marshall's immediate reaction to violence was very much like that of other rural Blacks—he left home to hide in the woods.

---

[29]Ibid.
[30]Ibid., March 31, 1879.
[31]C. H. Tandy, *Senate Report 693*, III: 43.
[32]Ibid., p. 53.

When the trouble passed, he returned home. He did not immediately take his family to the riverbanks and flee to Kansas. He left months later, citing terrorism as one of his main reasons for going. For Frederick Marshall, as for most Exodusters, bulldozing was a basic, but not immediate, cause for leaving Mississippi. The immediate cause was a vivid fear of future violence, stemming from remembrance of past terrorism. The memory of bulldozing combined with the memory of slavery to produce the threat of evils to come. That threat goaded the Exodusters forward with urgency.

Their fear of future evil and their dread of renewed slavery were intertwined. The Reverend W. D. Lynch, who worked extensively with Exodusters in Kansas, believed that "the mainspring of all this exodus movement" lay in the conviction of Blacks in the South that "slavery is not dead, but sleeping in disguise, as [if] it were a wolf in sheep's clothing."[33] Other freedpeople felt that the Democrats would reinstitute slavery, making it impossible for Blacks ever to leave the South. Henry Adams voiced this common fear that "the Democrats, as the Slave Holders, of the South will fix it so that we can not get from the South to the North unless we run away, for we Believed that not any colored man will be allowed to Leave the South without a Pass."[34] One migrant saw the resurgence of the Democratic party as motivating the Exodusters' urgent flight:

Dere wan't no time to lose. A little while back de Democrats got hold o' one end o' Congress, an' now dey's got de odder end. The Democrat party was de party dat kep' us in slavery, an' de Republican party was de party dat sot us free. When de party dat set us free goes out, an' de party dat kep' us in slavery comes in, it's time for de nigger to look out for himself. Constitutional Amendments an' all dem things us very nice for de white man to talk about, but it's mighty risky business for us.[35]

---

[33]The Reverend W. D. Lynch, Topeka, Kansas, New Orleans *Southwestern Christian Advocate*, July 22, 1880.

[34]Henry Adams to William Coppinger, New Orleans, Louisiana, April 28, 1879, *Am. Col. Soc. Papers*, Ser. IA, 234: 78. Apropos of having to steal away out of the South, a letter from Topeka, Kansas, printed in the Chicago Daily *Inter-Ocean* of December 30, 1879, reported the following: "The negroes who arrive here daily now almost all report that they did not dare make their intentions known before leaving the South, and in many cases that they have traveled by night on foot until the limits of their State were reached, fearing to travel by public conveyance."

[35]New York Daily *Herald*, April 17, 1879.

Bulldozing, slavery, Democratic government, Blacks knew all three from hard experience, and that knowledge propelled the Exodus.

The Kansas Fever idea offered a helping hand to the very poor, who would otherwise languish in the South, condemned to damnation; for no matter how urgently Blacks sought to leave the South, without money they were doomed to stay. An itinerant Black preacher described their frustrations: "We colored people have heard from that country [Kansas], and we are very anxious to go there." Even though they had labored since the end of the war, he explained, "we never realize a nickle from our cotton. The white folks take all."[36] Blacks had been saying this for years. A young Black woman in Mississippi summarized their predicament: "The way we are paid for labor in Miss. there will be very few of us that will be able to come without aid."[37] The Kansas Fever idea provided the promise of that aid.

The various rumored permutations of the Kansas Fever idea puzzled observers who were often at a loss to understand the causes of the Exodus.[38] They went wrong in examining the content of the rumors and the idea, and in trying to match them to the movement that seemed to follow. But the import of the Kansas Fever idea was not to be found in the exact nature of its promises, but in their function. The existence of the idea provided a means for leaving the South that impoverished Exodusters otherwise would have lacked entirely. It served as an enabling factor, supplying the missing link between renewed slavery and assured freedom, and closing the yawning chasm between what some Exodusters deemed the "young hell" of Mississippi and Louisiana and the "promised land," Kansas. This explains why when Exodusters

---

[36]The Reverend Henry Smith to Governor St. John, Marshall, Texas, May 7, 1879, CRSF, St. John, box 10, KSHS.

[37]Roseline Cunningham to Governor St. John, West Point, Mississippi, June 1, 1879, ibid.

[38]A rumor reported from Vicksburg, Mississippi, in March 1879 said that "the negroes in this part of the country have the 'Kansas Fever.' They have, in a manner, quit work, and are preparing to go to Kansas with Gen. Sherman, who is now in New Orleans with his troops, so they say. The report is that the United States Government has set Kansas apart as a negro State, and will give every family free land and $500 in money, build houses, etc., and all that are here after the 15th of March will be killed by order of President Hayes, who has turned Democrat." (New York *Tribune*, quoted in St. Louis *Globe-Democrat*, March 21, 1879.)

learned on the Mississippi River banks or in St. Louis that there was no free transportation, no free land, no General Sherman, and no Negro state, it made no difference whatsoever. They still meant to leave the South, and once disembarked in St. Louis, they would not go back.

St. Louis occupied a pivotal position in the mythology of the Exodus. It linked the two parts of the idea, negative and positive, slavery and freedom. The first step, and the most decisive, took Exodusters out of the South, beyond the grasp of re-enslavement. Arriving in Kansas, where there had never been any slavery and where salvation awaited, represented the final step. If they only got out of the South, Exodusters would automatically reach Kansas on the strength of their belief in the idea. The crucial point was St. Louis. When Exodusters reached that city they were out of danger: they had done their part. St. Louis was like the Red Sea, explained an Exoduster, drawing a parallel between Southern Black people and the Israelites:

. . . we's like de chilun ob Israel when dey was led from out o' bondage by Moses. De chilun ob Israel was a promised to be sot free by Pharoah, but wen Pharoah got over his skear he sot 'em back agin to makin' bricks out o' straw. Den Moses he said dat shouldn't be de case, an' he took 'em out o' bondage, and wen dey was all awaverin' an' mighty feared he took 'em 'cross de Red Sea an' den dey was safe. Now chile, jes' listen to me. Dis is our Red Sea, right hyah in St. Louis, atween home an' Kansas, an' if we sticks togeder an' keeps up our faith we'll git to Kansas and be out o' bondage for shuah. We's been sot free by Massa Linkum, but it war jes' sich another sot free as Pharoah gib de chilen of Israel. You heah me, chile, dem as is awaverin' an' is a'feared is goin' to sink in dis hyah Red Sea. . . .[39]

To reach safety, they needed only to stick together and keep up their faith.

The Old Testament analogy has long held special significance for American Black people, and the identification of Afro-Americans with the Children of Israel transcends the Kansas Fever Exodus. The themes of "Black Moses," "Go Down Moses," "Let My People Go," "The Land of Bondage," and so forth are still familiar and evocative. In the Kansas Fever Exodus, Kansas was often termed the "Negro Canaan," or the "Promised Land." Beyond

[39]St. Louis *Globe-Democrat,* March 19, 1879.

providing colorful terminology for the Exodus, the identification between Blacks and the biblical Chosen People enhanced many Blacks' conviction that the time had come for them to be taken out of the South. Many anticipated that day's arrival as simply a matter of time. A white Texan termed this conviction "religious fanaticism" and said many hard-working Black men he knew refused to buy real property in the South "because they have believed since their emancipation some general movement would eventually be made to take them out of the South. . . . all freedmen seemed to be embued with the idea that God has foreordained that they shall be made a great people whereby he will manifest to all nations His great power, etc."[40] These beliefs and expectations reinforced Kansas Fever, for they laid the groundwork for the time when the move would be possible. The Kansas Fever Exodus was the fruit of faith in an idea, but the Exodusters' belief was functional, selective, and strong. Yet it was no match for the determination of white Southerners and St. Louis merchants to stem the tide of migration before the region was emptied of its traditional work force and its agricultural economy ruined.

From the first moment Exodusters appeared on the banks of the Mississippi River on their way to Kansas, Southern whites tried to halt the movement. Newspapers ran letters from railroad companies insisting that they offered free transportation to the purchasers of their land but to no others. Later, letters from migrants unhappy in Kansas filled column after column. But this propaganda effort was no more effective than face-to-face conversations with Exodusters.

To keep Exodusters at home, white Southerners resorted to several techniques, most of which were not as gentle as verbal persuasion. Yet the planters' two favorite methods, imprisonment for debt and brute force, did not significantly impede the Exodus. In the end, only the refusal of riverboats to stop for Exodusters and their slow starvation on the banks of the Mississippi broke the movement's momentum.

For the entire duration of the Exodus, Blacks arriving in St. Louis and Kansas described coercive measures used to frustrate their departure. In March, for instance, an Exoduster testified that

---

[40]S. A. Hackworth to Governor St. John, Brenham, Texas, August 11, 1879, CRSF, St. John, box 10, KSHS.

early in the month two Black men were waiting near Greenville, Mississippi, to take a steamboat to St. Louis. They were accosted by a number of whites who talked to them about their going away. "The leading man among the whites was one Charlie Smith," said the Exoduster, "and they killed one of the colored men and the other ran off; they killed him because he wanted to go to Kansas."[41] Exodusters repeatedly reported incidents of this nature, but while they lamented the misfortunes of their comrades, they were not deterred from leaving. Similarly, Exodusters whose property was attached for trumped-up debts came away property-less rather than remain in the South. One Exoduster said that his mules had been taken by a deputy sheriff and twenty-five armed men, but he nevertheless boarded the boat—ten miles below his original point of departure.[42]

Arresting a would-be Exoduster for breach of contract was another procedure commonly used to disrupt the Exodus, according to a north Louisiana Black man, J. H. Cox. (Contracts ran from January to January, and the Exodusters were leaving in March, April, and May.) When an Exoduster was taken to jail, the jailer stripped him of his money and did not return it on his release. Since he would have been carrying all his money in anticipation of paying his family's passage to St. Louis, this method was unquestionably effective in keeping individual families at home, at least for the time being. Two of Cox's personal acquaintances suffered this fate, and he reckoned that about a dozen other men were in the same straits in the Tensas Parish jail.[43]

While this piecemeal obstruction could not bar thousands from going to Kansas, their utter inability to get passage to St. Louis did. In late April and May, steamboats simply refused to pick up Exodusters. This policy lasted no more than about a month, but it disturbed the impetus of the salvationist movement. Prospective Exodusters were stranded for weeks on end on the river; local white merchants refused to sell them food, and health authorities harassed and dispersed them. In late April an observer counted twenty-four different camps of Blacks "with their poor, battered and tattered household goods stacked up, waiting for a boat to give

---

[41]Thomas Carroll, *Senate Report 693*, III: 57.

[42]George Halliday, quoted in Frank H. Fletcher, *Negro Exodus*, n.p., n.d. [Topeka, Kansas, April 1879], p. 20.

[43]J. H. Cox, quoted in ibid., p. 15.

them the transportation they were capable of paying for." Many of them evidently had come long distances to reach the Mississippi; "with barely enough money to pay their steamboat passage, and the white people along the shore refusing them the ordinary necessaries of life, and they having no provisions of their own capable of lasting them a day or two, they are scattered along the banks of the broad Mississippi, famishing." The Exodusters' efforts to hail riverboats were futile:

The encampments all had hailing-signals up for the north-bound steamboats, and when these wildly, frantically waved signals were cruelly ignored while the boat proceeded complacently on its way, I saw colored men and women cast themselves to the ground in despair, and heard them groan and shout their lamentations.

What is to become of these wretched people God only knows. Here were nearly half a thousand, refused, scattered along the banks of the mighty Mississippi, without shelter, without food, with no hope of escaping from their present surrounding, and hardly a chance of returning whence they came.[44]

Despite the difficulty of stopping the St. Louis packets, the Exodusters waited and hoped. On April 23, a group of about ten families from the area of Lake Concordia, just inland from the Mississippi River, camped at the landing at Vidalia. Their numbers increased as other families joined them, but three weeks later they still had not succeeded in stopping a boat to St. Louis. Across the river at Natchez-under-the-hill, a camp of about 150 people suffered similar frustrations.[45] On the Mississippi side of the river, camps of 100 to 150 Exodusters each waited at Skipwith's Landing and Bullit's Bayou; on the Louisiana side, equally large camps waited at Delta, Waterproof, and Good Hope.[46] Up and down both sides of the Mississippi, from Greenville to Natchez, "the number of would-be Kansas emigrants increase," reported a witness. "Almost every landing has its camps of devoted colored people looking longingly down the river for the approach of a steamer that will carry them to the promised land."[47]

In mid-May, Thomas W. Conway estimated that the largest

---

[44]Cincinnati *Commercial,* quoted in Chicago Daily *Inter-Ocean,* April 25, 1879.

[45]Natchez Daily *Democrat,* April 24, 27, and May 10, 14, 1879.

[46]Chicago Daily *Tribune,* May 4, 10, 23, 1879.

[47]Ibid., May 23, 1879.

numbers of Exodusters camped at five landings: 200 at Vidalia, 300 at Buttonwood Bayou, 500 at Bass Bayou, 250 at Bonant, and 300 at New Carthage. Many others still waited in smaller camps.[48] From Concordia Parish, Louisiana, an Exoduster wrote to the postmaster of Topeka that members of his camp had "hailed boats but they wont stop. The Democrats have monopolized the thing."[49] At the Leota and Carolina landings in Washington County, Mississippi, about one hundred miles above Vicksburg, 150 Exodusters armed themselves to seize a northbound steamer to take them to Kansas.[50] And at Natchez, Exodusters had the Republican collector of customs write the United States attorney general on their behalf.[51]

Exodusters stranded on the riverbanks for long periods suffered terribly from exposure, and J. H. Cox noted that "some who have had a right smart of money have disposed of a good deal of it in taking care of themselves."[52] Conway's scheme of chartering boats to go up the river aimed to correct this pitiable situation. Then the boats finally relented, threatened with the Conway plan and lawsuits against their discriminatory actions (the steamboats were common carriers regulated by provisions of the Civil Rights Act of 1875). Nevertheless, the burdens imposed by weeks of waiting forced many hundreds to seek subsistence near the banks of the river and postpone migration to Kansas. The millenarian Exodus subsided, its momentum interrupted, and nearby planters wasted no time in tapping the pools of needy working-class Blacks. They sent recruiters and labor agents, whom Cox considered unprincipled hypocrites, to lure or force the disappointed Exodusters to work:

These people [the Exodusters] are visited every day by people of their own race, who are employed by planters and merchants to persuade them to stay and go back on the plantation. The refugees have put up rails and ropes to keep these agents out of their camps. I know of one or two

---

[48]Daily Memphis *Avalanche,* May 13, 1879.

[49]Ellis Jones to postmaster of Topeka, Kansas, Point Pleasant, Louisiana, May 18, 1879, CRSF, St. John, box 10, KSHS.

[50]New Orleans *Times,* May 6, 1879; Nashville Weekly *American,* May 8, 1879; Marshall (Texas) Tri-Weekly *Herald,* May 10, 1879.

[51]E. J. Castello, Collector of Customs, Natchez, to U.S. Attorney General Charles Devens, Natchez, Mississippi, May 14, 1879, Record Group 60, Department of Justice Source-Chronological Files, Southern Mississippi, box 497.

[52]J. H. Cox, quoted in Fletcher, *Negro Exodus,* p. 15.

instances where, after refugees had started, their wagon and clothes were taken away, but were returned to them on condition that they would remain South. These very agents would leave themselves, if they did not expect to make money from the planters and merchants by keeping the emigrants back.[53]

What stopped the Kansas Fever Exodus was not the discovery that there was no free transportation or land in Kansas, nor the fulminations and proclamations printed in Southern newspapers, nor the advice of "representative colored men," nor the suffering that Exodusters experienced on the banks of the Mississippi River, in St. Louis or in Kansas. Trickery and murder could not stay the Exodusters. Only the physical impossibility of keeping body and soul together during the long wait broke the back of the Kansas Fever Exodus. Once the boats began picking up migrants again later in the summer, the movement revived. But the urgent, millenarian Kansas Fever Exodus had closed. Migration steadily continued well into 1881, but never again was it as massive or sudden as it had been in the spring of 1879.

After the intensive spring migration, Exodusters trickled out of Mississippi and Louisiana by the tens, instead of by the hundreds. Except for a spasm of Kansas Fever activity in late July and early August in Louisiana, Mississippi, and Texas (and in Texas in the winter of 1879–80), the millenarian aspect of the migration ended in May 1879. Migrants flowed from the three states into Kansas and the Midwest for over a year, but they planned their moves. In August 1879 there was a reflux of Exodusters from Mississippi and Louisiana to Texas, via Kansas.[54]

Migration from Texas exhibited the same characteristics as the earlier migration from Mississippi and Louisiana, in both its millennial and nonmillennial phases. Exodusters left the heavily Black ("Senegambian") counties of east-central Texas: Washington, Burleson, Grimes, Nacogdoches, Walker, and Waller. From Texas, Exodusters either went by railroad from Denison and Sherman to Parsons, Kansas, or by wagon across Arkansas and part of the Indian Territory. Since the distance was only about three hundred miles from northern Texas to Kansas, Texas Exodusters suffered rather less than did their predecessors who had passed

[53]Ibid.

[54]Dallas *Herald-Commercial,* quoted in Brenham Weekly *Banner,* August 15, 1879; St. Joseph *North Louisiana Journal,* August 30, 1879.

through St. Louis. Between November 1879 and March 1880, an estimated three to four thousand Texas Exodusters arrived in Kansas.[55]

The Kansas Fever Exodus very possibly represents the first massive millenarian movement in this country.[56] The extraordinary magnitude of the Exodus, its lack of central leadership, and the nationwide charity efforts it called into play all combined to bring it tremendous publicity. The nation's public figures and newspapers were forced to take positions on the Exodus if they had any connection with partisan politics or with Blacks at all. A Senate select committee investigated the causes of the move. The Exodus also spurred nonmillenarian Blacks to consider seriously migrating to Kansas to better their condition. In sharp contrast to the Kansas Fever Exodusters, they proceeded deliberately and cautiously.

---

[55]New Orleans *Southwestern Christian Advocate*, December 4, 1879; Henry King, "A Year of the Exodus in Kansas," *Scribner's Monthly* XX, no. 2 (June 1880): 216.

[56]The movement of slaves to Union lines during the Civil War possibly had some of the same millenarian overtones; certainly it was massive and looked to a millennial era of freedom that would totally change the lives of the followers.

16

Contemporary Reactions
to the Exodus

The sensational Kansas Fever Exodus sparked strong reactions from its very beginning, but its greatest impact occurred in the summer of 1879. Nonmillenarian Southern Blacks responded to the Kansas Fever myth with enthusiasm, curiosity, and skepticism. Above all, they were anxious to learn more about Kansas, how the Exodusters fared there, and whether they, too, should go. They organized Kansas clubs and solicited information about Kansas through the same channels migrants had used before the Exodus. But now the volume of inquiry dwarfed pre-Exodus investigation. Prospective migrants also held meetings to formulate policy and rationalize future migration.

The planned migration that spun off from the Exodus differed markedly in tenor and aim from the millenarian movement. Deliberate migrationists sharply distinguished themselves from the Kansas Fever millenarians by questioning the advisability of migrating. (Millenarian Exodusters were convinced they had no choice but to flee.) Migrants began to answer that paramount question by seeking information about conditions in Kansas, especially the possibility of their acquiring land. Migrants moved, in large part, toward economic advantage, and for some, deciding whether to move to Kansas put them in a quandary; said one prospective migrant, "i have a littel Place and i Dont Wont to Brake up to Do better and Do Worse."[1] Calling a mass meeting

---

[1]Wallace Partee to Governor St. John, Nashville, Tennessee, August 23, 1879,

was often the first step toward determining if they could do better in Kansas.

During the summer of 1879 Blacks met all over Mississippi, Louisiana, Texas, and Tennessee to discuss the Exodus, in several instances sending representatives to Kansas to survey the situation. Delegates represented mass meetings, Kansas clubs, or just a few families. From Plaquemine, Iberville Parish, Louisiana, the chairman of the Committee to Visit Kansas wrote to the governor of Kansas for information preparatory to the committee's visit:

We the colored citizens of the Parish of Iberville having called a mass meeting for the purpose of sending a committee to Kansas next March to investigate into the condition of your State, and report back to us whether it would be favorable for us to emigrate to that State or not; desire to have your excellency write to us giving us your advise.[2]

Meetings usually took up collections to underwrite the delegates' expenses, but sometimes planters bore a substantial part of the burden.

Threatened with crop disruptions while workers waited to hear from their delegates to Kansas, planters more than once tried to cut their losses—if the tenants would finish out the season, they could choose a representative and the planter would send him to Kansas on their behalf. In some cases this arrangement bought the planter precious time; by winter the enthusiasm for Kansas had diminished. In Hazelhurst, Mississippi, local merchants tried the experiment on a larger scale. They organized an excursion to Kansas for both whites and Blacks, for which each man paid his own way, ten dollars. In mid-August 1879, their eleven-car train traveled from Mississippi to Kansas City and back, carrying men from Hazelhurst, Canton, and Oakland, Mississippi, and Jackson, Tennessee.

The sponsors of the trip expected that once the visitors witnessed the appalling suffering of the Exodusters in St. Louis and Kansas, they would lose all interest in leaving Mississippi once and

---

CRSF, St. John, box 10, KSHS. The only distinction between millenarians and nonmillenarians that clearly emerges from the sources is the strength of their belief. Millenarians, of essentially the same social and economic class as nonmillenarians, of the same states and the same churches, held a faith solid enough to travel on. Nonmillenarians did not.

[2]Samuel Muse to Governor St. John, Plaquemine, Louisiana, August 12, 1879, ibid.

for all. (Throughout the Exodus, white Southern newspapers had given extensive coverage to the Exodusters' miserable plight, stressing the utter hopelessness of their move. Blacks read the papers, but, cognizant of white Southern opposition to the movement, they sought information on their own, from independent sources.) In an interview in St. Louis, one Black excursionist noncommittally affirmed that "we merely go there to take a look at the country and see for ourselves whether we can better our condition there; likewise to find out how those who are there already have fared and prospered."[3] At first the results seemed mixed. Most of the Mississippians returned; about a quarter stayed in Kansas. But several months later the real import of the trip emerged. In December a whole colony set out from Hazelhurst. They went to occupy lands in southern Kansas that had been purchased for them by members of the August excursion.[4] Unfortunately, for most prospective migrants, on-the-spot intelligence was impossible.

Like Louis Poplar of Louisiana, who wrote asking for a map of Kansas for himself and his colony of twenty other men and their families, large numbers of migrants depended entirely on the mail for information.[5] They wanted first and foremost to know about purchasing land. A "poor colored teacher's" list of questions to Governor St. John of Kansas typifies the migrants' preoccupations:

1. Are all the government land in that state entered?
2. Would you encourage a good and industrious colored man to come there?
3. How is the facilities for education?
4. Send me the name of some prominent Colored Citizen that I might correspond with him . . .[6]

These inquiries about land were also calculated to test the Kansas Fever idea.

Letters expressing interest in migration repeatedly voiced skepticism in regard to the Kansas Fever idea, even though corre-

---

[3]St. Louis *Globe-Democrat*, August 14, 1879.

[4]St. Louis *Globe-Democrat*, August 14 and December 20, 1879; New Orleans *Southwestern Christian Advocate*, September 11, 1879.

[5]Louis Poplar to Governor St. John, Berwick City, Louisiana, July 5, 1879, CRSF, St. John, box 10, KSHS.

[6]J. B. Witherspoon to Governor St. John, Columbus, Mississippi, September 1, 1879, ibid.

spondents often said they could not hope to leave the South without monetary aid. They were not millenarians, however, and their faith in the idea, without knowledge of conditions in Kansas, was not sufficient to take them to the riverbanks. Others were doing well, but were intrigued by the Kansas Fever idea:

Owing to the Great Exodus of Colord People From the South to Kansas and to the Effect that those who go there are Furnished Transportation and are supplied with land   Farming Implements and Provision for the 1st year etc I Address you with a view to Ascertaining the Facts on [the] Subject of the Kansas immigration Please let me know upon what Terms land can be had . . . as I am living Tolelbuley [tolerably] well here I would like to Know if by moving to Kansas I would be Able to Do Better. . . .[7]

But serious doubts about the idea were not confined to the post-Exodus period.

While the Kansas Fever Exodus bore the special hallmark of millennialism, not all the migrants coming up through St. Louis between March and May 1879 were millenarians, panic-ridden and destitute. After the middle of April, reporters began to notice that some of the arrivals were seemingly of the "better class" of rural Blacks, and one reporter saw them as solid family men who had left the South "not so much with the special desire and intention of going to Kansas as to reach some point, no matter where, at which point they can make a fair livelihood and earn a little money over and above what is absolutely required to keep body and soul together."[8] His observation was substantially correct.

Nonmillenarians, in fact, scoffed at Kansas Fever and at the whole idea that the government would supply them with free transportation, land, and supplies. When millenarians learned in St. Louis that there was no free transportation, etc., they were at a loss as to where to go and what to do. They were convinced only that they wanted to go to Kansas and would not under any circumstances return to the South. Nonmillenarians, in contrast, were better informed and knew the provisions of the Homestead Act— which offered nearly free land to settlers, with certain qualifications concerning residence and improvements. At Wyandotte, when a migrant was asked if he expected to find land and a mule

---

[7] J. N. Harris to Governor St. John, Muldon, Mississippi, May 24, 1879, ibid.
[8] St. Louis *Globe-Democrat*, April 14, 1879.

team waiting for him in Kansas, he laughed and said, "Oh, now boss, who bin tellin' yo' dat dam nonsense! No sech thing! I heah dat Uncle Sam give eb'ry sojer 160 acres o' lan', 'n' I got my discha'ge papahs in my pocket. But I never 'xpeck' anybody t' give me a mule team."[9] Others who could not profit from soldiers' preemption benefits were nevertheless apprised of conditions for purchasing railroad lands. Another migrant, asked if he had come North expecting to inherit his forty acres and a mule from the government, answered emphatically, "Bress de Lord! no, massa. We wouldn't be sich fools as to bleve dat, nohow." Then he explained what he knew of the terms under which land could be acquired in Kansas: "De papers sed we could buy de best of land for $6 an acre, not so good fur $4, and de poorest fur $2; and dat we could get 160 acres out West ob de Guberment by being on it five years and paying $18 to de Guberment fur fees."[10] These were the terms of purchase that had been quoted in the Topeka *Colored Citizen* in answer to streams of correspondence from Southern Blacks inquiring into the possibility of buying land in Kansas.

Newspapers provided an information network linking St. Louis, Kansas, and the Southern states. The Topeka *Colored Citizen* was only one of the journals that prospective migrants consulted. The New York *Tribune* generally carried news about Blacks and Republican politics, and many literate Blacks in Louisiana, Mississippi, and Texas had subscribed to it for years. The weekly editions of the New York *Tribune* and the Chicago *Inter-Ocean*, both Stalwart papers, were popular with Blacks in the South. The New Orleans *Southwestern Christian Advocate,* one of the many regional *Christian Advocates* published by the Methodist Episcopal Church, was also a forum for news about the Exodus. These papers, and the *Kansas Agricultural Report* and the Philadelphia *Christian Recorder,* provided migrants with information basic to their planning. Finally, conductors and agents, such as Singleton, DeFrantz, and Johnson, helped migrants decide where to settle in Kansas. Among the conductors, only Benjamin Singleton salvaged a reputation that endured a hundred years.

The Kansas Fever Exodus brought Singleton fame as the "Father of the Colored Exodus." While Singleton and his coworkers over the years stimulated and channeled the migration from mid-

---

[9]Chicago Daily *Inter-Ocean,* May 9, 1879.
[10]Atchison (Kan.) *Tribune,* quoted in Chicago Daily *Tribune,* May 17, 1879.

dle Tennessee to Kansas in the late 1870s, he was not the "Father" of the 1879 Kansas Fever Exodus from Mississippi, Louisiana, and Texas. Nor was he, as he claimed, "the whole cause of the Kansas immigration!"[11]

Benjamin Singleton took credit for the Kansas Exodus of 1879 in part because he had printed and circulated several hundred posters advertising his and the Edgefield Real Estate and Homestead Association's stake in Kansas migration. (Many of these fliers are still extant, but they are of purely local interest.) This is not to say that Singleton's handbills did not form part of the general background that disposed people to migrate to Kansas, for he sent them into the states from which the Exodus of 1879 flowed. But he also sent handbills to states that contributed only negligible numbers of Exodusters to the movement: Alabama, North and South Carolina, Georgia, and Virginia.[12] Migration flowed from Kentucky over the whole period, and there is, in fact, some evidence that at least part of that movement was stimulated by Singleton's circulars. Nonetheless, the Kansas Fever Exodus, which brought Singleton nationwide fame, was not the movement from Kentucky, in spite of the latter's numerical importance.

Singleton's cardinal reason for naming himself Father of the Exodus lay in his sense of divine appointment. While post-Exodus forecasts predicted that every Black person in the South would finally leave for Kansas, Singleton took up the mantle of seer and gloried in his prophetic powers. Citing reports that eighty to one hundred thousand Blacks would leave in 1880, Singleton proclaimed: "I am the very man that predicted that. It was me published it. . . . It was me done it; I published it; they say other folks did it. No, Governor St. John or other folks, they did not do it; it was me; I did it."[13] But Singleton was no more able than whites or "leading colored men" to see that the Exodus needed no single great leader. He appropriated the movement, proclaiming himself the instrument of God: "Right emphatically, I tell you to-day, I woke up the millions right through me! The great God of glory has worked in me. I have had open air interviews with the living

[11]Benjamin Singleton, *Senate Report 693*, III: 382.

[12]Ibid., pp. 381–82.

[13]Ibid. Governor St. John refused to bar Exodusters' entry and figured prominently in the Freedmen's Relief Association in Topeka. For this he was widely accused of causing the Exodus.

spirit of God for my people; and we are going to leave the South."[14] Mention of the Exodus to Kansas even to this day recalls the name of "Pap" Singleton, but his fascinating Senate testimony, rather than any actual connection with the Kansas Fever Exodus from Mississippi and Louisiana, won him this fame.

The Exodus had other, less savory consequences that flowed from its sensational nature and the wide-scale publicity it attracted. After the millenarian phase of the Exodus had passed, con men and sharpers hastened to take advantage of people who lacked faith in the Kansas Fever idea but who also knew nothing of conditions for settlement in Kansas. In St. Tammany Parish in southern Louisiana, a parish that did not contribute significant numbers to the Exodus, an "emissary" called together a mass meeting at which he "harangued the colored population." He announced that General Grant had ordered that "the colored people should at once emigrate to this land [Kansas] set aside for their special use, where white men could not interfere with them, and where gold in any quantity could be dug out of the ground." The "emissary" repeated that free transportation, land, and provisions would be furnished to the migrants. Then he took up a collection from what the reporter called a "large and credulous audience."[15]

Peddling certificates that supposedly entitled the bearer to transportation to Kansas was an oft-repeated swindle in Texas and Louisiana. In Hays County, Texas, a "Negro preacher calling himself William Johnson" did a rousing business selling certificates at five dollars each, which he said guaranteed the purchaser transportation to Kansas worth nine dollars. "William Johnson" reportedly made two thousand dollars in Hays County alone.[16] Again, Hays County did not send a notable number of migrants to Kansas.

Not all the con men profiting in the wake of the Exodus excitement were Black, however. One of the most publicized frauds occurred in north Louisiana, where a white man sold toy flags to prospective Exodusters, to be used in Kansas, he said, to mark off

---

[14]Ibid., p. 381.

[15]New Orleans *Times*, May 9, 1879. There was a brief and modest gold rush in Cowley County, Kansas, in early 1879. (Chicago Daily *Inter-Ocean*, April 25, 1879.)

[16]New Orleans *Southwestern Christian Advocate*, April 15, 1880.

the land that the government would give to the migrant.[17] Several other impostures, ranging from the sale of bogus railroad passes and boat tickets to merely taking up collections in exchange for nonsensical lectures about Kansas, occurred in the three Gulf States affected by Kansas Fever.[18] Although some Blacks who ultimately ended up in Kansas were taken in on the way, con men for the most part avoided the areas of heavy migration. In those places, more Blacks corresponded with Kansas and received answers to their questions directly from the source. And working people there were in a better position to take advantage of the Exodus economically.

Sporadic labor unrest followed in the wake of the Exodus. In scattered areas of the states affected by the loss of sizable contingents of their workers, real if ephemeral economic benefits were accrued by the labor force. The first attempted strike by agricultural laborers after the Exodus took place in northeastern Louisiana, where hands on a plantation struck for seventy cents per day wages. The strike was easily broken, primarily because the plantation bordered the banks of the Mississippi River. The plantation owner threatened the strikers with replacement by would-be Exodusters marooned at Point Pleasant and "starved out waiting for a boat."[19] Thus, in riverine areas, the results of the Exodus's withdrawal of part of the labor force were canceled out by a glut of workers unable to get boats to St. Louis.

In Concordia Parish, Louisiana, an area hard hit by the Kansas Fever Exodus, agricultural laborers threatened to leave the parish if their rents were not scaled down. The reasons they cited as necessitating reduced rents echoed the generally accepted "causes" of the Exodus: "insecurity of life and property, the low rate of wages, exorbitant prices for provisions and leases, the utter impossibility of providing for old age, sickness, for our children's welfare. . . ." The workers asked that rents for current contracts be reduced to one four-hundred-pound bale of cotton per eight acres, or the equivalent of five dollars cash per acre. In Concordia Parish this would have entailed a substantial savings, for rents hovered around ten dollars per acre, among the most expensive

[17]Brenham Weekly *Banner*, June 6, 1879.
[18]Ibid., June 6 and July 4, 1879.
[19]New Orleans *Times*, May 6, 1879.

in the lower Mississippi Valley. Should this adjustment not be conceded, the laborers said, they faced destitution and had no alternative but "to seek homes elsewhere."[20] This incident, of undetermined success, grew directly out of the Exodus and occurred in an area from which Exodusters departed in massive numbers.

In Texas, the Exodus temporarily benefited Blacks who remained. Planters in Washington County grew alarmed as they watched Exodusters quitting the county for Kansas. By the end of 1879 some one thousand Blacks had left, and planters moved to keep the working people who remained. Instead of giving only one-year rentals at approximately five dollars per acre, planters now leased their lands for three-year terms at about three dollars per acre annually. They subdivided some plantations into fifty-acre farms selling for fifteen to twenty dollars per acre on ten-year mortgages. These still were high prices, but the terms allowed Black tenants far more advantage than they had had before the Exodus. The more favorable economic climate was ascribed directly to the Exodus and occurred in an area hit hard by the loss of laborers.[21]

In other parts of the three Gulf States affected by the Kansas Exodus, Black working people were reported entering into contracts only on a month-by-month basis. They reputedly refused to invest in real estate or make substantial improvements on what they already owned. This shrinking from long-term commitments was ascribed to the Exodus.[22] Whites summed up the situation as the "demoralization of labor."

During the following year, 1880, labor unrest affected the southernmost parishes of Louisiana. However, the strikes in St. Charles, St. John, and Plaquemines parishes may not have been directly related to the Exodus. Although interest in Kansas had spread into southern Louisiana in 1880, it had not produced any measurable migration by the time the strikes occurred in March, April, and May. In March, laborers in St. Charles Parish struck after their demands for wage increases of twenty-five cents per day (from seventy-five cents to a dollar) were refused. They

---

[20]Natchez Daily *Democrat*, May 11, 1879.

[21]S. A. Hackworth to Governor St. John, Brenham, Texas, August 11, 1879, CRSF, St. John, box 10, KSHS.

[22]New Orleans *Southwestern Christian Advocate*, August 7, 1879.

marched through the parish, attracting additional support. The strike was broken when the planters appealed to Governor Louis A. Wiltz, who sent in the state militia, complete with a field piece.[23] As a result of the violence triggered by the strike and the state government's reaction to it, Blacks reportedly were considering migration.[24] In this case, as in Plaquemines and St. John parishes, the strikes were not closely related to the Exodus or resulting labor shortages, but Black reaction afterward drew inspiration from the Exodus. Even though they discussed migration as a remedy to their situation, no great numbers of Black people left the southern Louisiana parishes. A few migrants to Kansas quit the neighboring parish of Iberville.

In the short term, the Exodus effected a reduction in rents and prices, bringing a real but fleeting amelioration in the economic lives of limited numbers of Blacks. Planters even promised to remedy the insecurity of life that the Exodusters complained of so persistently. In May 1879 a Chicago *Tribune* correspondent guardedly expressed sanguine hopes for real change in the conditions under which Blacks lived in the South. "Who that has read the proceedings of the Vicksburg Convention," he asked rhetorically, "in which many concessions and pledges were made to the negroes, can doubt that the exodus has had a good effect as far as it has gone?"[25]

---

[23]Ibid., March 25, 1880; Brenham Weekly *Banner*, March 26 and May 21, 1880.
[24]New Orleans *Southwestern Christian Advocate*, April 22, 1880.
[25]Chicago Daily *Tribune*, May 17, 1879.

17

Meetings and Conventions in the Wake of the Exodus

Unique among the scores of meetings held across the South to discuss the Exodus, the Vicksburg convention was white-run. All the others were Black undertakings, since the movement captivated Blacks far more than whites. In addition to the Vicksburg convention, major assemblages sat in the late spring and summer of 1879 in New Orleans, Nashville, and Houston.

In contrast to the local meetings that sent delegates to Kansas, the big conventions articulated public—usually eminently respectable—opinion on migration. Then local meetings, in turn, ratified, modified, or implemented those positions. The New Orleans and Vicksburg conventions grew directly out of the Exodus, but the two others were planned long before the movement took center stage.

The New Orleans meeting in mid-April crossed a conference of "representative colored men" with a local migration meeting. Variously termed the convention of colored preachers, social leaders, refugees, demagogues, or politicians, it proved a disorderly and heterogeneous gathering. Among the many political refugees taking part in the meeting, the Reverend A. R. Blount of Natchitoches and Henry Adams of Caddo figured prominently, showing special sensitivity to the issue of terrorism in the parishes. David Young and P. B. S. Pinchback, elected members of the Louisiana constitutional convention, still functioned as politicians, but

Blount and A. M. Newman, well-known ministers and de facto politicians, self-righteously considered themselves merely concerned citizens.

As the meeting progressed, two sides emerged, one conservative, whose most visible proponents were Pinchback, Young, and J. D. Kennedy, and the other radical, with the journalist George T. Ruby and Henry Adams its spokesmen. The Ruby-Adams view carried the day easily, for it supported the exceedingly popular Exodus. Ruby served as guiding spirit in the committee on address, drawing heavily on the information and opinions of Henry Adams's north Louisiana Colonization Council. The Pinchback group basically opposed the Exodus, favoring political and economic solutions to the problems of insecurity of life and property in the countryside.

At the outset the New Orleans *Times* noted the meeting's division between "the politicians" and "the better classes of colored people." By the time the meeting ended, the *Times* reclassified participants as either "demagogues" or "politicians."[1] Pinchback's newspaper, the *Louisianian,* expressed its editor's chagrin at the meeting's having shoved aside and ignored both him and his young disciple, Kennedy. Pinchback characterized it as "a mass meeting run and controlled almost wholly by small fry politicians." These "inexperienced hands, and gassy, curbstone politicians refused to hear the more intelligent class of the race generally." The organizers, he said, showed no interest in airing all points of view; they strove only for publicity, having seen "in the popular wave of emigration flowing over the South a chance to swim into cheap notoriety." The lone bright spot in the otherwise useless proceedings, according to Pinchback, was Kennedy's speech.[2]

But J. D. Kennedy made no headway whatever speaking against the spirit of the meeting. When he read some remarks of Frederick Douglass, whose implacable opposition to the Exodus he shared, a member of the audience asked whether Douglass himself had not run away from the South and why he should now oppose others following his example. Kennedy's advice to the colored people, to husband their resources and educate their children instead of migrating, fell on deaf ears.

---

[1] New Orleans *Times,* April 18, 20, 1879.
[2] New Orleans Weekly *Louisianian,* April 26, 1879.

Pinchback, too, was interrupted, at times by A. R. Blount, who called politicians "false leaders." While Blount's position was calculated to identify him with the working people, not with their supposed exploiters, he nevertheless put his finger on two central truths about the Exodus, whether by accident or design. He underscored the Exodusters' fear of a second slavery, which they must escape at all costs, and the inexorable nature of the movement; the "false political leader" could not hold it back. On both counts he was exactly right. Yet, one wonders if his opposition to the New Orleans professional politicians (such as Pinchback) does not go a long way toward explaining his statements on their impotence.[3]

Another prominent political figure who encountered opposition at the New Orleans convention was David Young of Concordia Parish. Well-to-do and conservative, Young was a member of the constitutional convention and an invitee to the upcoming Vicksburg planters' conference. His resolution that the chair appoint a committee of "seven discreet members" to confer with the planters at Vicksburg set off a wild uproar in which Young was howled down as a "bloated capitalist."[4]

The meeting's strenuous and vocal opposition to Young, Pinchback, and Kennedy—the self-appointed voices of reason—earned it the opprobrium of "leading colored men" and the white press in the South. The New Orleans *Times* reflected the pique of the conservative participants, quoting their view that the meeting had brought shame on the race and the Exodus movement. The sheer pandemonium, said the *Times,* harmed the whole colored cause; indeed, many observers, white and Black, considered the meeting's disorder and noise a disgrace.[5] They took sides on the resolutions (and on the entire Exodus question) on the basis of the outward appearance of the meeting. However, the caliber of the deliberations and the truths expressed in the address belonged to another order entirely.

The address of the New Orleans meeting captured the causes and tone of the Exodus more accurately than did that of any other

---

[3]New Orleans *Times,* April 18, 19, 1879.

[4]Ibid., April 20, 1879; Natchez Daily *Democrat,* April 22, 1879. As a state senator in the mid-1870s, Young was indicted for embezzling $31,000 of school funds. He was later acquitted.

[5]New Orleans *Times,* April 20, 1879.

convention. Perhaps the very confusion of the meeting reflected its vitality and proximity to the opinions of ordinary people; it mirrored popular enthusiasm for migration. The address had been drafted by George T. Ruby, a former schoolteacher and editor of the New Orleans *Observer*, but it clearly articulated the preoccupations of the migrationists in the parishes. The address saw persistent rural lawlessness as the fundamental cause of the Exodus, while it underscored the Exodus's more immediate motive: the "absorbing and constantly increasing distrust and alarm among our people through the State." In two paragraphs the address showed that migration was the only alternative left to the colored people in the bulldozed parishes. "The fiat to go forth is irresistible," the address proclaimed, and continued:

The constantly recurring, nay ever present fear, which haunts the minds of these our people in the turbulent parishes of the State, that slavery in the horrid form of peonage is approaching; that the avowed disposition of the men now in power is to reduce the laborer and his interests to the minimum of advantages as freemen, and to absolutely none as citizens, has produced *so absolute a fear that in many cases it has become a panic. It is flight from present sufferings, and the wrongs to come.*

Kansas with her freedom and broad prairies, with the memories of John Brown and his heroic struggle, seems naturally the State to seek. There is a natural halo of liberty, and justice and right about its very name which gives the untutored minds of our people in their miserable condition the same longing and all-pervading desire to leave here and to go there as the magic name Canada gave in that time to the slave. The feeling is identical, occasioned, too, by nearly like conditions.[6]

Without identifying Adams by name, the address cited the influence of the Colonization Council, whose cohesion and strength the address attributed to its underground nature. The address also mentioned the Timber Claims Act of 1874 and its provisions for

---

[6]New Orleans Weekly *Louisianian*, April 26, 1879. (Emphasis added.)

George T. Ruby was born in New York City in 1841 and migrated to Louisiana in 1864. He worked with the Freedmen's Bureau in 1865–66 organizing schools and teaching. In 1866 he moved to Galveston, Texas, where he taught until 1868. Elected a member of the Reconstruction constitutional convention in 1867, he subsequently served in the Texas state senate until 1873. He published the Galveston *Standard* until 1867, and became editor of Pinchback's *Louisianian* in 1874 after moving back to New Orleans. He started his own publication, the New Orleans *Observer*, in May 1878. Ruby was one of a significant number of Black carpetbaggers who represent a phenomenon well deserving serious study.

homesteading. Closing with an appeal for an orderly migration without undue haste, the address foresaw the people's ultimate success: "Under safe, judicious, leaders with strong wills, earnest purpose and an abiding trust in God, and the people's own right arms, we will achieve our liberties, secure peace and homes, and obtain Christian independence and citizenship in its broadest sense."[7]

The utter disorder that marked the meeting's deliberations earned it ridicule in the news columns of the New Orleans *Times* and the *Louisianian,* yet the *Times*'s editorial page commented more soberly. Writing off the meeting was foolhardy, the editorial said. The address would sway national opinion, for it "expressed the complaints and fears and apprehensions of their race and the real explanation of the exodus."[8] The *Times* overestimated the impact of the New Orleans meeting on the rest of the country. (Although a portion of the address was included in the minority report of the Senate Committee Report of the Exodus in 1880, it lay buried there for nearly one hundred years.) Black opinion, however, was generally favorable to the convention, with local mass meetings voicing their approval. While the New Orleans meeting only minimally affected the public beyond the lower Mississippi Valley, editorial opinion North and South hailed the Vicksburg Labor Convention as the dawn of a new day in Southern race relations.

Advertised as a coming together of the representatives of the planting and laboring interests of the lower Mississippi Valley, the Vicksburg convention attracted both Blacks and whites. Blacks, in fact, outnumbered whites by at least six to one. The governor of Mississippi, the president of the Vicksburg Cotton Exchange, and other planting and mercantile figures proposed the convention in mid-April. They also invited a number of "leading colored men" to represent the views of the Black laboring population. However, the Black invitees, such as Senator Blanche K. Bruce of Mississippi and David Young of Louisiana, were scarcely working men, and they all opposed the Exodus. John R. Lynch of Natchez, Mississippi, was invited but did not attend; at best, he was ambivalent toward the Exodus. Given the composition of the convention—

---

[7]Ibid.
[8]New Orleans *Times,* April 24, 1879.

conservative, comfortable whites and conservative, comfortable Blacks—it is hardly surprising that the two-day meeting passed off with barely a hitch.

Euphemism characterized the convention from the moment of its conception. The invitation asked citizens of the lower Mississippi Valley to "meet in convention at Vicksburg . . . to take into consideration the present agitation of the labor question."[9] It originally hoped to halt the Exodus or procure new sources of cheap labor. During the last part of April, however, the Exodus appeared to slacken (although it revived in early May). With the aid of the Southern press, the planners persuaded themselves that the Exodus was practically over and therefore no longer critical to the region's economic survival. Between the middle and end of April, they shifted emphasis from confronting the Exodus to effecting a permanent association of Mississippi Valley cotton planters. In the end, the convention's resolutions spoke hollowly to the Exodus and its causes; its other work—going into permanent organization—seemed of more consequence.[10] After several weeks of protest from Louisiana Blacks, the New Orleans *Times* conceded that while the convention was "good enough in its way," frankness compelled admitting that "it must have looked to the colored people too much like a 'set up job.' "[11] The *Times* was correct.

Most of the Black delegates to the Vicksburg convention were conservatives, particularly those who held office, but even they were skeptical of the convention's good faith. Before the meeting, the Black members caucused and decided not to vote on the resolutions, reasoning that the convention's more powerful white members would of necessity bear responsibility for implementing those resolutions.[12] The deliberations passed off with a smoothness characteristic of proceedings that skirt essential issues and thorny

---

[9]Vicksburg (Miss.) *Herald,* April 15, 1879, quoted in Natchez Daily *Democrat,* April 17, 1879.

[10]New Orleans *Times,* April 28, 1879. The planters' association seems to have died away almost immediately after the Exodus.

[11]Ibid., May 23, 1879.

[12]Nashville Weekly *American,* May 8, 1879; Daily Memphis *Avalanche,* May 13, 1879. Governor Henry S. Foote charged later that Black delegates were prevented from voting, but in all probability they had reached prior agreement not to vote on conclusions that did not realistically promise to ameliorate the condition of Blacks.

realities. General W. R. Miles acted as permanent president of the meeting, and four Black men, including David Young, served as vice-presidents. The chairman of the resolutions committee set forth the causes of the Exodus as he saw them:

1st. The low price of cotton and the partial failure of the crop of the past year.

2d. The irrational system of planting adopted in some sections . . .

3d. The vicious system of credit . . .

4th. The apprehension on the part of many colored people, produced by insidious reports circulated among them, that their civil and political rights are endangered, or are likely to be.

5th. The hurtful and false rumors . . . that by emigrating to Kansas, the colored people would obtain lands, mules and money from the government . . . and become independent forever.[13]

The resolutions addressed the economic causes of the Exodus, suggesting the abolition of crop mortgaging in advance (crop lien). To their credit, the resolutions recognized the necessity of assuring Blacks their personal security; the planters pledged themselves to protect "their labor." The first resolution voiced the fundamental ideology of the meeting: "the interests of planters, landlords and tenants, are identical; and . . . they must prosper or suffer together."[14] This view suited planters and merchants better than the absent laborers, who could register no protest.

Henry S. Foote, the Reconstruction governor of Mississippi, precipitated the single disturbance in the otherwise unruffled proceedings. Foote insisted that planters first shoulder the blame for much more than just the economic abuse of Black workers. Then they should take concrete steps to protect Blacks' personal safety as well as their civil rights. In place of vague pledges, Foote advocated the formation of local boards of arbitration in each county or parish with power to advise in labor disputes and to prosecute breaches of contract or law.[15]

---

[13]*Journal of Negro History* IV, no. 1 (January 1919): 51–52. "Low cotton prices" and "failure of the crop" were favorite conservative red herrings. Prices and yields varied among the counties and parishes affected by the Exodus. Yields depended on soil and cultivation, and prices had tended downward for the previous several years, overall.

[14]St. Joseph *North Louisiana Journal,* May 10, 1879.

[15]James B. Runnion, "The Negro Exodus," p. 230; F. R. Guernsey, "The Negro Exodus," p. 389; New Orleans *Times,* May 23, 1879.

In effect, he proposed bypassing existing government and law-enforcement agencies, which had shown themselves criminally negligent in regard to Blacks, and erecting in their place a parallel government responsive to the needs of Black people. The amendment was much too radical for the convention, and two of the Black vice-presidents spoke against it. Foote had only briefly jarred the dominant, conciliatory sentiment of the meeting. No forum for hammering out realistic and effective solutions to Southern racial tensions, the Vicksburg convention genteelly whitewashed real abuses.

Reaction to the Vicksburg Labor Convention ranged from guarded optimism to veiled skepticism among whites, and from guarded optimism to outright condemnation among Blacks. The New York *Herald* regarded the convention as a "promising sign of the times," but thought it made its greatest contribution by discrediting Southern politicians: "We have long been convinced that if public affairs in the South were controlled by its planters, merchants and bankers . . . race jealousies and antipathies would soon disappear. . . . The wise and considerate action of the Vicksburg Convention demonstrates the superiority of Southern wealth and intelligence to the stubborn Bourbonism of their section." The editorial also excoriated Governor Foote as an "uneasy and disturbing spirit" who was intent on inserting a " 'countercheck quarrelsome' " into the proceedings.[16] Despite its sharp criticism of Foote, the *Herald* concurred with his suggestion of bypassing elected state and local governments and relying on political amateurs—planters and merchants—to insure peace. Like Foote, the *Herald* registered a vote of no confidence in the elected governments of the Redeemed South.

The New Orleans *Times,* less sanguine than the *Herald,* took Foote to task for impugning the sincerity of the gentlemen meeting at Vicksburg, while it nonetheless agreed with him that the convention sidestepped the real issues surrounding the Exodus.[17] The Natchez *Democrat,* even less encouraged, doubted that much good could come of a meeting of men who neither worked nor owned capital. The *Democrat* rejected outright the convention's identity-of-interest platitudes: "This thing of resolving labor and capital into harmonious relations, is one of the popular fallacies

---

[16]New York Daily *Herald,* May 8, 1879.
[17]New Orleans *Times,* May 23, 1879.

which affords a fair field for display to those who can be placed in neither category."[18] Dismissing the convention as nugatory, the *Democrat,* too, reserved a few hard words for professional politicians.

Although a few Blacks, like William Murrell, who had been at Vicksburg, placed a measure of faith in the planters' pledges of protection, a New Orleans meeting in Lafayette Square represented more typical reactions to the Vicksburg convention. Some two hundred Negroes listened to speeches opposing the recommendations of the Vicksburg meeting and explaining the true causes of the Exodus. Governor Foote detailed his rejected amendments, asserting that Black delegates had been barred from voting. The resolutions adopted at the Lafayette Square meeting addressed the Vicksburg resolutions directly and rejected them point by point. They denied the allegation that circulars and agents lured the colored people away and pointed to violence and the fear of renewed violence as the causes of the Exodus. Its final verdict on the Vicksburg meeting found that "simple pledges for protection and fair play are not enough." The resolutions spoke directly to the planters and merchants: "We have had fifteen years of pledges. You have the courts in your hands, you make the public sentiment, you own the soil and control the capital, and no remedy for the evils of which we have spoken, can be inaugurated or made effective unless it be planned and carried out by you."[19]

In the parishes, working-class Blacks reiterated the sentiments of the Lafayette Square meeting. They found the planters' promises "too thin." Pledges had been "tried too often," they said, and "we have got nothing for it; promises won't go down any more."[20] Whether they meant to leave the South or stay, the planters' good intentions in no way influenced their decisions. "Representative colored men" were generally less skeptical, but they invested their hopes in a united stand among respectable Blacks, which they thought would emerge from the National Conference of Colored Men that met in Nashville the day after the Vicksburg convention. The Nashville conference, like the Vicksburg convention, affected only a narrow stratum of the race, the

---

[18]Natchez Daily *Democrat,* May 13, 1879.
[19]New Orleans *Southwestern Christian Advocate,* May 29, 1879.
[20]William Murrell, *Senate Report 693,* II: 529.

assimilated and the prosperous. Poor, rural Blacks were barely touched by it.

The Nashville conference gathered "leading colored men" from across the country. It partly satisfied the need that elected representatives normally would have filled in Congress or in state legislatures had it been possible for Blacks to elect their own representatives. The Nashville conference offered a forum for the exchange of opinions and a platform for articulating the colored people's views to the rest of the country. It was the Negro shadow government.

In terms of Afro-American political thought, the colored men's conference was of considerable moment, for it addressed a multitude of problems confronting the race throughout the nation. It paid special attention to difficulties stemming from Redemption in the South, taking an uncompromising stand against election violence and Black disfranchisement. It began to face the basic questions that would long mark post-Reconstruction race relations in the South. In terms of the Exodus, however, its importance was minimal. The Exodus infringed on the planned political deliberations, and neither the Exodus nor Southern politics received adequate attention.

Since January 1878, P. B. S. Pinchback had been writing in favor of reassembling the Nashville conference of 1876, particularly the Southern members. He intended the meeting to belie the common journalistic cant circulating across the nation that "the colored people of the South have no complaints to make of murder, violence, intimidation and unlawful deprivation of rights, that all is peaceful and serene, the colored people are happy and simply desire to be let alone." Pinchback felt that the "criminal silence" of the Southern colored men lent credence to these untruths.[21]

The elections of 1878 further emphasized the need for Blacks to mount a telling protest against bulldozing, and Pinchback's views gained greater acceptance. In late February 1879 a number of "representative colored men," including Pinchback, John R. Lynch, Richard T. Greener, and F. L. Cardozo, met in Cincinnati to discuss the feasibility of holding another national convention,

---

[21]New Orleans Weekly *Louisianian,* December 7, 1878. Unfortunately, the misconceptions that Pinchback sought to correct remained the common white view of Blacks in the South well into the twentieth century.

agreeing on Nashville as the site. The State Executive Committee of Tennessee (which had been designated at the 1876 meeting) officially recalled the convention for May 6, 1879, to consider "the present condition of the race, especially in the Southern States, and everything that pertains to their welfare and future prosperity as a people. . . ."[22] This already represented a compromise between several other views and the Pinchback position favoring a meeting of Southern Blacks to consider the particular problems Blacks now faced in the Redeemed South. John Cromwell, editor of the Washington (D.C.) *People's Advocate,* deprecated the entire convention idea, suggesting that the national government be asked to protect Southern Blacks' suffrage rights. National conventions, he said, were mere vehicles for publicity seekers.[23] Other prominent Blacks feared that a Southern convention would divide the race, which actually suffered from common ills all across the nation.[24] The compromise conference was to be national in scope, according special emphasis to Southern conditions.[25] In the period between the planning of the convention in February and its actual meeting in May, the Exodus broke out.

The event of the Exodus and the predisposition of many delegates toward migration combined to produce a strong sentiment in favor of Kansas on the floor; as a result, the deliberations veered toward the Exodus. Meanwhile, the leaders of the conference were caught off guard and were not prepared to take an unequivocal stand. John R. Lynch, the chairman of the meeting, admitted that its callers had not originally planned to give migration special attention.[26] From the tug-of-war between reluctant, conservative leadership and enthusiastic, insistent delegates emerged a moderate report from the committee on migration, which took three hours to adopt. While it did not admit that the Exodusters had followed the wisest course in fleeing from the South, it resolved that the "great current migration . . . should be encouraged and kept in motion until those who remain are accorded every right and privilege guaranteed by the Constitution and laws." Another

---

[22]Nashville Weekly *American,* February 20 and March 13, 1879.

[23]New Orleans Weekly *Louisianian,* December 28, 1878.

[24]Philadelphia *Christian Recorder,* March 28, 1878.

[25]*Proceedings of the National Conference of Colored Men of the United States* (Washington, 1879), pp. 3, 4.

[26]Daily Memphis *Avalanche,* May 7, 1879; Nashville Daily *American,* May 7, 1879.

resolution recommended "great care on the part of those who migrate. They should leave home well prepared with certain knowledge of localities to which they intend to move; money enough to pay their passage and enable them to begin life in their new homes with prospect of ultimate success." The report provided for cooperation with the National Executive Committee on Migration in Washington. It offered no direct support, aid, or encouragement to the Exodusters.[27]

A vituperative and highly critical resolution on the Vicksburg convention met rejection, and a mild, conciliatory statement appeared in its place.[28] In short, the proceedings of the Nashville conference were respectable and deliberate—even more propitiatory toward the planters than were the Southern white newspapers.

The last 1879 convention considering the Exodus met in Houston in July. The Kansas Fever Exodus overtook the Houston convention much as it had the Nashville meeting, recasting the terms of discussion. At Houston, emigration to Liberia was to have been the subject, but the Exodus distorted the deliberations, and the Northwest emerged as the preferred destination. The resolutions approved of migration, but only on a planned, gradual, and self-reliant basis.[29]

At the height of the Kansas Fever Exodus from Texas, in February 1880, another conference of colored men convened in Dallas, forming itself into the Texas Farmers' Association to homestead in the Texas panhandle.[30] The Reverend S. H. Smothers, the prime mover of the Dallas meeting, was convinced that Texas had

---

[27] *Proceedings of the National Conference of Colored Men,* pp. 100, 104–05.

[28] Ibid., pp. 95–96; Nashville Daily *American,* May 8, 10, 1879. The resolution as it was finally adopted read: "We view with gratification the recent efforts of the planters of Mississippi and Louisiana, at the Vicksburg Convention, to effect an adjustment of the labor troubles existing in that section of the country. Believing that through such movements it is possible to establish friendly relations, adjust all differences between the races, and secure a final and satisfactory settlement of the grave causes underlying the unsettled and inharmonious condition of affairs now obtaining among them at the South, we would respectfully recommend to both classes the adoption of similar action in the future. . . ." (*Proceedings of the National Conference of Colored Men,* pp. 95–96.)

[29] Galveston Daily *News,* July 3, 4, 5, 1879.

[30] Dallas *Herald-Commercial,* February 17, 18, 1880; Galveston Weekly *News,* February 19, 1880; Galveston Daily *News,* February 22, 1880.

a bright future and that Blacks could do as well there as in Kansas. At Dallas and at Houston, "leading men" futilely sought to organize and channel migration to free it from the stigma of pauperism. In fact, this characterization of Black migration especially embarrassed "representative colored men" from one end of the country to the other. Like their white counterparts, they placed considerable store on the nineteenth-century virtues of independence and hardy individualism. But behind their Victorian values lurked a well-founded fear that any reliance on charity would only feed the fires of white supremacy. However, in St. Louis, churchgoing Black people ignored all that, heeding only the Exodusters' desperate need and generously sharing what little they had.

18
Refugee Relief

No one in St. Louis expected the Exodusters in March 1879.[1] A modest Black politician, Charleton H. Tandy, found them first, and taking them in hand, he solicited aid from the Mullanphy Emigrant Relief Board. Administered by the city of St. Louis, the Mullanphy board was set up to aid migrants and immigrants on their way West, but it refused Tandy's first request on behalf of the Exodusters. He finally wrung one hundred dollars from the board for the hundreds of Exodusters in the city.[2] Within the next few days, the Black community circulated an appeal for "temporary relief" for the "suffering humanity" marooned in St. Louis. At this early stage, the Exodusters were provisionally lodged with Negro families.[3] But the continuous stream of arrivals soon necessitated long-range planning.

The March "temporary relief" appeal also called for a mass meeting of "our citizens," which met at St. Paul's African Methodist Episcopal Church. That meeting appointed a committee, which grew into the Committee of Twenty-Five, or the Colored Relief Board, as it was known in St. Louis. C. H. Tandy, the Reverend John Turner, and the Reverend Moses Dickson, who figured centrally in the St. Louis aid effort for the rest of the year, were

---

[1] St. Louis *Globe-Democrat*, March 13, 1879; C. H. Tandy, *Senate Report 693*, III: 36. In his 1880 testimony before the Negro Exodus Senate Investigating Committee, Tandy dates this occurrence in late February, but contemporary newspaper accounts support the middle of March.

[2] St. Louis *Globe-Democrat*, March 13, 1879. Tandy said that in the past, the board had allowed $300 to single white families. (St. Louis *Globe-Democrat*, March 21, 1879.)

[3] Ibid., March 14, 16, 1879.

all prominent at the meeting. Each colored society in St. Louis contributed five dollars to the Exodusters, and the collection netted over fifty dollars.[4] One of the speakers urged the colored people to aid the "refugees" from Southern oppression, and the term entered St. Louis usage permanently.[5] The Black community of St. Louis bore the brunt of the burden of caring for the Exodusters. It sent them on to Kansas, as most of them arrived at St. Louis unable to pay their passage any farther. The task was enormous, and the Colored Relief Board never managed to get very far ahead of its obligations.

The first necessity was shelter, and after the March 17 meeting, the Eighth Street Baptist Church, the Lower Baptist Church, and St. Paul's Church (A.M.E.) housed Exodusters. Approximately 1,400 Exodusters arrived in St. Louis in the week and a half preceding March 21, and they were put up in the three churches. On March 21, 400 had already gone on to Kansas through the aid of the Colored Relief Board; about 1,000 remained in St. Louis, of whom 250 were at the Eighth Street Baptist Church, 250 at the Lower Baptist Church, and 150 at St. Paul's Church; about 350 stayed in Black homes across the city. St. Louis Blacks had donated two hundred dollars in cash and substantial amounts of food and clothing. Until well into April, the Exodusters depended almost entirely on the St. Louis Black community for subsistence, shelter, and passage.[6] By that time, the news of the Exodus had spread to the rest of the nation; charitable whites and Black communities all over the country then began to contribute supplies and money to the Exodusters.

As the aid effort spread beyond St. Louis, the Colored Relief Board came under the fire of a conservative "representative colored man," J. Milton Turner of St. Louis. Between April 15 and 20, Turner assembled a counterorganization. He filed papers of incorporation and attempted to gather an advisory board of prominent whites to put his association on a businesslike footing, he said. His

---

[4] Ibid., March 18, 1879.

[5] Ibid.

[6] Ibid., March 20, 21, 23, 25, 26, and April 2, 8, 15, 1879. Tandy's statement in 1880 to the Senate Investigating Committee that St. Louis Blacks contributed nothing to the refugee relief effort is directly contradicted by day-to-day newspaper reports. On March 26, the St. Louis *Globe-Democrat* reported that there were 2,500 Exodusters in the city at that moment; St. Louis Blacks had contributed the entire $1,500 spent on Exodusters in the previous three weeks.

new organization was necessary, Turner claimed, because the church-based Colored Relief Board had operated "in a very random and irresponsible way, and . . . now they were wholly disorganized and could not be got together."[7] Turner's criticisms rang true, but only from an exceedingly narrow point of view. The Colored Relief Board had always operated hand-to-mouth; nonetheless, it met regularly and its meetings were announced and reported in the *Globe-Democrat.* The board also periodically listed contributions and disbursements in the *Globe-Democrat*'s columns. More than anything else, Turner objected to the lack of respectability of the original, ad hoc group; he could not complain of its indefatigable effectiveness.

The Colored Relief Board helped far more Exodusters than did any other body in St. Louis, including Turner's estimable but short-lived organization. (The latter group's sole usefulness comprised a contribution of $250, which it turned over to the original Colored Relief Board.[8]) However, J. Milton Turner's challenge moved the ad hoc board to go into permanent organization.

On April 22, 1879, the Colored Relief Board, or Committee of Twenty-Five, organized under the name "Colored People's Board of Emigration of the City of St. Louis" (but it was still known as the Colored Relief Board). In its continuing work, two members had visited Kansas in April to look after the Exodusters it had sent there. Kansas lacked a centralized aid organization, so individual cities and Black communities, such as that in Wyandotte, provided intermittent aid.[9] Meanwhile, C. H. Tandy visited the East and New Orleans, soliciting money for the Exodusters. Tandy's trip was financially successful, but he stirred a good deal of criticism. The complaints were of the same order as J. Milton Turner's quarrel with the Colored Relief Board. According to critics, Tandy was unpolished and small-time.

He joined Richard T. Greener in Washington in mid-April, and together they addressed several aid meetings. Frederick Douglass gave him "a very cold reception in Washington," according to the description of their meeting Tandy gave at a New York benefit. At the mention of the name Douglass, the predominantly Black audi-

---

[7]Ibid., April 15, 20, 1879. Turner was a former American minister to Liberia.
[8]Ibid., July 22, 26, 27, and August 5, 1879.
[9]Ibid., April 17, 20, 1879.

ence broke into hisses.[10] The New York *Herald* made no comment
on Tandy's bearing or credibility, but two New Orleans papers
spared him few kind words. "VINDEX," in the *Louisianian,* agreed
with Frederick Douglass and termed Tandy an "unfortunate"
choice for spokesman for the relief effort. He thought Tandy a
good man, but "illiterate, inexperienced and unknown . . . a mere
ward politician."[11] The New Orleans *Times,* even less generous,
charged Tandy with "trying to make himself conspicuous," advancing "his own interests . . . at the expense of the ignorant blacks
of the South. . . . a demagogue of the first class."[12] Nevertheless,
Tandy materially assisted the cause, even though he was not, in
the words of VINDEX, a man of "recognized ability and character."
He and the other hard-working members of the Colored Relief
Board came to the Exodusters' aid first, and their actions were
spontaneous. In the eyes of charitable white groups in the East,
however, the existence of two seemingly identical colored aid
societies in St. Louis created confusion. To sort out the situation,
Thomas W. Conway went to St. Louis.

Conway visited St. Louis in the middle of May on behalf of
Philadelphia Quakers and other "philanthropic people" in the
East. In St. Louis he conferred with the Colored Relief Board in
particular and eventually took the Reverend John Turner to
Washington, where they presented a plan to President Hayes for
rescuing stranded Exodusters. Turner supported Conway's pro-
posal to charter Ohio River boats because the Colored Relief
Board had received several letters from marooned Exodusters in
Mississippi and Louisiana.[13]

The first newspaper report of the meeting between Conway,

[10]New York Daily *Herald,* April 24, 1879.

[11]New Orleans Weekly *Louisianian,* April 26, 1879. "VINDEX" was the pseudonym Senator Blanche K. Bruce used in the columns of the *Louisianian.* (Blanche
K. Bruce Papers, Moorland-Spingarn Collection, Howard University Library:
P. B. S. Pinchback to Bruce, New Orleans, Louisiana, May 19, June 12, and October
23, 1879.)

[12]New Orleans *Times,* May 19, 1879. No evidence whatsoever supports the
charges made by the *Times.*

[13]T. W. Conway, *Senate Report 693,* III: 433; *Nation* XXVIII, no. 728 (June 12,
1879): 395; St. Louis *Globe-Democrat,* May 12, 13, 1879. Conway had been a commissioner of the Freedmen's Bureau and the Louisiana State commissioner of education until 1872. He was violently hated in the South, and the *Nation* called him "an
adventurer." (Conway, *Senate Report 693,* III: 435; *Nation* XXVIII, no. 727 [June
5, 1879]: 377.)

Turner, and President Hayes emphasized the president's warm support of the Exodus and the rescue plan. He was said to have endorsed the charter-boat project as a move of "justice and humanity." When asked whether the federal government could be relied upon to grant protection in the event the mission was opposed by violent means, the president reportedly replied, "with considerable spirit and earnestness, 'such resistance to a lawful business carried on on a national highway, such as the Mississippi is, would be rebellion, and there would be no doubt but that the government would afford its protection.' " The following day, however, spokesmen for the president retracted the original version of the interview, which they ascribed to General Conway. Hayes had been misrepresented, they said, for he had not supposed that thousands of Blacks actually waited on the riverbanks, and "he did not advise chartering or sending steamboats to carry them away."[14]

White Southerners considered the Conway plan inflammatory. Congressman J. R. Chalmers of Mississippi wrote a well-publicized letter to Mississippi Governor John M. Stone, advising that he arrest everyone on board any steamboat attempting to take Blacks from the riverbanks. This militant white reaction coupled with the president's back-pedaling entirely killed the scheme.[15]

Although Conway and the St. Louis Colored Relief Board never implemented the rescue plan, Conway was satisfied that it had served its purpose. Under the threat of chartered transportation, the Anchor Steamship Line agreed to carry Exodusters to St. Louis again.[16] Conway returned to the East (a few months later he involved himself in migration from North Carolina to Indiana). During his Exodus work, several backers, including Colonel Robert Ingersoll and his associates in Boston and Newburyport, covered Conway's expenses.[17] Although Conway had contacts with the Emigrant Aid Association in Washington, he did not funnel significant financial support from that body to the St. Louis Colored Relief Board, which limped along for the rest of the year.

[14]Chicago Daily *Inter-Ocean,* May 26, 27, 31, 1879; St. Louis *Globe-Democrat,* May 27, 29, 1879; see also the St. Louis *Globe-Democrat,* June 26, 1879, for Wendell Phillips's reaction to the Conway charter scheme.

[15]Chicago Daily *Tribune,* May 29, 1879; *Nation* XXVIII, no. 727 (June 5, 1879): 377.

[16]T. W. Conway, *Senate Report 693,* III: 442.

[17]Ibid.

The board still existed in 1880, but it provided minimal aid to the migrants. The public had lost interest in the Exodus, and contributions were negligible. A slight taint of scandal brushed the Reverend John Turner, but more than anything else, the Kansas migration had outlived public concern.[18] Migrants arrived in spurts after May 1879, and fortunately, a larger proportion got to Kansas on their own. In June, the Colored Relief Board reported that the heavy reliance on the Black community that had marked the mid-March to mid-April period had shifted; now "several benevolent gentlemen" were contributing much of the Exodusters' food. The report listed $7,374 worth of rations distributed to Exodusters, $4,330 worth of clothing, and 5,535 Exodusters sent from St. Louis to Kansas and other states. The board had received $8,078 in cash and spent $9,178.[19] The debt persisted, but the board continued to function, providing whatever aid it could. After the middle of April, other relief societies shared the task in Washington and Topeka.

In mid-April 1879, the Emigrant Aid Association organized in Washington, with Senator William Windom and Richard T. Greener taking central roles. The group attracted the vituperation of white Southerners and other Democrats, but it made little direct impact on the refugees in St. Louis. It cooperated with the Topeka Freedmen's Aid Association and, in December, sent Greener to Kansas to survey the condition of the Exodusters there.

At about the same time the Washington Emigrant Aid Association effected its permanent organization, the scattered relief efforts in Kansas gave way to a centralized association, headquartered in Topeka and led by the state's highest officers. On April 20 and 21, two parallel aid societies held their first meetings. On the twentieth, the colored people of Topeka, centered around a nucleus of associates of Benjamin Singleton, Columbus Johnson, and Alonzo DeFrantz, met to help the Exodusters who were there.[20] The Reverend T. W. Henderson also figured in the April 20 meeting, and he was detailed to work closely with the Freedmen's Aid Association that organized the following evening.

The mass meeting of April 21, held at the Topeka Opera House, recalled the abolitionist era. In warm support of Exodus-

---

[18]St. Louis *Globe-Democrat,* November 23, 24, 1879.
[19]Ibid., June 11, 1879.
[20]Topeka *Commonwealth,* April 22, 23, 1879.

ters' cause, Governor St. John commemorated Kansas's historic love of freedom and the glorious days of the Civil War. The Exodusters came to Kansas, he said, cognizant that "Kansas has a history devoted to liberty." Kansas could not deny the Blacks asylum, for "when the life of the Nation was in danger, the blood of the negro mingled with our blood to sustain the Union. When our boys escaped from the Southern prison, they were helped through the enemies' lines by the negro."[21]

This Unionist fervor and sense of Kansas's special destiny as the land of freedom marked the entire freedmen's aid campaign in Kansas. In comparison to the negative and grudging attitude of the St. Louis city officials, all Topeka seemed fired with enthusiasm for the cause. One member of the Opera House meeting, a "well known and respected citizen of Topeka," described its deep fellow feeling: "How wonderfully affairs do turn in this world of ours! Kansas was the territory where the battle for freedom began. . . . Now it seems that Kansas is destined to decide the question by furnishing homes for all the colored people who can get here."[22] The most outstanding citizens of the state, the governor, who chaired the meeting, the attorney general, the chief justice, several prominent businessmen, and Susan B. Anthony—who was visiting in Topeka at the time—all worked with the Exodusters' aid movement.[23] A handful of Black men, particularly the Reverend Mr. Henderson, belonged to the Freedmen's Aid Association, but for all practical purposes it was a white, abolitionist organization.

As time passed, the state officers resigned and the relief work devolved upon Quakers, especially Elizabeth L. Comstock and Laura S. Haviland. The Kansas Freedmen's Aid Association drew upon philanthropists across the nation and in England, and between its formation in April 1879 and its disbandment in May 1881, it distributed over ninety thousand dollars in cash and supplies.[24] It collaborated with Isaiah T. Montgomery in settling Exodusters

---

[21]Ibid., April 22, 1879.

[22]New Orleans *Southwestern Christian Advocate*, May 1, 1879.

[23]St. Louis *Globe-Democrat*, April 22, 1879. Susan B. Anthony, originally from Massachusetts, was not related to Governor Anthony, governor of Kansas between 1876 and 1878, although her two brothers Daniel and Merritt settled in Kansas in 1865, the same year that George Anthony came from his home in New York State.

[24]Laura S. Haviland, *A Woman's Life Work*, 4th ed. (Chicago, 1889), p. 512; Henry King, "A Year of the Exodus in Kansas," *Scribner's Monthly* XX, no. 2 (June 1880): 213.

in a colony in Waubaunsee County, helped start a common school at Dunlap, an old Singleton Colony in Morris County, and aided countless Exodusters in finding employment in Kansas and other Northern states.[25]

In contrast to the situation in Kansas, St. Louis officials discouraged the Exodusters whenever possible. Early on, Mayor Henry Overstolz moved to prevent steamboats from bringing Exodusters to the city; he threatened to enforce an ordinance fining any person up to $300 for bringing a pauper into the city. The Federal Civil Rights Act of 1875 governing common carriers prevented the enforcement of the statute, however.[26] After that setback, the mayor telegraphed a proclamation to local authorities all along the Mississippi, warning colored people, in extremely discouraging terms, against coming to St. Louis.[27] Though it did not in the least affect the Exodus, the proclamation annoyed the Black community in St. Louis. City officials ultimately realized the futility of the obstructionist effort and simply made St. Louis as miserable and vexatious to the Exodusters as possible. The City Board of Health, for instance, refused the Colored Relief Board's request for accommodations in the quarantine station, on the grounds that Exodusters would rest too comfortably there and would not want to leave.[28] The St. Louis Western Sanitary Commission constantly irritated the Colored Relief Board. First it announced that all aid funds in St. Louis were exhausted and that Exodusters should not request any more relief; then it overrode the Colored Relief Board's directions and sent a group of Exodusters to Kansas City, only to have them sent right back again. The Exodusters were stranded until the board's original plans were reimplemented.[29] Finally, the city-administered Mullanphy board begrudgingly contributed $450 toward the Exodusters' subsistence and fares to Kansas, but only under extreme pressure from Tandy and the board.[30] Unofficial white St. Louis proved no more supportive.

As soon as the Exodus assumed perceptible proportions, the

---

[25]Haviland, *A Woman's Life Work*, pp. 482–532.

[26]St. Louis *Globe-Democrat*, March 14, 1879. The Civil Rights Act of 1875 stipulated that passengers could be refused place on a common carrier with available space only if they lacked their fare.

[27]Ibid., March 16, 1879.

[28]Ibid.

[29]Ibid., July 22, 26, 27, and August 5, 1879.

[30]C. H. Tandy, *Senate Report 693*, III: 37.

Anchor Steamship Line announced that its boats would transport any Exoduster back South free of charge.[31] While countless migrants were utterly lost at finding no free transportation to Kansas at St. Louis, a negligible number took advantage of the Anchor Line's proposition. This offer, with the exception of modest individual contributions of cash and food, constituted the entire extent of white private aid to the Exodusters in St. Louis. Amid the heaviest flow of refugees from the South, the Reverend John Turner doubted the St. Louis Black community's financial ability to succor the thousands of Exodusters arriving in the city. With some bitterness, he noted that white ministers showed no concern at all for the Exodusters. One exceptional Episcopalian visited him, but other ministers, Turner said, "have evinced no desire to be charitable on this occasion, though they should lose all sight of the prejudices which they may have toward our race. . . . We have received no donations from white congregations. . . . Verily," the Reverend Mr. Turner concluded, "I believe there is yet a strong color line in this city."[32]

The federal government offered Exodusters no more comfort, for efforts initiated in Kansas to secure military or Congressional aid failed.[33] To the end, the burden of aiding the Exodusters was borne according to nineteenth-century views of minimum governmental activity. Private charity contributed the money and clothing that eased the Exodusters from St. Louis to Kansas and helped them settle there. But private charity fell short of preventing suffering and occasional loss of life among the refugees—especially the children, from respiratory diseases, exposure, and dysentery. Nonetheless, few Exodusters doubted that the trip was worth the sacrifices. Whites and "representative colored men" were less certain.

---

[31]St. Louis *Globe-Democrat,* March 16, 1879.

[32]Ibid., March 27, 1879.

[33]Ibid., April 17, 1879; St. Joseph *North Louisiana Journal,* May 24, 1879. The mayor of Kansas City asked the secretary of war for the release of rations from Fort Leavenworth for the 2,000 hungry Exodusters camped nearby. The secretary refused this request for temporary help, saying that Congress was in session and had jurisdiction over all disbursements. In its turn, the House Committee on Appropriations declined to extend assistance to the Exodusters.

19
National Reaction
to the Exodus

In March and April 1879 the Exo-
dus flashed across front pages from one end of the country to the
other, to disappear just as suddenly from most newspapers shortly
afterward. But in its brief moment it compelled the attention of
Republicans and Southerners, Black and white. For most white
Southerners the Exodus countermanded all they had been repeating to themselves and to Northerners about post-Reconstruction
Black life. They could understand the Exodus only as an artificial
creation, and they remained convinced that Blacks left the South
for no sound reasons whatever. In an opinion that characterized
this view, J. Floyd King, congressman from north Louisiana, wrote
that the flourishing and contented colored people had been persuaded to leave by "the scattering of lying circulars among the
most ignorant to induce them to desert their homes and seek a
new land of Canaan."[1] Senator Lucius Q. C. Lamar of Mississippi
filled in the details of the scoundrels' motivations: the agents—
politicians or preachers—were "moved by pure cussedness, hatred of the South," and many of them only sought to "make money
out of the negroes."[2] The New Orleans *Democrat* discovered Exodus agitators among the exiled political figures from the parishes
who had sent stealthy representatives back into the countryside.

---

[1] St. Joseph *North Louisiana Journal,* May 17, 1879.
[2] Ibid., August 30, 1879. Vernon Lane Wharton reports that in private, Lamar
thought Negro emigration would benefit the South economically. (*The Negro in
Mississippi, 1865–1890,* Torchbook ed. [Chapel Hill, 1947], p. 114.)

According to the *Democrat,* emissaries of A. R. Blount, financed by assessments taken on employees of the New Orleans Customs House and the New York Anti-Slavery Society, circulated in the parishes and spread Kansas Fever.[3]

Whereas the *Democrat* accused Black politicians in New Orleans, Congressman King blamed national politicians and the press in general for inflating the importance of the movement. In reply to the great play Stalwart journals gave to the Exodusters' accounts of bulldozing, King downgraded the violence and raged against Reconstruction, which, he said, had dislocated social and economic life in the South. The Exodus was greatly exaggerated, King intoned in his "Vindication of the People of Louisiana," and this insignificant little movement was directly traceable to "political leaders" in Washington, "who for personal and party ends have instigated this negro exodus":

It is said by mendacious presses, and re-echoed by equally mendacious persons in this Capitol, that the colored man is being driven from Louisiana by oppression and political persecution.

Nothing is easier, Mr. Chairman, than for the imagination to build on isolated cases a theory utterly false in fact. At every corner of this city [Washington, D.C.] able-bodied colored men stretch out the hand of mendacity with pitiful tales of distress. There are more negroes begging their bread between the White House and the Capitol than between Arkansas and the Gulf of Mexico.[4]

The Nashville *Christian Advocate,* an organ of the Methodist Episcopal Church (South), also saw politics at the core of the Exodus. In perhaps the most mindless editorial of all, the *Advocate* explained the three central lessons of the Exodus:

1. That the Presidential canvass has begun. It is perfectly obvious that this is the mainspring of this negro migration.
2. That a set of greedy land agents are speculating upon the credulity of Southern negroes, and the excitability and prejudices of a large class of persons in the Northern States.
3. That there is a class of shiftless and vicious people in all communities that will respond to such appeals as have been made to the negroes in the South.

The editorial closed with the blind allegation that "here in Nash-

---

[3] New Orleans *Democrat,* March 31, 1879, quoted in New York Daily *Herald,* April 3, 1879.
[4] St. Joseph *North Louisiana Journal,* May 17, 1879.

ville there is no trouble, no friction, no excitement, no 'hegira.' "[5] Even among white Southerners who disparaged the Exodus, the Nashville *Christian Advocate* stood out as a paragon of self-deception.

Among white Southern newspapers, the New Orleans *Times* offered a singular exception to the prevailing attitude. The *Times* shifted its position on the Exodus as the spring wore on, yet its initial reactions were at one with its fellow white Southern papers. The colored people, said the *Times*, were really contented; they were merely misled:

There are demagogues who are endeavoring to make them [the Exodusters] believe that they are denied their political rights and, for that reason, ought to abandon their homes. . . . Their wrongs are imaginary rather than real. Some few there are, perhaps, who are anxious for office and whose desires in this respect have not been cordially responded to by the white people. The masses of the colored people, however, are not troubled particularly about politics.[6]

While the *Times* and most other white Southerners tended to discount the significance of the Exodus, a minority of Southern whites welcomed the movement, seeing in it a means of improving the work force. With Black malcontents skimmed off, Southern labor would be more productive, whether European immigrants or satisfied Blacks. From this position, a white Mississippian wished the Exodusters God-speed: "Let them go among their special friends, the champions of their rights; let those people try the medicine they prescribe for us; it will do them as well as the negroes great good; will bring them to their proper senses. We can live without them, and then white immigration, now kept back by negroes, will come this way."[7]

This good-riddance attitude toward the Exodusters enjoyed especial popularity among whites in Texas. The Brenham *Banner* and the Marshall Tri-Weekly *Herald* exhorted the "bad element" of Blacks to leave immediately, for they were "idle, discontented,

---

[5]Nashville *Christian Advocate*, quoted in Nashville Daily *American*, May 8, 1879. The sizable Black migration from central Tennessee, stimulated by men such as Benjamin Singleton from 1876, continued during the entire life of the Kansas Fever Exodus and well afterward.

[6]New Orleans *Times*, March 15, 1879.

[7]Natchez Daily *Democrat*, May 22, 1879.

and malignant," and demoralized the rest of the colored people.[8] The issue of attracting European immigrants loomed particularly large in Texas, for the state already included a sizable body of German immigrants, and boosters wanted still more.[9]

White Southerners showed extra sensitivity about their states' failure to attract large numbers of European immigrants, whose presence indicated industry and modernity in postwar American thinking. Accordingly, the South's inability to draw Europeans proved its backwardness and misgovernment in comparison to the immigrant-rich North and West. White Southerners could hardly deny what everybody knew—that the South was backward—but they blamed Blacks for keeping away progress and sturdy, industrious Europeans. Common among white Southerners of modern views was the belief that European labor would cultivate Southern lands better, more cheaply, and more efficiently than did the shiftless and indolent Blacks. *Any* other labor, they said, would be more desirable than that of thriftless colored people; thus, some planters first welcomed the Exodus as a unique opportunity to substitute the frugal and dependable Chinese for Blacks. (Others, however, found the Chinese proposition threatening—considering the Chinese reputation for thriftiness and hard work, planters felt that they might well find themselves displaced in the not-too-distant future by this "race of Oriental Yankees."[10])

The Chinese Six Companies in San Francisco soon quashed the planters' hopes and fears; in reply to inquiries, they said that they would not send Chinese laborers South for the remuneration that Blacks received and that had been offered to the Chinese—fifty cents a day without board.[11] In the end, schemes to replace Blacks never received serious trial, for the Exodus did not create a perceptible labor shortage. But the eventual outcome was not apparent until well into the summer of 1879. Meanwhile, many white Southerners indulged their fantasies.

By the time most white Southerners admitted that the Exodus really existed, they had taken another step toward rationalizing it away. The Exodusters fared miserably in Kansas, they insisted, and

[8]Marshall Tri-Weekly *Herald,* July 10, 1879.

[9]The Germans in Texas, while contributing to the state's economy tremendously, bedeviled Texas politics. They often voted Republican, combining with Blacks, as in Washington County in 1878, where they split the white vote.

[10]F. R. Guernsey, "The Negro Exodus," p. 388.

[11]Chicago Daily *Tribune,* May 17, 1879.

besides, they were all coming back, having learned that the South was the best place for the colored people, their natural home. Great publicity attended the Exodusters' every hardship in St. Louis and Wyandotte, and the proclamations and statements of St. Louis and Kansas officials all seemed to relay the same messages in the white Southern press. In Kansas the Exodusters were "suffering from exposure and pangs of hunger," Kansas did not want them, the officials of the state did nothing for them, and "there seems to be no opening for them, and while the State authorities are profuse in promises of assistance and employment, thus far little or nothing has been done."[12] The St. Joseph *North Louisiana Journal* reported Senator Preston B. Plumb of Kansas as saying that "Kansas does not want any negro emigration from the South," for the state was "not suitable for negroes."[13] In fact, however, both Plumb and Congressman Thomas Ryan of Topeka were ambivalent about the Exodus. Plumb actually said, "We do not desire them to come to us, for the reasons which I have given [the Exodusters' destitution and dependence on charity], yet we do not wish to appear as if shutting our door in their faces." Congressman Ryan expressed similar sentiments: ". . . you will not understand me as saying a word in discouragement of the exodus of the blacks, especially those who are in any way prepared to provide for them-

---

[12]St. Joseph *North Louisiana Journal,* May 3, 1879.

[13]Ibid., April 19, 1879. An English visitor to Kansas City, Missouri, and Kansas found Blacks very well treated there at the end of 1878. Sir George Campbell, M.P., characterized Wyandotte (Kansas City, Kansas) as "intermediate between black and white countries, where the blacks evidently have no difficulty." Campbell was informed that Blacks were doing reasonably well, both in eastern Kansas and in the interior. He wrote in his journal: "In Kansas City, and still more in the suburbs of Kansas proper, the negroes are much more numerous than I have yet seen. On the Kansas side they form quite a large proportion of the population. They are certainly subject to no indignity or ill-usage. They ride quite freely in the trams and railways alongside of the whites, as I myself experienced, and there seems to be no prejudice whatever against personal contact with them. . . . Here the negroes seem to have quite taken to work at trades; I saw them doing building work, both alone and assisting white men, and also painting and other tradesman's work. On the Kansas side I found a negro blacksmith, with an establishment of his own; he was an old man, and very 'negro,' and I could only extract a little from him. He grumbled just like a white man—he made a living. . . . He came from Tennessee, after emancipation; had not been back there, and did not want to go. . . . I also saw black women keeping apple-stalls, and engaged in other such occupations." (Sir George Campbell, *White and Black: The Outcome of a Visit to the United States* [New York, 1879], pp. 225–26.)

selves. What I do not care to see encouraged is the inducement to come among us before they are prepared to provide for themselves."[14] Senator John J. Ingalls was far more supportive of the Exodus. Yet, according to the white Southern reading of their sentiments, Kansas did not accept the Exodusters and Blacks really wanted to return South.

Very few Blacks returned. The New Orleans *Democrat* said that more actually wanted to come home, but they were "bull-dozed" into staying in Kansas. Several Exodusters had reportedly agreed to return to Tensas Parish, but "as soon as the other colored emigrants heard of this they became very violent, maltreated and beat the negroes who proposed to return to Louisiana."[15] The white Southern newspapers always insisted that Exodusters who wished to return were talented men of sterling character, even though this line of reasoning strained the consistency of their stance toward the Exodusters over several months. Whereas when they left the South the Exodusters supposedly represented the most slothful and improvident class of Blacks, either duped by lying circulars or after something for nothing in Kansas, on their return they always belonged to the very best sort of colored people. In the Southern press, returnees were decent and hard-working, and they invariably had owned property in the South before their flight. The Carroll (Louisiana) *Conservative* offered the case of William George, a returned Exoduster, a man of "more than ordinary intelligence, a carpenter by trade, and a sober industrious man." He had been doing well when "the Kansas craze struck him last Spring, he having an acre of land, with a comfortable house on it, all paid for, and was making a little money, but the golden prospects portrayed in Kansas pictures which flooded the South made him discontented." George had left Louisiana with $160.00 and returned with only $2.50. The article posed the question "What think ye of the picture, colored men?"[16] And the obvious lesson showed that Blacks were infinitely better off in the South.

Instructive examples notwithstanding, the Exodus continued

---

[14]New York Daily *Herald*, April 4, 7, 1879.

[15]New Orleans *Democrat*, quoted in St. Joseph *North Louisiana Journal*, May 10, 1879.

[16]Carroll (La.) *Conservative*, November 22, 1879, quoted in St. Joseph *North Louisiana Journal*, November 29, 1879.

to draw Blacks away from the river parishes and counties, threatening, apparently, to desolate those areas completely. Some white Southerners grew alarmed, cognizant that in the labor-intensive Southern agricultural system, land without labor lay useless and barren. Should a significant portion of the Black laborers desert the South, the planters, merchants, and cotton factors in New Orleans and St. Louis would find themselves impoverished. With this desolate future staring them in the face, the New Orleans *Times* and the St. Joseph *North Louisiana Journal* began to press for the creation of planters' organizations to protect their tenants and laborers from bulldozers, an implicit recognition that the Exodusters' grievances stemmed from real evils.[17]

The *Times* went even further. Gradually it shifted from dismissing the Exodus as Negro foolishness to taking it very seriously indeed. By late May the *Times* not only advocated the sale of land to Blacks—as did the "radical" Chicago *Tribune*—but it staunchly criticized white Southerners for self-delusion. "Why in the world can we not be honest and truthful to ourselves about the matter?" the *Times* asked its readers:

It is a characteristic of our people to constantly deceive themselves. We have been doing it in this grave matter as in everything else. Our newspapers all through the lower [Mississippi] valley; our Washington, St. Louis and Kansas correspondents, for a month past have been repeating that the exodus has ceased; that the negroes are miserable in Kansas and are coming home; that everybody now admits that the movement was induced by land speculators and all such twaddle and nonsense. The truth is that the threatened departure of the great body of the colored laborers from several portions of the State is still impending. The truth is that there were more who left this city last week than have returned to the entire South from Kansas.

In this rare exhibition of Southern straight talk, the *Times* challenged its readers to admit to reality and take meaningful steps to remedy abuses: "Why not recognize the evil, acknowledge its causes, appreciate its seriousness, understand the necessity of averting and checking the movement which threatens to impoverish the fairest portions of the State."[18] How could the Exodus be halted? The *Times* had already set out the measures it saw as the

---

[17]St. Joseph *North Louisiana Journal*, April 12, 1879; New Orleans *Times*, April 22, 1879.

[18]New Orleans *Times*, May 23, 1879.

best remedies—planters' organizations to secure to Blacks "perfect protection in their lives and property, and in their civil and political rights . . ." and long lease or sale of farms to Black farmers. "In some way let the colored man understand that, after all he may yet secure, here in the south where he was born, among those whom he has known from childhood, these 'forty acres and a mule.'"[19] The *Times*'s unheeded and much-reviled advice smacked too much of the Freedmen's Bureau and Radical Reconstruction.

By late May, then, one thoughtful white Southern newspaper had come to the conclusion ultimately reached by Northern Republican journals. They, too, had required time to absorb the meaning of the Exodus, which at first baffled Stalwart papers such as the New York *Herald,* the Chicago *Tribune,* the Chicago *Inter-Ocean,* and the New Orleans *Southwestern Christian Advocate.*[20] As they continued to cover the movement, however, the papers sympathized with the plight of the Exodusters, if not with the Exodus. Among American newspapers, the Stalwart press gave the Exodus the best coverage, and of these radical Republican journals, the Chicago *Tribune* stood first. It sent two correspondents South to investigate the Exodus as it took place. They wrote trenchant reports of the movement and the conditions that bred it but failed to affect significantly the *Tribune*'s editorial stance. Like those of most other Republican organs, the *Tribune*'s editors viewed the Exodus first as a rebuke to the white South for its mistreatment of the freedpeople, and ultimately as a warning of the section's impending ruin unless its rulers changed their ways. *Tribune* editorials discussed the condition of Blacks at length, but their lives always remained a secondary consideration. The *Tribune*'s primary concern lay with the economic health of the South.

In an early editorial the *Tribune* likened the Exodusters to the fugitive slaves of prewar days, and blamed the migration on the whites of the South:

One does not have to search very far for the reasons that are actuating the negroes to turn their faces Northward, and they are not very different

---

[19]Ibid., April 22, 1879.

[20]The *Southwestern* was a radical newspaper editorially, although it was located in New Orleans. An organ of the Methodist Episcopal Church (North), its editor was a Northern white, the Rev. J. C. Hartzell. The vast majority of the *Southwestern*'s readers were Blacks in Mississippi, Louisiana, and Texas.

from those which induced them to take the North Star for their compass in the days of slavery. . . . The first of these motives is the refusal of the whites to allow them to have the rights guaranteed them by the Constitution. . . . Second, having no rights of citizenship, they are at the mercy of their employers. . . . The two motives may be summed up in one. It is the right to live that is urging the negroes to abandon the South. . . . If it were not that the South seems incapable of comprehending its own interests, it could easily check the emigration. If it were not that the South is determined to keep the negro in a servile condition, the latter would be contented. . . . The South may learn after a time that ordinary humanity and the existing customs of civilization are not only right but remunerative.[21]

A later editorial quoted the correspondents but still spoke to white Southerners' blindness to their own self-interest. In May the *Tribune* again commented on the Exodus, citing Black landownership in the South as the only way to stop the migration. The gist of its remarks stressed the economic aspects of the Exodus, which, should it continue, would ruin the South. The Exodus ought therefore to be halted:

This Mississippi gentleman [a planter with whom a *Tribune* correspondent had spoken], while professing a total inability to account for what he regards as little less than lunacy on the part of the blacks, unconsciously furnishes to the Northern mind a very clear reason not only why the blacks desire to leave, but why they will leave unless there be a radical change of policy on the part of the planters. . . . These planters at the South must open their eyes to the inevitable fact *that free labor must own the land it cultivates.* . . . The danger which threatens the Southern land-owner is not alone that the laborer is about to leave, but that the tenants will also leave, if, indeed, they do not precede, the less enlightened and ambitious field-hands. . . . The blacks are free. They must and will have land. If they cannot have forty acres per family in Mississippi by purchase on fair terms, they will seek it by eighty and 160 acres in the North free. The Southern planters must part with their land or part with the labor which cultivates it.[22]

No other Stalwart paper dealt with the Exodus in such detail, but the discussions ran along similar lines. The Boston *Traveller* saw the Exodus from Mississippi and Louisiana as "the sequel to that monotonous headline—'Louisiana Outrages.' "[23] The *Southwest-*

---

[21]Chicago Daily *Tribune,* March 29, 1879.
[22]Ibid., May 2, 1879. (Emphasis in original.)
[23]New Orleans *Southwestern Christian Advocate,* April 3, 1879.

ern Christian Advocate viewed it as an avenue of self-improve-
ment for migrating Blacks, but the movement "meant financial
distress if not temporary financial ruin" to the whites of the
South.[24] In short, Stalwart newspapers seized the occasion to chas-
tise white Southerners for bulldozing and for the crop-lien system,
while at the same time they exhorted them to reform for the good
of the region. In the interest of the South as a whole, white Republicans concluded, the Exodus ought to be stopped. In this final
verdict, Stalwarts and white Southerners reached agreement.
Blacks, however, generally focused their concern more sharply on
the interests of the colored people of the South, not on the South
as an economic entity.

Although Black opinions on the Exodus varied considerably,
they centered on the people and therefore covered a narrower
range than did white views. Many "representative colored men"
found themselves in a quandary. They approved of migration out
of the South, for they could not dismiss the weight of political
violence and economic oppression, yet the pell-mell aspect of the
Kansas Fever Exodus appalled them. In contrast to the whites,
most Blacks welcomed the movement.

Respectable Blacks' opinions on the Exodus ran the gamut
from conditional criticism, through conditional approval, to enthusiastic acclaim. Aside from Frederick Douglass, who stood almost entirely alone in his views, the two most deprecatory com-
mentators were Blanche K. Bruce and J. Milton Turner. Using his
pseudonym "VINDEX," Bruce wrote the New Orleans *Louisianian*'s
Washington column, in which he vituperatively opposed the
Exodus. Exasperated by the Exodusters' disorder and their reliance on charity, he took aim at the "mischief-makers among us
who stir up this discontent" and boldly attempted to call a halt to
the Exodus by fiat. When the Exodus continued nonetheless, he
damned the movement, which, he said, "springs out of a passion
rather than a performance, and that is pursued impulsively and
thoughtlessly, depending upon luck and charity rather than
preparation, for its success, it can be justified on no ground, and
can bring good to no one, who is engaged in it." VINDEX fixed the
"fault" of the Exodus on the "influence of an illiterate and mis-
guided clergy, billeted upon these people . . . to serve selfish

---

[24]Ibid., April 17, 1879.

ends."[25] This estimate might well have been written by a white Southerner, and it stands uniquely barren of sympathy or comprehension.

Another conservative, J. Milton Turner, at least recognized the legitimacy of the Exodus. Enumerating its basic causes, he listed the great destitution among Blacks resulting from the partial failure of crops the previous year, Black overpopulation in the cotton states, and "adverse political pressure." Like Bruce and white Southerners, whose views he often shared, Turner took refuge in alleged causes only tangentially related to the real state of affairs, but unlike them, he approved of the Exodus. His reasons, nevertheless, recalled much of their thinking; he thought the Exodus would thin out the Black population and thereby prove highly advantageous to "the country, the planter, and the colored race." Better yet, it would ameliorate race relations in the South:

. . . it would necessitate more industry among the colored people, give them better social organization and more steady and remunerative employment. Beyond doubt the indolent and aimless lives of many of the Southern blacks, their improvidence and slothfulness, have the effect of promoting and maintaining a strong aversion between the two races, and constant discord and more or less intimidation is the result.[26]

P. B. S. Pinchback, former lieutenant governor of Louisiana and editor of the *Louisianian,* took a long and discursive look at the Exodus, and his conclusions fell well within the range of Black opinion. He sympathized with the Exodusters and felt that the movement stemmed from real grievances. The basic causes, in Pinchback's mind, were political and economic, but he saw bulldozing, "political outrages," as "the main motor in giving activity to the . . . movement." Nonetheless, he believed that economic reforms were necessary to terminate the Exodus. Without explicitly wishing to keep Blacks in Louisiana, he projected a better future for them in a reformed South:

Do away with the country store, encourage thrift and economy in the laborers, not in a missionary and philanthropic spirit, but as a matter of sound policy. Sell land to such of the laborers who are most industrious and give promise of being successful planters. In a word, deal with our people precisely as the oppressed peasants of the old world who flock to

[25]New Orleans Weekly *Louisianian,* March 29 and April 12, 1879.
[26]New York Daily *Herald,* April 7, 1879.

our Western wilds, are dealt with by residents there. Our people must become large tax payers, but they can only be such by being owners of the soil.[27]

Perhaps in reaction to the attitudes of the preceding decade that they now classed as sentimental, Bruce, Turner, and Pinchback took positions they could defend as being hardheaded and economically sound. They applauded planned, reasonable action and decried precipitate conduct, whether or not they approved of the Exodus.

Most articulate Blacks, even if they harbored grave misgivings about the unbridled quality of the Kansas Fever Exodus, commiserated with the oppressed Exodusters and wasted few tears on the best interests of the South or of white Southerners. J. H. Rainey, Henry Highland Garnet, George T. Ruby, Sojourner Truth, George T. Downing, John M. Langston, and Richard T. Greener all warmly supported the Exodus. Perhaps not all of them shared Garnet's sanguine enthusiasm, but his views were reasonably representative. For Garnet, the Exodus was "the best thing they could do. It is one of the most important movements that has ever been undertaken." He was confident it would succeed because it was "entirely voluntary . . . undertaken without extraneous help or leadership."[28] Stressing the Exodusters' common sense and self-direction, J. H. Rainey concurred with Garnet:

The freedman may lack education, but I'll assure you he is not quite the fool imagined. They have complained frequently of rights denied and appealed to the country for redress and protection, but all without avail. . . . Humanity forbids that this patient people should longer remain

---

[27]New Orleans Weekly *Louisianian,* April 5, 1879. In line with these respectable Black views, Booker T. Washington in 1911 compared the migration of Southern Blacks into Oklahoma around the turn of the century with the Exodus of twenty years earlier. He found that the later migrants "came with a definite notion of where they were going; they brought a certain amount of capital with them, and had a pretty clear idea of what they would find and what they proposed to do when they reached their destination." The difference between the two migrations, for Washington, marked the degree to which the race had progressed. (*My Larger Education* [New York, 1911], pp. 184–86.) In an earlier work, *The Story of the Negro* (New York, 1909), Washington had presented a garbled account of the Exodus, leaning heavily on the views of Frederick Douglass.

[28]New York Daily *Herald,* April 3, 1879. Other opinions are to be found in the *Herald* of April 10, 11, 1879.

in the midst of their persecutors, if they are disposed to move. They have too long been made targets of for Christmas pastime and election amusement.[29]

In New Orleans, Ruby wrote with great compassion of the Exodusters' flight from political terrorism. An April 1879 editorial in his New Orleans *Observer* said: "The migration of colored laborers from all the bulldozed and adjoining parishes in Louisiana and Mississippi is then a natural movement, begotten from the lawless acts and avowed purpose of the class misgoverning and ruining these States as self-announced exemplars of intelligence and integrity."[30] In the following month Ruby ran a column entitled "What Has Induced the Exodus." In sharp contrast to Pinchback's closely worded, nonpartisan disquisition, Ruby's editorial bore neither reasoning nor argument. It consisted of a stark enumeration of the names of the victims of the recent "troubles" in Tensas and Concordia parishes, with a brief description of the circumstances of each shooting or hanging.[31]

Ruby's bleak indictment of the post-Reconstruction South cut too close to the quick for most whites, but two old abolitionists expressed similar feelings. William Lloyd Garrison and Wendell Phillips unreservedly criticized the white South. Garrison called for a new imperative, "a trumpet-tongued" edict, "that there shall be a speedy end put to all this bloody misrule." He saw in the Exodusters a despairing people fleeing for their lives: "Self-prompted as a movement it tells its own story of years of unrequited toil, merciless exaction and persistent brutality of treatment; of blasted hopes and broken spirits in their several localities where the victims were born and raised, and to which they tenaciously clung until longer endurance became intolerable. . . ."[32] Like Garrison, Wendell Phillips cheered the Exodusters on, and like most Blacks, he refused the planters any consolation: "Leave the tyrants and bullies to till their own soil or starve while they do nothing but wrong and rob their laborers."[33] Fourteen years after the war, Phillips and Garrison faithfully took ad-

---

[29]Ibid., April 11, 1879.

[30]New Orleans *Observer*, quoted in ibid., April 3, 1879.

[31]Chicago Daily *Tribune*, May 23, 1879.

[32]New York Daily *Herald*, April 24, 1879. Garrison died within the year.

[33]Ibid. See James M. McPherson's *The Abolitionist Legacy from Reconstruction to the NAACP* (Princeton, 1975), pp. 102–04, for a discussion of the Exodus within the broader context of white abolitionists after Reconstruction.

vanced abolitionist positions in their views on former slaves and former masters.

Another figure from the antebellum struggles turned up in Kansas in the fall of 1879, "laboring for her race in Kansas, waking, watching, waiting for the salvation of her people," Sojourner Truth, by then very old. She traveled about the country lecturing and "stirring up a feeling of sympathy for the colored oppressed." Sojourner Truth considered the Exodus "the greatest movement of all time," and she composed a verse in tribute to it:

> The word it has been spoken; the message has
> been sent:
> The prison doors have opened, and out the prisoners
> went.
> To join the sable army of African descent, for God
> is marching on.[34]

The radical abolitionists of the antislavery crusade—Sojourner Truth, William Lloyd Garrison, Wendell Phillips, Henry Highland Garnet, George T. Downing—all championed the Exodusters' flight from oppression. But Frederick Douglass, now far and away the most famous Black American, took a maverick stance.

Despite the large area of agreement among articulate Blacks in support of the Exodus, the prominence accorded Douglass's views skewed public discussion of the movement toward his position. Douglass's critics were well respected but not so widely known: John Mercer Langston, George T. Downing, and Richard T. Greener. Douglass, unlike Bruce, did not consider the Exodus entirely artificial. He admitted that if the Exodusters' stories of mistreatment were only half true, "the explanation of the Exodus and the justification of the persons composing it, are full and just."[35] But Douglass, in Greener's words, was not an "inactive opponent" of the Exodus: "He has written elaborate resolutions, made at least six speeches, spoken at the Methodist Conference, and been interviewed on the Exodus . . . the *morale* of his influence is in opposition."[36]

---

[34]St. Louis *Globe-Democrat*, April 24, 1879. See also Chicago Daily *Inter-Ocean*, October 25, 1879.

[35]Philip S. Foner, ed., *The Life and Writings of Frederick Douglass* (New York, 1955), 4: 330–31.

[36]Richard T. Greener, "The Emigration of Colored Citizens from the South-

Indeed, Douglass did oppose the Exodus. He deprecated Blacks' cultivating "the habit of roaming from place to place," because "the way of an oppressed people from bondage to freedom is never smooth. . . . Suffering and hardships made the Saxon strong,—and suffering and hardships will make the Anglo-African strong."[37] Enlarging on the salutary effects of suffering, Douglass censured the "swarm of Conways and Tandys" crisscrossing the country, begging for charity in the name of the Exodusters.

Douglass's two central criticisms stemmed from his estimation of conditions in the South. Optimistic that Blacks would soon see an end to their distress, he insisted that they must remain where they were. The present victimization of Blacks in the South was "exceptional and transient":

. . . we cannot but regard the present agitation of an African Exodus from the South as ill-timed, and in some respects hurtful. We stand today at the beginning of a grand and beneficent reaction. There is a growing recognition of the duty and obligation of the American people to guard, protect, and defend the personal and political rights of all the people of the States. . . . At a time like this, so full of hope and courage, it is unfortunate that a cry of despair should be raised in behalf of the colored people of the South. . . .[38]

Looming perhaps even larger in Douglass's view was the danger of renouncing the cardinal principle of citizens' rights. In his eyes, the Exodus constituted a surrender,

. . . a premature, disheartening surrender, since it would make freedom and free institutions depend upon migration rather than protection; by flight, rather than by right; by going into a strange land, rather than by staying in one's own. It leaves the whole question of equal rights on the soil of the South open and still to be settled, with the moral influence of Exodus against us; since it is a confession of the utter impracticability of equal rights and equal protection in any State, where those rights may be struck down by violence.[39]

Douglass pointed to the basic issues of racism and civil rights,

---

ern States," *Journal of Social Science* XI (May 1880): 27. Greener was one of the first Black graduates of Harvard College (1870) and had taught at the University of South Carolina during Reconstruction. In 1879 he was dean of the Howard University Law School and among the most respected Black men of his time.

[37] Foner, *Frederick Douglass*, 4: 331.
[38] Ibid., p. 334.
[39] Ibid., p. 336; New York Daily *Herald*, April 3 and May 13, 1879.

which would be settled (or at least confronted, with some measure of success) in the twentieth century by raising the level of violence against nonviolent Black protesters to a level intolerable to the rest of the country.[40] But in the late 1870s, the rest of the country seemed able to tolerate a greater measure of anti-Black violence than the Blacks themselves could; the Compromise of 1877 symbolized the deaf ear Northerners turned to the victims of bulldozing.[41] "When the President's Southern policy was announced," said George T. Downing in this connection, "we realized that we were offered up." Whereas Douglass's logic presupposed some limits to Southern white violence against Blacks, or to Northern tolerance of it, Downing felt no such assurance. In Downing's view, the South, with its "perverseness," had worn out a weary North "anxious for peace and prosperity." Abandoned by fagged-out Northerners, Southern Blacks ought not to be expected to remain among whites whom Greener had found to be "utterly untrustworthy and incapable of generous or humane instincts."[42]

Greener entertained none of Douglass's solicitude for the good of the South as a whole. Instead, he looked to the good of Blacks: "As a negro I have no sympathy to waste on perfidious politicians and Confederate sympathizers, and I would gladly remove the negro entirely from their baneful influences to a region where a man is measured not by the color of his skin, but by his worth as a peaceful, law-abiding citizen."[43] Comparing the South to the West, Douglass's critics saw no reason why, when European immigrants were homesteading on the American plains and prairies, Afro-Americans should languish in the South to be butchered for the sake of principle. Greener spoke in the name of "the deliberate judgment of the more intelligent colored men who are identified with the South" when he wholeheartedly endorsed the Exodus, even in its disorder and reliance on charity. "There must necessarily be some hardships, and perhaps isolated cases of suffering, arising from improvidence, in this movement," he said, "but they will be lost sight of in the greater good which will accrue to

---

[40]I owe this interpretation of the civil rights struggles of the 1960s to my colleague Carl Brauer.

[41]Radical Benjamin Wade of Ohio privately confessed that he was already "sick of niggers" in 1873. (Joe Gray Taylor, *Louisiana Reconstructed*, p. 273.)

[42]New York Daily *Herald*, April 5, 11, 1879.

[43]Ibid., April 5, 1879.

the greatest number."[44] Where Greener hoped the Exodus would continue until "bearing proudly onward . . . there bursts upon its sight the sea, the broad sea of universal freedom and protection," Douglass, if he could, would have stayed Black emigration from the South.[45]

Frederick Douglass's public pronouncements had been gradually falling farther and farther out of line with the drift of postwar Northern Black opinion; thus, the Exodus controversy simply marked another step in his estrangement. Although Douglass still received the best hearing among whites, and the American Association of Social Scientists solicited his opinion of the Exodus, George T. Downing spoke for most Afro-Americans when he said, "Do not let colored men who are enjoying better opportunities, themselves fugitives, who have place and position, put themselves in the way of their struggling brethren who are being robbed and murdered."[46] Douglass forfeited Black support for his lack of sympathy toward the Exodusters. But whites applauded and praised him, and as 1879 drew to a close, his opposition to migration and charity drives echoed through the United States Senate.

Nationwide appeals for refugee relief lent the Exodus a political dimension: Senator John J. Ingalls of Kansas and Representative James A. Garfield of Ohio each introduced substantial appropriation bills for refugee aid.[47] While Exodusters piled up in

---

[44]Ibid.

[45]Greener, "Emigration of Colored Citizens," p. 35.

[46]New York Daily *Herald,* May 12, 1879. In the autobiography he revised in 1892, Douglass recognized his isolation on the Exodus issue: "In all my forty years of thought and labor to promote the freedom and welfare of my race, I never found myself more widely and painfully at variance with leading colored men of the country than when I opposed the effort to set in motion a wholesale exodus of colored people of the South to the northern states. . . ." His interpretation of the movement displayed a breathtaking ignorance of its mechanics and an extraordinary acceptance of Democratic twaddle: "Influenced, no doubt, by the dazzling prospects held out to them by the advocates of the exodus movement, thousands of poor, hungry, naked and destitute colored people were induced to quit the South amid the frosts and snows of a dreadful winter in search of a better country. I regret to say that there was something sinister in this so-called exodus, for it transpired that some of the agents most active in promoting it had an understanding with certain railroad companies." (*Life and Times of Frederick Douglass,* rev. ed. [1892], p. 428.)

[47]*Congressional Record,* Senate, 46th Cong., 1st sess., pp. 620, 661. Both bills died in committee.

Topeka and Wyandotte, a complication arose from the need to disperse them to other states. In this regard, Thomas Conway supplied an additional irritant. Conway had already antagonized white Southerners and Democrats with his Mississippi River expedition plan when he returned East via Indianapolis, spending three days discussing the possibilities of diverting some of the Exodusters from Kansas to Indiana. A group of Republicans, including a newspaper editor and the chairman of the state Republican committee, welcomed the idea, and it was put into effect in the fall, when a group of migrants from North Carolina encountered financial difficulty reaching Kansas and settled in Indiana instead.[48]

Conway was not directly involved in the North Carolinians' move to Indiana, but Democrats thought him a radical troublemaker anyway. He made no effort to conceal his partisanship and said that Southern Blacks were useful, hard-working people, all the more valuable for voting Republican:

Of course they vote the Republican ticket; I am glad they do; I hope they always will; I have, and I always expect to. To whatever part of the country they may go, I hope they will continue to vote the Republican ticket, because it is in the interests of their race, and in the interests of the country at large—in the interests of a higher civilization.[49]

To Democrats in closely balanced Indiana, however, the entry of Southern Republican Blacks introduced a partisan as well as a racial threat. When Southern Black migration to Indiana was merely a point of debate, the Columbus (Indiana) *Democrat* had already fulminated against any scheme that would place white Indianians "completely at the mercy of this ignorant black horde, led by a few unscrupulous politicians." The migration of Blacks to Indiana was repugnant, for they were "no ornament to society, because the bulk of them are ignorant and vicious."[50]

---

[48]T. W. Conway, *Senate Report 693*, III: 440–42.

[49]Ibid., p. 443.

[50]Columbus (Ind.) *Democrat*, quoted in Chicago Daily *Inter-Ocean*, April 2, 1879. The satirical character Petroleum V. Nasby went to Indiana "to assist in keeping that state from being Africanized." Signing himself "Cawcashen," Nasby said, "I come to Plugville [Indiana] the minit I heerd that a dozen uv niggers, wich hed got the noshen uv leevin ther nateral homes in the sunny South, perposed to settle here. I felt it my dooty to aid the strugglin whites uv this seckshun to repel this invashun, that Injeany shood be saved from the horrors uv nigger dominashen. Cood Injiany redoose em to ther normal condishen uv servitood, we shood wel-

As 1879 ended and the North Carolina–Indiana migration materialized, the Exodus acquired an irradicably partisan taint. Democrats had never lent much credence to Exodusters' complaints of racial and political victimization; by the end of the year, these considerations were completely overshadowed by politics. In the Democratic optic, Governor St. John of Kansas especially invited Negroes into Kansas and Republicans supported Conway and the refugee relief committees in order to promote the Exodus, colonize Blacks in swing states in the North, and assure a Republican victory in the presidential election of 1880. A Senate investigating committee took testimony and deliberated against this partisan backdrop. The majority of the Senate select committee on Negro migration was Democratic; its report reflected its views and provided a concise summary of the Democratic interpretation of the Exodus and Black migration in general.

The majority report bore only on the North Carolina–Indiana migration that had occurred just prior to the committee's selection. (The Mississippi-Louisiana-Kansas Exodus was almost a year old when the committee began taking testimony.) More important, two of the three Democratic senators represented states directly involved in the 1880 movement: Daniel W. Voorhees of Indiana and Zebulon B. Vance of North Carolina. Voorhees was anxious to halt Black migration into Indiana by demonstrating that it grew out of Republican machinations entirely. Vance, for his part, defended Democratic Redemption in North Carolina. They fashioned the report to satisfy both of their requirements. The condition of the colored people in the South was good,

. . . not only as good as could have been reasonably expected, but is better than if large communities were transferred to a colder and more inhospitable climate, thrust into competition with a different system of labor, among strangers who are not accustomed to them, their ways, habits of thought and action, their idiosyncracies, and their feelings. . . .

Examining particularly into the condition of the colored men in North Carolina, it was disclosed by the testimony of whites and blacks, Republicans and Democrats, that the causes of discontent among those

come em, but when they come ez free men it is altogether too disgustin." (Chicago Daily *Inter-Ocean,* February 10, 1880.)

people could not have arisen from any deprivation of their political rights or any hardship in their condition.[51]

These happy Blacks had been induced to leave their homes in North Carolina, and, by extension, elsewhere in the South, by the aid societies, which "operated to *cause the exodus originally,*" and further "stimulated it directly by publishing and distributing among the colored men circulars artfully designed and calculated to stir up discontent."[52]

Your committee is further of the opinion that all the attempts of legislation; that all the inflammatory appeals of politicians upon the stump and through the newspapers; that the wild and misdirected philanthropy of certain classes of our citizens; that these aid societies, and all other of the influences which are so industriously brought to bear to disturb the equanimity of the colored people of the South and to make them discontented with their position, are doing them a positive and almost incalculable injury, to say nothing of pecuniary losses which have thus been inflicted upon Southern communities.[53]

The relief societies were the exact opposite of disinterested, philanthropic bodies, intoned the majority report; they cherished partisan goals, inveigling Exodusters North for their votes:

Every single member, agent, friend, or sympathizer with these societies and their purposes were ascertained to belong to the Republican party, and generally to be active members thereof. . . . They thought it would be well to remove a sufficient number of blacks from the South, where their votes could not be made to tell, into close States in the North, and thus turn the scale in favor of the Republican party.[54]

In contrast to the fanciful and baseless report issued by the Democratic majority of the Senate select committee on the Exo-

---

[51]*Senate Report 693,* I: iii–iv. The third Democrat, George H. Pendleton of Ohio, was often either absent or silent. Vance and Voorhees clearly dominated the Democratic side of the committee.

[52]Ibid., p. iv. (Emphasis added.)

[53]Ibid., p. vii. Here the report doubtless referred to the *Principia Papers,* number 11, by the president of the National Farmers' Association, Boston. During the fall, excerpts of the *Principia Papers* had reached the national press and were seen as inflammatory. But the pamphlet exhorting Blacks to leave the South was published in October 1879, too late to have caused the Exodus. Further, no Exoduster ever indicated any knowledge of the National Farmers' Association or its publications.

[54]Ibid., p. iv.

dus, the minority report, by Senators William Windom of Minnesota and Henry W. Blair of New Hampshire, discussed the Exodus with unusual sensitivity. The minority report leaned heavily on Southern Black testimony, quoting portions of Henry Adams and Benjamin Singleton's remarks and the text of George T. Ruby's address of the New Orleans Convention of Colored Men. It concurred with the views of Ruby, Adams, and a St. Louis petition to Congress that concluded "that the great migration of Negroes from the South is itself a fact that overbears all contradiction and proves conclusively that great causes must exist at the South to account for it." These causes were crimes against "the citizenship, lives, and the personal rights of these people," and "a faithful and honest discussion of this subject compels a reference to the darkest, bloodiest, and most shameful chapter of our political history."[55] Democrats, Northern and Southern, refused to admit to the fact of Southern lawlessness because many of the crimes had been perpetrated by Democrats, usually for their party's own advancement. Windom and Blair cited the committee's majority report as proof of their allegation:

In the presence of [the] most diabolic outrages clearly proven; in the face of the declaration of thousands of refugees that they had fled because of the insecurity of their lives and property at the South, and because the Democratic party of that section had, by means too shocking and shameful to relate, deprived them of their rights as American citizens; . . . in the face of all these facts the majority of the committee can see no cause for the exodus growing out of such wrongs, but endeavor to charge it to the Republicans of the North.[56]

The minority report found that aid societies had not caused the Exodus—Southern lawlessness had. "The only remedy for the exodus," Windom and Blair concluded, "is in the hands of Southern Democrats themselves."[57]

Perhaps because they were Republicans and identified with the victims, Senators Windom and Blair freely accused the Democrats on the committee of covering up and excusing the violence that underlay the Exodus. But for whatever reason, the findings of the Republican members of the committee were accurate; those of the Democrats, wrong-headed. The Democratic view, never-

---

[55]Ibid., pp. xxiii–xxiv.
[56]Ibid., p. xv.
[57]Ibid., p. xxv.

theless, gained popular acceptance. Congress drafted no legislation to aid the Exodusters, with the single exception of a bill passed
in 1883 to exempt the Topeka Freedmen's Aid Association from
paying duty on a shipment of used clothing sent to the Exodusters
in late 1879 from England.

In the context of the political thinking of the late nineteenth
century, it is not surprising that Congress appropriated no aid to
the Exodusters. But views that prized individual self-reliance
could not excuse the narrow-minded partisanship and racism that
blinded the majority of the Senate Committee to palpable evils of
post-Reconstruction race relations in the South. Their report further lulled American opinion into disregarding Black cries of distress, while simultaneously according the spokesmen of the Redeemed South a credibility they did not merit. The Senate
Committee's majority report marked another step in American
self-delusion about Southern politics. It was all the more unfortunate for its having been taken at Black Southerners' expense.

Epilogue

No more than a hazy picture emerges of the Exodusters in Kansas after 1879.[1] But letters, oral testimony, newspaper articles, census data, and two reports support tentative conclusions about the Exodusters' fate. In early 1880 roughly fifteen thousand migrants still remained in Kansas. Of that number, one estimate counted between four and five thousand who had come during the spring 1879 Kansas Fever Exodus. Most of the fifteen thousand migrants worked as laborers, on farms, in industry (especially on the railroads or in the mines), or as domestics and washerwomen. Another reporter estimated that about one third were on farms, one third in towns, working and saving to purchase land, and one third employed on a daily or weekly basis. Exodusters had bought or entered approximately twenty thousand acres of land, of which about three thousand acres were broken. Discounting the unusually severe weather over the Christmas holidays, the mild winter of 1879–80 proved a great boon for the Exodusters, for they were ill-clad and had few teams. "God seed dat de darkeys had thin clothes," remarked an Exoduster preacher, "an' He done kep' de cole off." It was possible to plow most of the time, and in Graham County, Black settlers plowed virgin prairie with ordinary spades.

About one fourth of the migrants arriving between the summer and winter of 1879 came with some money, and they took up land immediately. The minority of migrants able to put in crops

---

[1]Thomas C. Cox's Princeton dissertation, "Blacks in Topeka, Kansas, 1865–1900," analyzes one of Kansas's largest Black communities in considerable detail and includes coverage of the post-Exodus period.

before the 1879 growing season closed fared reasonably well the following year, purchasing land and sometimes even putting aside small savings. During the first year, the Exodusters accumulated property and money worth roughly $40,000, or, had it been evenly spread, some $2.25 per person. While this was an encouraging figure, it was little enough. Additionally, that sum was unevenly divided, with those migrants who arrived penniless (and such migrants continued to arrive through the winter of 1879–80) likely to continue in precarious financial straits.[2]

Economically, the Exodusters remained relatively poor, but many of them thought themselves better off than they had been in the South. And as early as January 1880 a correspondent surveying the Exodusters' fortunes discovered that they found in Kansas "the first real prosperity which has ever come to their race in America."[3] By 1886, according to a Kansas Bureau of Labor and Industrial Statistics report, a small sample of Exoduster heads of household in Wyandotte (Kansas City, Kansas) were earning an average of $262.75 annually, while comparable white laborers were averaging $333.09 per year. Nearly all the Exoduster wives worked, usually as washerwomen, and the combined incomes of husband and wife brought the yearly average to $363.28. About three quarters of the families owned their own homes. Yet, several of the Exodusters reported difficulties in finding steady work, and this may explain the tremendous mobility of the Exodusters in the years immediately following 1879.[4]

---

[2]Chicago Daily *Inter-Ocean*, October 10, 24, and December 31, 1879; January 2, 22, and February 7, 10, 1880. Manuscript census of 1880, passim. Henry King, "A Year of the Exodus in Kansas," *Scribner's Monthly* XX, no. 2 (June 1880): 213–15. This figure does not include what was given the Exodusters through charity, which touched approximately 8,000 migrants.

[3]Chicago Daily *Inter-Ocean*, January 2, 1880.

[4]Kansas, *First Annual Report of the Bureau of Labor and Industrial Statistics* (Topeka 1886), p. 255. I am grateful to Thomas C. Cox for bringing this report to my attention.

Material cited in Stephan Thernstrom's *The Other Bostonians, Poverty and Progress in the American Metropolis, 1880–1970* (Cambridge, 1973), pp. 225–27, sheds some additional light on horizontal mobility: "The only marked deviation from this pattern [persistence rates in the 40 to 60 percent range] appeared in the earliest years of settlement on the frontier, in which population turnover was exceptionally rapid. No more than a third of the adult male residents of newly opened farm areas remained there as long as a decade—whether it was Wapello County, Iowa, in the 1850s, Trempealeau County, Wisconsin, and various townships in eastern and east-central Kansas in the 1860s, Roseburg, Oregon, in the 1870s,

. . .

George H. Hardy experienced the mobility and frustrations common to Exodusters in Kansas. In 1879 Hardy arrived in Kansas from Texas with $250. He settled first in Emporia, about fifty miles southwest of Topeka, then three months later he moved west and took up farmland. He left the farm in May 1880 ("I was not able to stane the famine,") and then went to Parsons, in the extreme southeast. In Parsons his children, like other Black Texan children, were consigned to a separate school. By 1882 Hardy wearied of the color line and wanted to "com home" to Liberia. He and another Exoduster from Texas started out for Africa, via New York, but they ran out of money in Chicago. Hardy went to work, his wife sickened and died, and he too grew ill. When finally he got on his feet again, he decided to stay in Chicago.[5] Hardy did not discover an interest in Liberia in Parsons by accident, for that city witnessed considerable emigration activity in the early 1880s. In fact, George Charles, a migration activist in Mississippi from 1876, corresponded with the American Colonization Society in 1881–82 and sustained interest in Liberia well into the 1880s.[6]

Former Exodusters in Parsons, Topeka, and Wyandotte encountered difficulty in obtaining steady work although they were fairly well paid when they found it. Some families were never able to save enough money to take up homesteads or buy land, for lack of long-range, remunerative employment. Others floundered in both attempts, and the agricultural depression that afflicted the New West in the late 1880s only aggravated their problems. The Nicodemus Colony in Graham County, for instance, knew its greatest business-flush times in the mid-1880s, with good rainfall and high expectations that the railroad would pass through the town. But the rain dried up, the railroad stopped short of Nicode-

---

Grant County, Wisconsin, between 1885 and 1895, or West Kansas from 1895 to 1905. After an initial period of extraordinary rapid reshuffling of the population, however, a distinct settling-in took place, and rural persistence rates tended to rise to the general level of those in cities."

[5]George H. Hardy to William Coppinger, Parsons, Kansas, April 26, July 4, and September 28, 1882; November 1, 10, 1882, Chicago, Illinois, *Am. Col. Soc. Papers*, Ser. IA, 247:54; 248: 10, 223; 249: 92, 108.

[6]Chicago Daily *Inter-Ocean*, January 1, 1880; George Charles to William Coppinger, December 4, 11, 1881; January 6, March 10 and April 17, 1882, *Am. Col. Soc. Papers*, Ser. IA, 245: 195, 208; 246: 24, 206; 247: 41.

mus, and the boom burst. Yet, the population of Nicodemus continued to grow slowly until 1910.[7] Nicodemus's growth, like that of the Black population in Kansas after the early 1880s, depended on natural increase rather than on new migration from the South.

After the very early 1880s there seems to have been a limited, secondary migration out of Kansas, especially to Nebraska and Oklahoma. A brief movement of Blacks from St. Louis and Kansas into Nebraska increased by nearly 2,000 the number of Southern-born Blacks in the state, according to the 1890 census, and this trend was followed in the succeeding decade by a decrease of some 1,100 of the Black Southern-born population. In the meantime, the same decade witnessed a sizable jump in Black Southern-born population in Oklahoma territory, about 3,350, some of whom came from Kansas.

In the 1890s the Indian Territory was opened for settlement, and E. P. McCabe, one of the leading Black figures of Nicodemus and Kansas, went to what would become Oklahoma in hopes of creating a Black, politically autonomous area—perhaps a state. He had been elected state auditor of Kansas but was eased out of office in the mid-1880s. McCabe and other migrants noticed that the rising tide of racism in the United States in the late nineteenth century affected Kansas, too.[8]

Racism in Kansas was not entirely novel in the 1880s and 1890s, for the massive influx of Blacks in 1879 had inspired some limited resentment among white Kansans. They feared that large numbers of Blacks would turn the tide of white migration from Kansas to Nebraska and Minnesota. (It did not have that effect at all.) Whites also thought Blacks were "immoral" and that the association of Black and white children in schools would somehow harm white children.[9] In the cities, but not in the rural areas, segregated

---

[7]Glen Schwendemann, "Nicodemus: Negro Haven on the Solomon," *Kansas Historical Quarterly* XXXIV, no. 1 (Spring 1968): 29–31.

[8]United States Bureau of the Census, *Negro Population, 1790–1915* (Washington, 1918), p. 68; Bittle and Geis, *The Longest Way Home: Chief Sam's Back-to-Africa Movement*, pp. 18–39; Rayford W. Logan, *The Betrayal of the Negro*, 2d ed. (London, 1965), p. 143; Mozel C. Hill, "The All-Negro Communities of Oklahoma," *Journal of Negro History* XXXI, no. 3 (July 1946): 260–62.

[9]F. R. Guernsey, "The Negro Exodus," p. 377.

In his comprehensive study of the *Brown* v. *Board of Education* decision of 1954, Richard Kluger notes that the state of Kansas provided for the separation of the races in schools at the first meeting of its legislature. Later sections limited segregated schools to the larger cities, then extended them to smaller ones in 1867.

schools had long been the rule, even before the Kansas Fever Exodus vastly increased the state's Black population.

By 1900 Blacks in Kansas were generally, if not overwhelmingly, more prosperous than their counterparts in the South; politically they were enormously better off. Although they might not enjoy their civil rights to the extent that white Kansans did, they were far freer and less discriminated against than were their peers in the South. Kansas was no Canaan, but it was a far cry from Mississippi and Louisiana. Relative to those states, Kansas was better in the 1880s and still better in the 1890s and early twentieth century. The sad fact was that first-class citizenship existed nowhere in this country for Afro-Americans. Any Black movement seeking real freedom within America was destined to realize no more than a relative measure of success. To the degree that the Exodusters aimed to escape the South and the specter of reenslavement, they succeeded. All in all, the Exodus to Kansas was a qualified but real success.

Although the Exodus of 1879 shared the effect of removing significant numbers of Blacks from the South with the Great Migration of the First World War years, the resemblance ends there. The Exodus was a rural-to-rural migration, at least in intent, whereas the later movement was rural-to-urban. After the turn of the century, the Afro-American quest for land subsided, or turned into a hunt for jobs. In a sense, then, the Exodus was atavistic, for the fundamental drift of American population in the late nineteenth and the twentieth century was toward the cities. Although the Exodus may have had limited demographic impact, politically it spoke volumes.

The Exodus presented proof that Afro-Americans did not quietly resign themselves to the political or economic order of the Redeemed South. They cared that their civil rights were extinguished; they missed public school education for their children; they minded that they were victimized economically unless they

---

Between 1876 and 1879, Kansas schools were desegregated, but in 1879, after the Exodus, they were resegregated on the elementary level in cities of more than 15,000. On the secondary level, however, integrated education remained the rule until 1905, when Kansas City was allowed to put Negro students in a separate high school. William Reynolds of Topeka brought the first (unsuccessful) suit against segregated schools in 1903. (Richard Kluger, *Simple Justice* [New York, 1976], pp. 371–72.)

bargained away some of their rights. But lacking the classic tool for public redress—the reasonably independent exercise of the vote—their best alternative was flight. Exodusters on their way to Free Kansas said no, we do not acquiesce in Redemption; we do not believe that this is the way of American democracy. Yet, of the more than six million Blacks subjected to Southern rule, only a few thousand acted on their faith that a Promised Land of freedom and equality might exist for them somewhere in this country.

Bibliographical Essay
Selected Bibliography
Index

Bibliographical Essay

The Exodus to Kansas has suffered from a threefold handicap historio-graphically, for it was not only a movement of Blacks, but of poor, rural, Southern Blacks not sufficiently Westernized to write their own histories. Until very recently, American historians entirely overlooked the move-ment because of long-standing and ultimately racist habits of scholarship. Only the activities of white Americans, particularly those who left per-sonal papers, found their place in print. But further, the Exodusters bore a double burden of class. Up to the 1960s, for the most part, the concerns and actions of ordinary Americans (Blacks, whites, immigrants, Amerindi-ans) languished while historians studied political figures—or at least fa-mous and influential men. The only Blacks worthy of mention were "rep-resentative colored men," the Frederick Douglasses and Booker T. Washingtons. They found favor in the eyes of articulate white Americans, who took them at face value.

But the Exodusters fared almost no better at the hands of Afro-Ameri-can historians. Black writers—and they have produced the great body, if not the most publicized works, of Black history—have sought extraordi-nary individuals to research in detail and with repetition. Racist denigra-tions of the incapacity of the race for civilization, leadership, and great-ness up to the mark of the white society prompted Black historians to disprove these charges with concrete examples. They have emphasized respectable individuals, "credits to the race," who have made "contribu-tions" to American life in general. "Contributing" to American history all too often has merely meant receiving the accolades of prominent whites for having mastered Euro-American culture and succeeded in its terms. This focus on heroes in Afro-American histories is entirely understand-able, but it has, unfortunately, veered toward considering isolated in-dividuals in a vacuum, or against a white rather than a Black backdrop, while extended families, friends, and colleagues faded into faceless and undifferentiated stereotypes of Negroes, or disappeared altogether. Old-fashioned sexism may have further contributed to this difficulty, for Black women were more likely than their white counterparts to be active on the grass roots level in the late nineteenth century, yet we learn very little about them. Not only was there a long tradition of Black women working alongside men, but in addition, the generations maturing after the Civil War acquired their Western education in coeducational institutions. Black women were likely to be as Westernized as Black men, a result in part of the common conviction that the race needed educators and as-similators too much to sacrifice half its young people to sexist discrimination.

The Exodus did not enter the annals of American history in the late nineteenth century because its protagonists were ordinary, rural folk, hardly the raw material for historical writing as conceived of at that time. Worse, their movement could point to no one famous leader nor boast of meticulous planning or hardy self-reliance. By the twentieth century, it had largely been lost sight of, reappearing sporadically in unpublished master's theses and articles, with each work starting from scratch. There has been no continuity from one work to another, and, strictly speaking, the Exodus has no historiography.

To no small extent, the obscurity of the Exodus is due to the lack of a strong Afro-American historiographical tradition, for one of the works that gives the Exodus extensive, sympathetic treatment is nearly un-known and uncited today: George Washington Williams, *History of the Negro Race in America* (New York, 1883). Later works by Black writers, such as Carter G. Woodson, *A Century of Negro Migration* (Washington, 1918), Emmett J. Scott, *Negro Migration During the War* (New York, 1920), and Benjamin Brawley, *A Social History of the American Negro* (New York, 1921), accord the Exodus three or four pages and rely heavily on printed sources, including Williams's account. Woodson's work is more an attempt to place the Great Migration of 1915–19 in historical perspective than a survey of Black migration before World War I; his treatment of the Exodus is cursory and gives most attention to the Vicksburg Labor Convention and Frederick Douglass's views. Later Black writers of an integra-tionist turn of mind give the Exodus even briefer treatment. W. E. B. DuBois's encyclopedic *Black Reconstruction in America, 1860–1880* (New York, 1935) is equipped with a splendid bibliographical essay whose words still ring true: "I write then in a field devastated by passion and belief. Naturally, as a Negro, I cannot do this writing without believing in the essential humanity of Negroes, in their ability to be educated, to do the work of the modern world, to take their place as equal citizens with others. I cannot for a moment subscribe to that bizarre doctrine of race that makes most men inferior to the few." (Meridian edition, p. 725.) But *Black Reconstruction in America* completely omits the Exodus. The stand-ard post-World War II Negro history (in a family copy of whose first 1947 edition I discovered Afro-American history), John Hope Franklin's *From Slavery to Freedom*, 4th ed. (New York, 1974), takes only the briefest look at the Exodus, citing Adams and Singleton as its leaders. Again the Exodus is forced into the procrustean bed of movements foreshadowing twentieth-century migrations.

Writers of American and Southern history generally give the Exodus no more attention. Thoroughgoing studies such as John Blassingame's *Black New Orleans, 1860–1880* (Chicago, 1973) and Joe Gray Taylor's *Louisiana Reconstructed, 1863–1877* (Baton Rouge, 1974) make no mention of the movement. In the definitive History of the South series, C. Vann Woodward's otherwise masterful *Origins of the New South, 1877–1913* (Baton Rouge, 1951) remands the reader to E. Merton Coulter's preceding volume. In his *South During Reconstruction, 1865–1877* (Baton Rouge, 1947), Coulter dispenses with the Exodus in one paragraph of accurate description and questionable interpretation. William Ivy Hair, in his useful *Bourbonism and Agrarian Protest* (Baton Rouge, 1969), provides the exception and devotes the better part of a chapter to the Exodus. Several other works, either state or race histories, mention the Exodus, but only briefly and on the authority of secondary sources—often fantastically and fundamentally mistaken—or of the reports of the United States Senate Committee on the Negro Exodus. As a result, the Exodus generally either receives superficial treatment or is given a standard discussion studded with recurring and inaccurate conclusions.

Usually the Exodus is dealt with as a movement led by Henry Adams and Benjamin Singleton, as in Rayford W. Logan's *The Betrayal of the Negro, from Rutherford B. Hayes to Woodrow Wilson,* 2d ed. (London, 1965), which is one of the most complete and accurate treatments of the subject. This error grew from the preeminence that the Senate select committee investigating the Exodus gave Singleton and Adams in its *Report and Testimony of the Select Committee of the United States Senate to Investigate the Causes of the Removal of the Negroes from the Southern States to the Northern States,* 3 vols. (Washington, 1880). Because of their reliance on the Senate report and lack of original research, historians, when they are even aware of the Exodus, perpetuate the same mistakes: they do not distinguish between planned migration and the Kansas Fever Exodus, nor between migration from Kentucky, Tennessee, and Missouri and that from Mississippi, Louisiana, and Texas. None of the historians mentions the millennial aspects of the Exodus, and further, they overlook the Colored Relief Board in St. Louis.

In preparing this book, I have relied almost entirely on primary sources, since the paltry secondary sources are riddled with errors. Two United States Senate investigations provided a total of four useful volumes of testimony on the Exodus and Black life in the South: the three-volume report and testimony on the Negro Exodus, mentioned above, and the *Report of the United States Senate Committee to Inquire into Alleged Frauds and Violence in the Elections of 1878,* 2 vols. (Washington, 1879), of which only the first volume was of use. Several newspapers also included invaluable material, especially the New Orleans *Southwestern Christian Advocate,* the New Orleans *Times,* the Natchez (Mississippi) Daily *Democrat,* the Chicago *Tribune,* the Chicago Daily *Inter-Ocean,* the St. Louis *Globe-Democrat,* and the New York Daily *Herald.* The Philadelphia *Christian Recorder* should have been a mine of information, but the 1879 volume has been absent, since the 1930s, from the files of both Mother Bethel A.M.E. Church in Philadelphia and Drew University; similarly, American Missionary Association correspondence is bare after 1878. The American Colonization Society Records in the Library of Congress Manuscript Division and the Justice Department Records in the National Archives are very rich. However, the core manuscript collection was that of the Kansas State Historical Society, which includes not only letters to the governors of Kansas and their correspondence, but also the Singleton Scrapbook. Once again, however, there is a lamentable lacuna in the Correspondence Received, Subject File of Governor John P. St. John for January–March 1879, the very time when a tremendous volume of Exodus mail from Southern Blacks must have reached Topeka. I suspect that the 1879 materials were removed shortly after the Exodus, perhaps to supply documentation for the Senate investigating committee.

In spite of unfortunate bald spots in the primary sources, especially the loss of most Black newspapers, enough documentation exists on this subject and others concerning ordinary Black folk to allow serious writing about their past.

Selected Bibliography

Primary Sources

Manuscript Collections

Dillard University
American Missionary Association Papers
  Kansas
  Mississippi

Fisk University Library
Special Collections
  Charles Waddell Chestnutt Papers
  John Mercer Langston Papers

Howard University Library
Moorland-Spingarn Collection
  Blanche K. Bruce Papers, boxes I, II, IV

Kansas State Historical Society (KSHS)
Governor Thomas A. Osborn, Correspondence Received
  Subject File, 1873–1877, box 2
Governor George T. Anthony, Correspondence Received
  Subject File, 1877–1879, boxes 1, 3, 5, 6
  Governors' Letters, 1878, vols. 10, 11, 12
Governor John P. St. John, Correspondence Received
  Subject File, 1878–1879, boxes 10, 11
  Governors' Letters, vols. 14, 15, 16
Singleton Scrapbook
Kansas Scrapbook
Negro Clippings, 7 vols.
County Clippings, Butler, Douglas, Graham, Morris, Shawnee

Library of Congress
Manuscript Division
  American Colonization Society Records, Series IA, vols. 227–256;
  Series VI, vol. 19

Louisiana State University Archives
  T. I. Galbrith Papers
  J. E. Hawkins Papers
  Daniel R. Carroll and Family Papers
  J. G. Kilbourne and Family Papers
  Police Jury Records, Vidalia

Mississippi Department of Archives and History
  Adelbert Ames Papers
  Governors' Papers
    Governor John Marshall Stone, 1876–1882
      Correspondence and Papers: Series E, vol. 122
    Governor Adelbert Ames, 1874–1876
      Series E, vol. 106

National Archives
  Record Group 60, Department of Justice Source-Chronological Files
    Kansas, boxes 409–410
    Louisiana, boxes 432–435
    Northern Mississippi, boxes 490–491
    Southern Mississippi, boxes 496–497
    President, boxes 6–7
    Tennessee, boxes 663, 666

The Historical Society of Pennsylvania
  William Still Letterbook, 1873–1874
  The American Negro Historical Society Papers—
    Leon Gardiner Collection
  James Still Correspondence
  Isaiah T. Wears Papers

Tennessee State Library and Archives
  Library
    Nashville and Edgefield Directory, 1876, 1877, 1878, 1879
  Manuscript Unit
    Robert H. Cartmell Papers
    Church Records, Methodist Episcopal
    Cooper Family Papers

Newspapers

District of Columbia
  Washington *People's Advocate*

Illinois
  Chicago Daily *Inter-Ocean*
  Chicago Daily *Tribune*

Kansas
Columbus *Border Star*
Fort Scott and Topeka *Colored Citizen*
Leavenworth Weekly *Times*
Oswego *Independent*
Topeka Daily *Blade*
Topeka Daily *Commonwealth*
Topeka Weekly *Commonwealth*

Louisiana
Lake Providence Carroll *Conservative*
New Orleans Weekly *Louisianian*
New Orleans Daily *Picayune*
New Orleans *Southwestern Christian Advocate*
New Orleans *Times*
St. Joseph *North Louisiana Journal*
Shreveport Daily *Standard*
Shreveport Evening *Standard*

Mississippi
Columbus *Patron of Husbandry*
Jackson Weekly *Clarion Ledger*
Natchez Daily *Democrat*
Raymond *Hinds County Gazette*
Vicksburg Daily *Commercial*

Missouri
St. Louis *Globe-Democrat*

New York
New York *Baptist Home Mission Monthly*
New York Daily *Herald*
New York *Times*

Pennsylvania
Philadelphia *Christian Recorder*

Tennessee
Daily Memphis *Avalanche*
Memphis *Baptist*
Nashville Daily *American*
Nashville Weekly *American*
Nashville *Christian Advocate*
Nashville *Republican Banner*
Nashville *Union and American*

Texas
Brenham Weekly *Banner*
Dallas *Herald and Commercial*

Texas (cont.)
  Denison Daily *News*
  Galveston Daily *News*
  Galveston Weekly *News*
  Marshall Tri-Weekly *Herald*
Virginia
  Hampton *Southern Workman*

Public Documents

Kansas, *First Annual Report of the Bureau of Labor and Industrial Statistics,* Topeka, 1886.

Kansas, State Board of Agriculture, *First Biennial Report, 1877–1879,* Topeka, 1878.

Texas, *Report of the Secretary of State for the State of Texas,* 1874, 1876, 1878, 1881, 1882.

U.S., Congress, *Congressional Record,* 45th Cong., 3d sess., 46th Cong., 1st and 2d sess.

U.S., Congress, House of Representatives, *The New Orleans Riots,* 39th Cong., 2d sess., House Report 16, Washington, 1867.

U.S., Congress, House of Representatives, *Report of the Joint Committee on Reconstruction,* 39th Cong., 1st sess., House Report 30, Washington, 1866.

U.S., Congress, House of Representatives, *Testimony Taken by the Sub-Committee of Elections in Louisiana,* 41st Cong., 2d sess., House Miscellaneous Document 154, Washington, 1870.

U.S., Congress, Senate, Committee on Agriculture and Forestry, *Condition of Cotton Growers,* Washington, 1895.

U.S., Congress, Senate, *Report of the United States Committee to Inquire into Alleged Frauds and Violence in the Elections of 1878, with the Testimony and Documentary Evidence,* 2 vols., 45th Cong., 3d sess., Senate Report 855, Washington, 1879.

U.S., Congress, Senate, *Report and Testimony of the Select Committee of the United States Senate to Investigate the Causes of the Removal of the Negroes from the Southern States to the Northern States,* 3 vols., 46th Cong., 2d sess., Senate Report 693, Washington, 1880.

U.S., Congress, Senate, *Report of the Committee of the Senate upon the Relations Between Labor and Capital, and Testimony Taken by the Committee,* 5 vols., 48th Cong., Washington, 1885.

U.S., Congress, Senate, *Testimony Taken by the Joint Select Committee to Inquire into the Condition of Affairs in the Late Insurrectionary States,* parts XI and XII, 42d Cong., 2d sess., Senate Report 41, Washington, 1872.

U.S., Department of Agriculture, Division of Statistics, Miscellaneous Series, Bull. 16, John Hyde and James L. Watkins, *The Cost of Cotton Production*, Washington, 1899.

U.S., Department of Commerce, Bureau of the Census, *Compendium of the Ninth U.S. Census*, Washington, 1872.

U.S., Department of Commerce, Bureau of the Census, *Compendium of the Tenth U.S. Census*, Washington, 1883.

U.S., Department of Commerce, Bureau of the Census, *Negro Population, 1790–1915*, Washington, 1918.

U.S., Department of Commerce, Bureau of the Census, *Statistics of the Population at the Tenth Census*, vol. I, Washington, 1883.

U.S., Department of Commerce, Census Office, *Report on Cotton Production in the United States*, part I, Washington, 1884.

U.S., Works Progress Administration, Federal Writers' Project, "Slave Narratives, A Folk History of Slavery in the United States from Interviews with Former Slaves," 1936–1938, vol. VI, Kansas; vol. IX, Mississippi; vol. XVI, 3 parts, Texas.

Articles

Douglass, Frederick, "The Negro Exodus from the Gulf States," *Journal of Social Science* XI (May 1880): 1–21.

Greener, Richard T., "The Emigration of Colored Citizens from the Southern States," *Journal of Social Science* XI (May 1880): 22–35.

Guernsey, F. R., "The Negro Exodus," *International Review* VII, no. 4 (October 1879): 373–90.

Hartzell, Joseph C., "The Negro Exodus," *Methodist Quarterly Review* XXXIX (October 1879): 722–47.

King, Henry, "A Year of the Exodus in Kansas," *Scribner's Monthly* XX, no. 2 (June 1880): 211–18.

The Nation XXVIII, no. 706 (January 9, 1879); XXIX, no. 755 (December 18, 1879), editorials.

"Proceedings of a Mississippi Migration Convention in 1879" [The Vicksburg Labor Convention], *Journal of Negro History* IV, no. 1 (January 1919): 51–54.

Runnion, James B., "The Negro Exodus," *Atlantic Monthly* XLIV (August 1879): 222–30.

Books and Pamphlets

Appleton's *Annual Cyclopaedia and Register of Important Events of the Year 1879*, New York, 1880.

Appleton's *Annual Cyclopaedia and Register of Important Events of the Year 1880*, New York, 1881.

Campbell, George, *White and Black, The Outcome of a Visit to the United States,* New York, 1879.

City Directories, Kansas
Emporia City Directory, 1883.
Hoye's *Kansas City, Kansas, City directory*, 1886–87.
Lawrence City Directory, 1871, 1879, 1883.
Edwin Green's *Leavenworth City Directory,* 1878–79, 1879–80, 1880–81.
Grimes's *First Annual Directory of Parsons,* 1878.
Grimes's *Directory of the City of Parsons,* 1880.
Parsons City Directory, 1882.
Radge's *Topeka City Directory,* 1878–79, 1880, 1881.

Convention of Colored Newspapermen, Cincinnati, 1875.

Dana, William B., *Cotton from Seed to Loom,* New York, 1878.

Fletcher, Frank H., *Negro Exodus,* n.p., n.d. [Topeka, 1879].

Foner, Philip S., *The Life and Writings of Frederick Douglass,* 4 vols., New York, 1950–55.

Hammond, M. B., *The Cotton Industry,* 2 vols., New York, 1897.

Haviland, Laura S., *A Woman's Life Work,* Chicago, 1889.

Kansas Freedmen's Relief Association, *Second Semi-Annual Report of the Kansas Freedmen's Relief Association,* Topeka, 1880.

Langston, John Mercer, *Freedom and Citizenship: Selected Lectures and Addresses,* Washington, 1883.

Lynch, John Roy, *The Facts of Reconstruction,* New York, 1914.
————, *Reminiscences of an Active Life, the Autobiography of John Roy Lynch,* Chicago, 1970.

Mossell, N. F., *The Work of the Afro-American Woman,* Philadelphia, 1894.

Penn, I. Garland, *The Afro-American Press and Its Editors,* Springfield, Mass., 1891.

Proceedings of the National Conference of Colored Men of the United States, held in the State Capitol at Nashville, Tennessee, May 6–9, 1879, Washington, 1879.

Redkey, Edwin S., ed., *Respect Black: The Writings and Speeches of Henry McNeal Turner,* New York, 1971.

Robert, Charles E., *Negro Civilization in the South,* Nashville, 1880.

Schurz, Carl, *Report on the States of South Carolina, Georgia, Alabama, Mississippi, and Louisiana,* Washington, 1865. Reprinted as *Report on the Condition of the South,* New York, 1969. (This document also appears in U.S. Congress, Senate, 39th Cong., 1st sess., Executive Document no. 2.)

Simmons, William J., *Men of Mark,* Cleveland, 1887.

Williams, George Washington, *A History of the Negro Race in America,* 2 vols., New York, 1883.

Secondary Sources

Unpublished Theses and Dissertations

Abramowitz, Jack, "Accommodation and Militance in Negro Life, 1876–1916," Ph.D. dissertation, Columbia University, 1950.

Aiken, Earl Howard, "Kansas Fever," M.A. thesis, Louisiana State University, 1939.

Belleau, W. J., "The Nicodemus Colony of Graham County, Kansas," M.S. thesis, Fort Hays Kansas State College, 1943.

Blake, Lee Ella, "The Great Exodus of 1879 and 1880 to Kansas," B.S. thesis, Kansas State College of Agriculture and Applied Science, Manhattan, 1942.

Brayne, Elisabeth M., "Journey to Canaan: The Negro Exodus from the South in 1879–1880," M.A. thesis, Smith College, 1967.

Cartwright, Joseph Howard, "The Negro in Tennessee Politics, 1880–1891," M.A. thesis, Vanderbilt University, 1968.

Chartrand, Robert Lee, "The Negro Exodus from the Southern States to Kansas, 1869–1886," M.A. thesis, University of Kansas City (Mo.), 1949.

Corlew, Robert Ewing, "The Negro in Tennessee, 1870–1900," Ph.D. dissertation, University of Alabama, 1954.

Hallman, Jacqueline Rankin, "A Calendar of the Memorials and Petitions to the Legislature of Texas from 1877 to 1937," M.A. thesis, University of Texas, Austin, 1938.

Jordan, Tyree, "The Negro in Tennessee during Reconstruction," M.A. thesis, Vanderbilt University, 1934.

McDaniel, Orval L., "A History of Nicodemus, Graham County, Kansas," M.S. thesis, Fort Hays Kansas State College, 1950.

Peoples, Morgan Dewey, "Negro Migration from the Lower Mississippi Valley to Kansas, 1879–1880," M.A. thesis, Louisiana State University, 1950.

Roberts, Mary Elizabeth, "The Background of Negro Disfranchisement in Louisiana," M.A. thesis, Tulane University, 1932.

St. Clair, Sadie, "The Public Career of Blanche K. Bruce," Ph.D. dissertation, New York University, 1947.

Schwendemann, Glen, "The Negro Exodus to Kansas, First Phase, March–July, 1879," M.A. thesis, University of Oklahoma, 1957.

Smith, L. G., "The Early Negro in Kansas," M.A. thesis, University of Wichita, 1932.

Waldron, Nell B., "Colonization in Kansas," Ph.D. dissertation, Northwestern University, 1932.

Webb, Allie Blaine, "A History of Negro Voting in Louisiana, 1877–1906," Ph.D. dissertation, Louisiana State University, 1962.

Williams, Corinne Hare, "The Migration of Negroes to the West, 1877–1900, with Special Reference to Kansas," M.A. thesis, Howard University, 1944.

Williams, Frank B., "Poll Tax as a Suffrage Requirement in the South, 1870–1901," Ph.D. dissertation, Vanderbilt University, 1950.

Articles

Abbott, Martin, "Free Land, Free Labor, and the Freedmen's Bureau," *Agricultural History* XXX, no. 4 (October 1956): 150–56.

Armstrong, Warren B., "Union Chaplains and the Education of the Freedmen," *Journal of Negro History* LII, no. 2 (April 1967): 105–15.

Babchuk, Nicholas H., and Ralph V. Thompson, "The Voluntary Associations of Negroes," *American Sociological Review* XXVII, no. 5 (October 1962): 647–55.

Chafe, William H., "The Negro and Populism: A Kansas Case Study," *Journal of Southern History* XXXIV, no. 3 (August 1968): 402–19.

Cook, Samuel DuBois, "The Tragic Conception of Negro History," *Journal of Negro History* XLI, no. 4 (October 1960): 219–40.

DeSantis, Vincent P., "The Republican Party and the Southern Negro, 1877–1897," *Journal of Negro History* XLV, no. 2 (April 1960): 71–87.

Dillard, Irving, "James Milton Turner: A Little Known Benefactor of His People," *Journal of Negro History* XIX, no. 4 (October 1934): 372–411.

Elliott, Claude, "The Freedmen's Bureau in Texas," *The Southwestern Historical Quarterly* LVI, no. 1 (July 1952): 1–24.

Erikson, Erik H., "The Concept of Identity in Race Relations: Notes and Queries," *Daedalus* 95, no. 1 (Winter 1966): 145–71.

Fichter, Joseph H., "American Religion and the Negro," *Daedalus* 94, no. 4 (Fall 1965): 1085–1106.

Fleming, Walter L., " 'Pap' Singleton, The Moses of the Colored Exodus," *American Journal of Sociology* XV, no. 1 (July 1909): 61–82.

Garvin, Roy, "Benjamin or 'Pap' Singleton and His Followers," *Journal of Negro History* XXXIII, no. 1 (January 1948): 7–23.

Gross, J. A., "Historians and Literature of the Negro Worker," *Labor History* X (Summer 1969): 536–46.

Hawkins, H. C., "Trends in Black Migration from 1863–1960," *Phylon* XXXIV, no. 2 (June 1973): 140–52.

Higgins, Billie D., "Negro Thought and the Exodus of 1879," *Phylon* XXXII, no. 1 (Spring 1971): 39–42.

Hill, Mozell C., "The All-Negro Communities of Oklahoma: The Natural History of a Social Movement," *Journal of Negro History* XXXI, no. 3 (July 1946): 254–68.

Kessler, Sidney H., "The Organization of Negroes in the Knights of Labor," *Journal of Negro History* XXXVII, no. 3 (July 1952): 248–76.

Kunkel, Paul A., "Modifications on Louisiana Legal Status, 1812–1957," *Journal of Negro History* XLIV, no. 1 (January 1959): 1–25.

Lamplugh, George R., "The Image of the Negro in Popular Magazine Fiction, 1875–1900," *Journal of Negro History* LVII, no. 2 (April 1972): 177–89.

Lentz, Sallie M., "Highlights of Early Harrison County Texas," *The Southwestern Historical Quarterly* LXI, no. 2 (October 1957): 240–56.

Logan, Frenise A., "The Economic Status of the Town Negro in Post-Reconstruction North Carolina," *North Carolina Historical Review* XXXV, no. 4 (October 1958): 448–60.

Martin, George W., "Early Days in Kansas," *Transactions of the Kansas State Historical Society* IX (1905–06): 126–43.

McPherson, James M., "Abolitionists and the Civil Rights Act of 1875," *Journal of American History* LII, no. 3 (December 1965): 493–510.

———, "White Liberals and Black Power in Negro Education, 1865–1915," *American Historical Review* LVII, no. 2 (June 1970): 1357–86.

Meier, August, "The Beginning of Industrial Education in Negro Schools," *The Midwest Journal* VII, no. 1 (Spring 1955): 21–44.

———, "The Negro and the Democratic Party, 1875–1915," *Phylon* XVII, no. 2 (2d Quarter 1956): 173–91.

Patterson, H. Orlando, "Slavery, Acculturation, and Social Change," *British Journal of Sociology* XVII (June 1966): 151–64.

Pellegrin, Roland J., and Vernon J. Parenton, "The Impact of Socio-economic Change on Racial Groups in a Rural Setting," *Phylon* XXIII, no. 1 (Spring 1962): 55–60.

Perkins, A. E., "James Henri Burch and Oscar James Dunn in Louisiana," *Journal of Negro History* XXII, no. 3 (July 1937): 321–34.

Pickering, I. O., "The Administrations of John P. St. John," *Transactions of the Kansas State Historical Society* IX (1905–06): 378–94.

Porter, Kenneth W., "Negro Labor in the Cattle Industry, 1866–1900," *Labor History* X (Summer 1969): 346–74.

Rainwater, Lee, "The Crucible of Identity: The Negro Lower-Class Family," *Daedalus* 95, no. 1 (Winter 1966): 172–216.

Riddleberger, Patrick W., "The Radicals' Abandonment of the Negro During Reconstruction," *Journal of Negro History* XLV, no. 2 (April 1960): 88–102.

Rose, Harold M., "The All-Negro Town: Its Evolution and Function," *The Geographical Review* LV, no. 3 (July 1965): 362–81.

Rose, J. C., "The Census and the Colored Population," *The Nation* LII (March 19, 1891): 232–33.

Savage, W. Sherman, "The Negro in the Westward Movement," *Journal of Negro History* XXV, no. 4 (October 1940): 531–39.

Schwendemann, Glen, "The Exodusters on the Missouri," *Kansas Histori-cal Quarterly* XXIX, no. 1 (Spring 1963): 25–40.

———, "Nicodemus: Negro Haven on the Solomon," *Kansas Historical Quarterly* XXXIV, no. 1 (Spring 1968): 10–31.

———, "St. Louis and the 'Exodusters' of 1879," *Journal of Negro History* XLVI, no. 1 (January 1961): 32–46.

———, "Wyandotte and the First 'Exodusters' of 1879," *Kansas Historical Quarterly* XXVI, no. 3 (Autumn 1960): 233–49.

Seagrave, C. E., "The Southern Negro Agricultural Worker: 1850–1870," *Journal of Economic History* XXI (March 1971): 179–92.

Shapiro, H., "Afro-American Responses to Race Violence During Recon-struction," *Science and Society* XXXVI (Summer 1972): 158–70.

Spindler, Frank MacD., "Concerning Hempstead and Waller County Texas," *The Southwestern Historical Quarterly* LIX, no. 4 (April 1956): 455–72.

Suttles, William C., Jr., "African Religious Survivals as Factors in Ameri-can Slave Revolts," *Journal of Negro History* LVI, no. 2 (April 1971): 97–104.

Tindall, George B., "The Liberian Exodus of 1878," *The South Carolina Historical Magazine* LIII, no. 3 (July 1952): 133–45.

Trebeau, C. W., "Some Aspects of Planter-Freedmen Relations, 1865–1880," *Journal of Negro History* XXI, no. 2 (April 1936): 130–50.

Van Deusen, John G., "The Exodus of 1879," *Journal of Negro History* XXI, no. 2 (April 1936): 111–29.

Wesley, Charles H., "Creating and Maintaining an Historical Tradition," *Journal of Negro History* XLIX, no. 1 (January 1964): 13–33.

Wilson, W. W. W., "The Methodist Episcopal Church in Her Relation to the Negro in the South," *The Methodist Review* LXXXVI (1894): 713–23.

Woodward, C. Vann, "Clio with Soul," *Journal of American History* LVI, no. 1 (June 1969): 5–20.

———, "The Political Legacy of Reconstruction," *Journal of Negro Edu-cation* XXVI, no. 3 (Summer 1957): 231–40.

Woolfolk, George R., "Turner's Safety-Valve and Free Negro Westward Migration," *Journal of Negro History* L, no. 3 (July 1965): 185–97.

Work, Monroe N., "Some Members of Reconstruction Conventions and Legislatures and of Congress," *Journal of Negro History* V, no. 1 (Janu-ary 1920): 58–119.

Books and Pamphlets

Alexander, Thomas B., *Political Reconstruction in Tennessee,* Nashville, 1950.

Andreas, A. T., *History of the State of Kansas,* Chicago, 1883.

Aptheker, Herbert, *A Documentary History of the Negro People in the United States*, 2 vols., New York, 1951.

Bittle, William E., and Gilbert Geis, *The Longest Way Home: Chief Alfred C. Sam's Back-to-Africa Movement*, Detroit, 1964.

Blackmar, Frank W., *Kansas, A Cyclopedia of State History*, 2 vols., Chicago, 1912.

Blassingame, John, *Black New Orleans, 1860–1880*, Chicago, 1973.

———, *The Slave Community*, New York, 1972.

Bleser, Carol, *The Promised Land*, Columbia, S.C., 1969.

Bogue, Allan G., *Money at Interest: The Farm Mortgage on the Middle Border*, Ithaca, N.Y., 1955.

Bontemps, Arna, and Jack Conroy, *Anyplace But Here* (rev. ed. of *They Seek a City*, 1945), New York, 1966.

Brandfon, Robert L., *Cotton Kingdom of the New South*, Cambridge, Mass., 1967.

Brawley, Benjamin, *A Social History of the American Negro*, New York, 1921.

Brewer, J. Mason, *Negro Legislators of Texas and Their Descendents*, Dallas, 1935.

Chambers, W. L., *Niles of Nicodemus*, Los Angeles, 1925.

Connelley, William, *Kansas and Kansans*, 5 vols., Chicago, 1928.

Davis, George A., and O. Fred Donaldson, *Blacks in the United States: A Geographic Perspective*, Boston, 1975.

DeSantis, Vincent P., *Republicans Face the Southern Question: The New Departure Years, 1877–1897*, Baltimore, 1959.

Dick, Everett, *The Dixie Frontier: A Social History*, New York, 1948.

———, *The Sod-House Frontier, 1854–1890*, New York, 1943.

Doyle, Bertram Wilbur, *The Etiquette of Race Relations in the South: A Study in Social Control*, Chicago, 1937.

Fite, Gilbert C., *The Farmers' Frontier, 1865–1900*, New York, 1966.

Franklin, John Hope, *From Slavery to Freedom*, 3d ed., New York, 1967.

Frazier, E. Franklin, *The Negro Church in America*, New York, 1964.

———, *Race and Culture Contacts in the Modern World*, Boston, 1957.

Fuller, Thomas O., *History of the Negro Baptists of Tennessee*, Memphis, 1936.

Genovese, Eugene D., *Roll, Jordan, Roll: The World the Slaves Made*, New York, 1974.

Hair, William Ivy, *Bourbonism and Agrarian Protest*, Baton Rouge, 1970.

Handlin, Oscar, *Boston's Immigrants* (orig. pub. 1941), rev. ed., Cambridge, Mass., 1959.

———, *The Uprooted*, New York, 1951.

Haskins, James, *Pinckney Benton Stewart Pinchback*, New York, 1973.

Haygood, L. M., *The Colored Man in the Methodist Episcopal Church*, New York, 1890.

Henri, Florette, *Black Migration: Movement North, 1900–1920*, Garden City, 1976.

Hirshon, Stanley, *Farewell to the Bloody Shirt: Northern Republicans and the Southern Negro, 1877–1893*, Bloomington, Ind., 1962.

Hobsbawm, E. J., *Primitive Rebels: Studies in Archaic Forms of Social Movement in the Nineteenth and Twentieth Centuries* (orig. pub. as *Social Bandits and Primitive Rebels*, 1959), 2d ed., New York, 1963.

Hood, James W., *One Hundred Years of the African Episcopal Zion Church on the Centennial of African Methodism*, New York, 1895.

Jordan, Lewis G., *Negro Baptist History, U.S.A.*, Nashville, 1930.

King, James L., ed., *History of Shawnee County, Kansas, and Representative Citizens*, Chicago, 1905.

Kluger, Richard, *Simple Justice: The History of* Brown v. Board of Education *and Black America's Struggle for Equality*, New York, 1976.

Kuznets, Simon, and Thomas, Dorothy S., eds., *Population Redistribution and Economic Growth: United States, 1870–1950*, 3 vols., New York, 1957–1964.

Lanternari, Vittorio, *The Religions of the Oppressed*, London, 1963.

Lewinson, Paul, *Race, Class, and Party: A History of Negro Suffrage and White Politics in the South*, New York, 1932.

Malin, James C., *A Concern about Humanity: Notes about Reform, 1872–1912, at the National and Kansas Levels of Thought*, Lawrence, Kan., 1964.

Mays, Benjamin E., *The Negro's God as Reflected in His Literature*, Boston, 1938.

McEntire, Davis, *Residence and Race*, Berkeley, 1960.

McGinty, Garnie W., *Louisiana Redeemed*, New Orleans, 1941.

McPherson, James M., *The Abolitionist Legacy from Reconstruction to the NAACP*, Princeton, 1975.

Meier, August, *Negro Thought in America, 1880–1915: Racial Ideologies in the Age of Booker T. Washington*, Ann Arbor, 1963.

Miller, Wallace E., *The Peopling of Kansas*, Columbus, Ohio, 1906.

Myrdal, Gunnar, *An American Dilemma*, 2 vols., New York, 1944.

Nunn, W. C., *Texas under the Carpetbaggers*, Austin, Texas, 1962.

Phillips, Charles H., *The History of the Colored Methodist Episcopal Church in America*, Jackson, Tenn., 1898.

Redkey, Edwin S., *Black Exodus: Black Nationalist and Back-to-Africa Movements, 1890–1910*, New Haven, 1969.

Rice, Lawrence D., *The Negro in Texas, 1874–1900*, Baton Rouge, 1971.

Saloutos, Theodore, *Farmer Movements in the South, 1865–1933*, Berkeley, 1960.

Scott, Emmett J., *Negro Migration During the War*, New York, 1920.

Scott, Mingo, Jr., *The Negro in Tennessee Politics and Governmental Affairs*, Nashville, 1964.

Shannon, Fred, *The Farmer's Last Frontier: Agriculture, 1860–1897,* New York, 1945.

Smith, Henry Nash, *Virgin Land: The American West as Symbol and Myth,* Cambridge, Mass., 1950.

Taylor, Alrutheus A., *The Negro in Tennessee, 1865–1880,* Washington, 1941.

Taylor, Joe Gray, *Louisiana Reconstructed,* Baton Rouge, 1974.

Thompson, E. P., *The Making of the English Working Class,* New York, 1963.

Thornbrough, Emma Lou, ed., *Black Reconstructionists,* Englewood Cliffs, N.J., 1972.

Thrupp, Sylvia L., ed., *Millennial Dreams in Action: Studies in Revolutionary Religious Movements,* New York, 1962.

Washington, Booker T., *The Story of the Negro,* 2 vols., New York, 1909.

Wharton, Vernon Lane, *The Negro in Mississippi: 1865–1890,* Chapel Hill, 1947.

Williamson, Joel, *After Slavery,* Chapel Hill, 1965.

Woodman, Harold D., *King Cotton and His Retainers,* Lexington, Ky., 1968.

Woodson, Carter G., *A Century of Negro Migration,* Washington, 1918.

Woodward, C. Vann, *Origins of the New South,* Baton Rouge, 1951.

————, *Reunion and Reaction, The Compromise of 1877 and the End of Reconstruction,* Boston, 1951.

Woofter, Thomas Jackson, Jr., *Negro Migration, Changes in Rural Organization and Population of the Cotton Belt,* New York, 1920.

Woolfolk, George Ruble, *The Cotton Regency: The Northern Merchants and Reconstruction, 1865–1880,* New York, 1958.

Worsley, Peter, *The Trumpet Shall Sound,* 2d ed., New York, 1968.

Wright, R. R., Jr., *Encyclopaedia of African Methodism,* 2d ed., Philadelphia, 1947.

Wynes, Charles E., ed., *The Negro in the South since 1865,* Tuscaloosa, Ala., 1965.

Zornow, Frank, *Kansas: A History of the Jayhawk State,* Norman, Okla., 1957.

Index

A Note About the Author

Nell Irvin Painter was born in Houston, Texas. She received a B.A. from the University of California, Berkeley, in 1964; an M.A. in African History from U.C.L.A. in 1967; and a Ph.D. in American History from Harvard in 1974. She has taught French at the Ghana Institute of Languages and is now an assistant professor of history at the University of Pennsylvania. She has published articles in the *New England Quarterly* and the *Journal of Social History*. During 1976/77 Ms. Painter was a Fellow of the American Council of Learned Societies and a Radcliffe Institute and Charles Warren Fellow at Harvard.

A Note on the Type

This book was set via computer-driven cathode ray tube in
Video Gael, an adaptation of Caledonia, a Linotype face
designed by W. A. Dwiggins. It belongs to the family of
printing types called "modern face" by printers—a term
used to mark the change in style of type letters that occurred about 1800. Caledonia borders on the general design
of Scotch Modern, but is more freely drawn
than that letter.

Composed, printed, and bound by The Haddon Craftsmen, Inc.,
Scranton, Pennsylvania.
Designed by Gwen Townsend

NEW ROCHELLE PUBLIC LIBRARY

Main Building   632-7878
662 Main Street

Film Service   576-2278
662 Main Street

Huguenot Park Branch   632-5747
794 North Avenue

Columbus Branch   632-5136
93 Seventh Street

For library hours
please call the numbers listed

PRO DART   PRINTED IN U.S.A.   23-263-002